BRISTOL

AND THE

CIVIL WAR

BRISTOL
AND THE
CIVIL WAR

for King and Parliament

J O H N   L Y N C H

The History Press

First published 1999
This edition first published 2009

The History Press
The Mill, Brimscombe Port
Stroud, Gloucestershire, GL5 2QG
www.thehistorypress.co.uk

British Library Cataloguing in Publication Data.
A catalogue record for this book is available from the British Library.

ISBN 978 0 7524 5214 2

Typesetting and origination by The History Press
Printed in Great Britain

For Rachael, Rebecca and Miriam
Remember the past is always with you

Contents

Acknowledgements

This book began as my dissertation at Ruskin in 1989 and therefore I must acknowledge the help and assistance of Victor Threadwell and Bob Purdy, two of the finest teachers I have ever been fortunate enough to meet. I would also thank Christopher Hill, the external examiner, for his kindness and encouragement on that occasion. I must mention the friends who supported me during my time in Oxford: Chris, Iris, Pete, Tim, Fiona and others, thank you all. Lastly, most importantly, I must mention Ann who made this possible.

I gratefully acknowledge the help of the staff of the local studies section of Bristol Central Library, the Bristol Records Office, Ruskin College and the Queen's University Belfast, whose tolerance and kindness were critical to the completion of this work. I also extend my thanks to the staff of the Department of Economic and Social History, Queen's University, particularly Valerie Fawcett, the Departmental Secretary, for their support and assistance.

I especially thank Alan Turton, James Russell, Jane Bradley, Stephen Howe and Simon Cox for their generous help in illustrating this book – a task I found more difficult than writing the text. I acknowledge a debt to members of the English Civil War Society in the late 1970s and early 1980s who shaped my view of these events.

CHAPTER 1

Introduction

During the war between Charles I and his Parliament the city of Bristol, to quote the old Chinese curse, 'lived in interesting times' and was almost ruined by military action and the exactions of both sides. The 'history' of Bristol during this period has assumed an almost mythical quality which distorts perceptions of these events. This is not unique to the city as the English Civil War in general has often been presented in terms reminiscent of Sellar and Yeatman.

> With the ascension of Charles I to the throne we come at last to the central period of English history (not to be confused with the Middle Ages, of course), consisting in the utterly memorable struggle between the Cavaliers (Wrong and Wromantic) and the Roundheads (Right and Repulsive).
>
> Charles I was a Cavalier king and therefore had a small pointed beard, long flowing curls, a large, flat, flowing hat and gay attire. The Roundheads, on the other hand, were clean-shaven and wore tall, conical hats, white ties and sombre garments. Under these circumstances war was inevitable.[1]

With the possible exception of Cromwell's campaign in Ireland, the war is often viewed as a romantic conflict, a gentlemanly affair fought between friends with the greatest of reluctance. A letter written by the Royalist Ralph Hopton to his Parliamentarian opponent William Waller illustrates this fellow-feeling between the two sides and incidentally provided the title for Ollard's history of the war.[2]

> The experience I have of your worth, and the happiness I have enjoyed in your friendship, are wounding considerations when I look upon the present distance between us. Certainly my affections to you are so unchangeable that hostility itself cannot violate my friendship to your person, but I must be true to the cause wherein I serve. . . . That great God, which is the searcher of my heart, knows with what sad sense I go upon this service, and with what a perfect hatred I detest this war without an enemy.[3]

Two weeks after the letter was written the armies commanded by these friends fought to a bloody stalemate at Lansdown. As with all civil wars this was a bitter, vicious conflict with up to 10 per cent of the adult male population under arms during the campaigning seasons of 1643, 1644 and 1645, and with 20–25 per cent serving in one army or the other during the conflict.[4] It is estimated that 85,000 people died as a result of military action during the civil war with another 100,000 falling victim to disease.[5] In addition excesses and atrocities were committed against civilians by both sides.[6] Bristol's citizens were to experience extortion, malicious damage, intimidation and murder during this 'war without an enemy', and would discover to their cost – on two occasions – what it meant to support the losing side in a civil war.

What was Bristol's role during in this bitter internecine conflict? Control of the city was of critical strategic importance, as Clarendon explained after the Royalists captured the city in 1643:

> This reduction of Bristol was a full tide of prosperity to the king, and made him master of the second city of his kingdom, and gave him the undisturbed possession of one of the richest counties of the kingdom (for the rebels had now no standing garrison, or the least visible influence upon any part of Somerset-shire) and rendered Wales (which was before well affected, except some towns in Pembroke-shire) more useful to him; being freed of the fear of Bristol, and consequently of the charge, that always attends those fears; and restored the trade with Bristol; which was the greatest support to those parts.[7]

However, there is, even in the most recent history of this war, a tendency to minimize the city's importance.[8] I shall adopt a wider perspective, placing Bristol within the national context to re-evaluate its significance. While this book focuses on a single area, and therefore is a 'local' history, it will not be parochial in its view of the war or of the importance of Bristol to the Royalist 'war machine'. Although their role was less romantic than that of Prince Rupert and his cavalry, the ordnance officials based in Bristol, the manufacturers who supplied them and the ships' captains who ran their vital cargoes past the parliamentary patrols were equally important to the survival of the Royalist cause.

A typical myth about Bristol during the civil war concerns its capture by Prince Rupert in July 1643. Traditionally it has been accepted that Bristol was attacked by a Royalist army of up to 20,000 men and that William Waller had irresponsibly reduced the garrison to 1,500 infantry and 300 mounted troops, insufficient to man the defensive lines surrounding the city. It is further accepted that these defences were inadequate and that their weakness was compounded by a serious shortage of ammunition. Despite these problems the Royalists breached the defences by the chance discovery of a weak point unknown to the defenders. Once the line was breached the city was indefensible and the garrison commander, Nathaniel Fiennes, surrendered the city to save his troops and civilian population. Although this account was shown to be inaccurate shortly after the event it has retained some credibility.

Fred Little's image of the capture of Bristol by Prince Rupert in 1643 illustrates the romantic view of these events that has tended to pass as history until recently. (Author's Collection)

The myth was the creation of the man who surrendered the city, Col. Nathaniel Fiennes, and is first found in his reports to the House of Commons and the Lord General.[9] Contemporaries were quick to challenge his version of events, as did a range of witnesses during his subsequent court martial.[10] Despite this historians have continued to rely upon Fiennes, in part at least because one of the main Royalist accounts of the siege lends Fiennes credibility by extensively quoting from his *Relation*.[11] Samuel Seyer, writing in 1823, based his account largely on contemporary documents and offered a range of estimates of the Royalist strength between 8,000 and 20,000.[12] He credits the garrison with greater strength than Fiennes admitted, but presents Rupert's success as almost a lucky chance and is so biased that much of the value of his work is undermined.[13] Writing in 1868, Robinson accepted Fiennes's statement as to the strength of the Royalist force and the governor's assertion that the city was indefensible, although he does suggest that the garrison was stronger than reported.[14] In Gardiner's (1893) description of events at Bristol both the accidental nature of the Royalist success and the indefensibility of the city after the first breach are emphasized.[15] Latimer, who made extensive use of both State Papers and City Archives, largely follows Robinson's argument although he displays a strong pro-parliamentary bias.[16] Wedgwood (1958) accepted that the garrison had been weakened to such an extent that it was no longer able to defend the city and that Fiennes was forced to surrender owing to lack of ammunition.[17] Many historians, such as Rodgers and Young, accepted the myth without the reservations of Seyer or Latimer and simply repeat the details from Fiennes's reports uncritically.[18] The myth appears in both popular histories and the footnotes of works of impressive scholarship.[19] The latest history at time of writing once again states that Fiennes had only 300 horse and 1500 foot against a Royalist force of between 14,000 and 20,000.[20]

Despite acceptance and repetition of this myth, the reality is more complex and intriguing. When he surrendered, Fiennes's troops had successfully repulsed almost all the main attacks and Rupert's men were bogged down in costly street fighting. The Royalists had suffered serious losses, particularly among brigade and regimental commanders, and the *attackers* were running out of ammunition. A new and intriguing question presents itself: why, in view of the military situation, did Col. Fiennes surrender one of the most important cities in England to the king's forces?

Another myth is that the city was not of any great significance to the outcome of the conflict. Robinson told his Bristol audience in 1868, no doubt to their great disappointment, that those studying these events 'must not attach undue importance to that city'.[21] Likewise McGrath in 1981 minimized the significance of the city in the wider conflict:

> Bristol in these years failed to play the important part that might have been expected from a large and rich port, and it had no relish for a civil war in which men were fighting for reasons which did not fill most Bristolians with any great enthusiasm.[22]

Once again this is a well-established tradition: as early as 1685 the pro-Royalist author of *Mercurius Belgicus* sought to minimize the significance to the Royalist cause of the recapture of Bristol by Parliament:

> Bristol delivered upon conditions by Prince Rupert, after three weeks' siege, part of the city won by assault; which the rebels gained not without some loss, so their loss no ways equivalent to the importance of the place.[23]

Conversely Clarendon, a member of the Royalist Council of the West, saw the loss of Bristol as a disaster:

> The sudden and unexpected loss of Bristol, was a new earthquake in all the little quarters the king had left, and no less broke all the measures which had been taken, and the designs which had been contrived, than the loss of the battle of Naseby had done.[24]

The importance of the city in the minds of some Parliamentarians was evident at Fiennes's trial.

> The Parliament, his Excellency, London and the whole Kingdom, looked upon Bristol as a place of greatest consequence of any in England, next to London, as the metropolis, key, magazine of the west, which would be all endangered and the kingdom too by its loss. As a town of infinite more consequence than Gloucester, by the gaining whereof the enemy could be furnished with all manner of provisions, and ammunition by land, with a navy and merchandise by sea and enabled to bring in the strength of Wales and Ireland for their assistance.[25]

How important was control of the city of Bristol in deciding the outcome of the Civil War? The city was more than a garrison; it was a communication, administrative and manufacturing centre. The value of the port with its shipping and overseas contacts should also be considered, particularly in view of Royalist dependence on imported arms supplies. I disagree with those who maintain that Bristol played only a minor role in the civil war and certainly dispute Edmund Turner's remark in 1803 that 'it does not appear from the annals of Bristol, that anything particular occurred during the government of Prince Rupert'.[26] Its capture by the Royalists in July 1643 allowed the king to continue the war, and its loss two years later dealt a devastating blow to his cause. It is also significant that both the commanders who surrendered the city were disgraced as a result, although both were well connected at the highest levels of their respective factions.

Another example of the confusion over Bristol's role in the civil war concerns the city's political allegiance. Contemporaries were confused, and confusing, in their descriptions of the loyalty of Bristolians in the 1640s. The Earl of Essex's Scoutmaster, Samuel Luke, certainly received contradictory reports; in February 1643 Ferdinando Atkins, one of Luke's agents who carried out reconnaissance missions behind Royalist lines, described the inhabitants of the city, which was under Parliamentary control, as 'three parts' malignants.[27] By December Ralph Norton reported that the city's Royalist garrison was convinced 'that the town will rise for they are all Roundheads (they say) except the mayor and 2 or 3 aldermen, and that the townsmen run to Colonel Massey, and acquaint him with all things that happen there'.[28] In the 1820s Seyer argued that the city was Royalist in sympathy, in part at least because of his own political opinions, while in the early years of the twentieth century, again influenced by his beliefs, Latimer argued that the city had favoured Parliament. In more recent times Patrick McGrath, in common with other researchers on the war, notably Underwood in his study of Somerset, argued that the political situation was far more complex and that neutralism was a significant feature.[29] Interestingly, Underwood has since argued that neutralism in this period may not imply the absence of support for one party or the other.

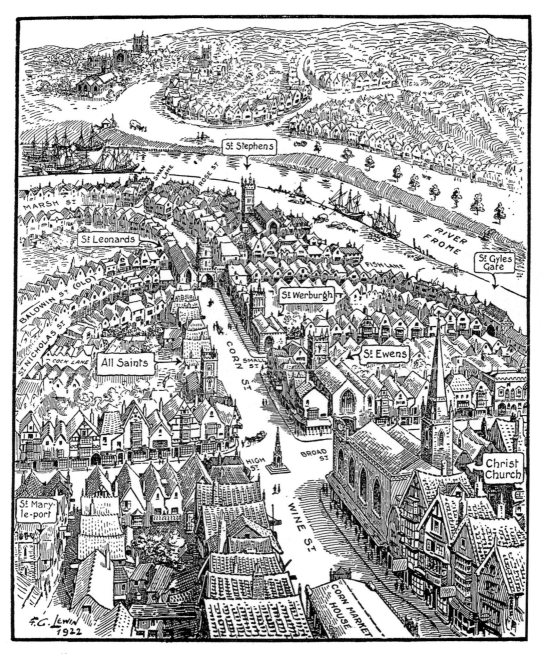

Above and opposite: These 1920s artist's impressions of Bristol during the civil war era contain some serious errors but give a good impression of what the city must have looked like. (Reproduced by kind permission of Bristol Central Library)

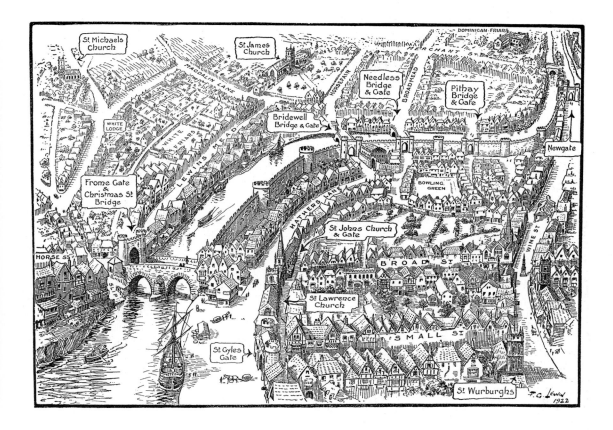

Neutralism, for example, was not always absolute. People might sensibly want to avoid risking life and limb, might wish to escape the war and till their fields in peace, and still prefer one side to the other. The preference might not be strong enough to provoke them into hopeless resistance to a dominant power, but in times of conflict it could be clearly visible in a reluctance or willingness to provide armies with supplies or intelligence. Neutralism could coexist with real differences of regional outlook. The vagaries of individual behaviour, too, can be allowed for.[30]

It is certainly the case that a person might hold a belief but that this might not induce him or her to take action. For example, today far more people habitually vote for political parties than make themselves available to canvass voters or help on polling day. In the case of a civil war where action could result in death or loss of property many would choose to 'keep their heads down'. It is debatable how far one can accept McGrath's arguments:

A study of the part played by Bristol in the First Civil War from 1642 to 1646 makes it clear that it was never a committed 'parliamentary' or 'royalist' city, still less a 'puritan' city. Of the two hundred or so merchants in Bristol, not more than thirty showed even minimal commitment to one side or the other, and of those about twenty were involved with the royalists.[31]

How typical were the merchant classes, and how many of the other 170 merchants supported one side or the other but chose not to make a public display of 'minimal commitment'? Was Bristol Royalist, Parliamentarian or merely indifferent to the war that raged around it for four years?

The history of Bristol during the civil war is a fascinating tale full of dramatic events and colourful characters, but there is also a deeper and less attractive aspect to the story. This account will look at the broader issues of the war in Bristol and their effects on everyday life, while attempting to produce a 'warts and all' portrait of the city in this period.

CHAPTER 2
Peace, Neutrality and War

To the modern Bristolian the city of the 1640s would appear tiny. The old medieval centre, bounded by the Rivers Frome and Avon, would today include Castle Green, the Centre and the area around Fairfax Street. South of the city, in the bend of the Avon between Temple Meads and Redcliff Backs, were the old suburbs of St Thomas, Mary Redcliff and Temple, the wall which marked their southern boundary following the line of the modern Redcliff and Temple Ways. The city was surrounded by high ground: Brandon Hill and Kingsdown to the north, Totterdown and Bedminster to the south. Millard's *Prospect of Bristol* published in 1673 shows a maze of crowded streets dominated by the towers and spires of the city's churches.

The early seventeenth century was a period of peace and prosperity for Bristol. Peter Mundy described the city at this time as 'a little London for merchants shipping and great well furnished markets etc., and I think second to it [*London*] in the Kingdom of England.[1] Owing to a huge increase in overseas trade the city was enjoying a recovery from the depressed conditions of the late sixteenth century. During 1598–9, 37 ships arrived in Bristol from French ports and 22 from Spain and Portugal; of the 61 ships that left the city in that period, 36 sailed to France, 1 to the Cape Verde Islands, 4 to Italy and 20 to Ireland.[2] By 1637–8 arrivals from France and Iberia were 70 and 38 respectively and the total number of ships outbound from the city had increased to 195.[3] The trade with Ireland during these years, owing to a combination of peace, plantation and the development of a large-scale trade in live cattle, increased from 28 arrivals in 1598–9 to 140 vessels.[4] Trade routes were also established with the new colonies in North America and the West Indies, which were to increase in importance as the century progressed.

Increasing trade stimulated expansion in manufacturing and processing industries, and by the early seventeenth century soap making, gunpowder milling, sugar refining, rope production and glass making were all noted local trades. Strangely for a city whose wealth was so closely linked to the sea and trade, shipbuilding was not significant. Farr argued that the main reason for this was an inadequate supply of suitable timber. In 1634 it was claimed that only one vessel of 100 tons had been built in the city during the previous nine years, although this was probably an exaggeration.[5] Easily accessible supplies of iron and charcoal from the Forest of Dean, coal from Kingswood, and lead

Visitors frequently compared Bristol Bridge with London Bridge. It was noted that those who lived in the houses along its sides were strongly parliamentarian in sympathy. It was also noted that the goldsmiths of Bristol tended to live here, perhaps for security reasons. (Author's Collection)

and copper from the Mendips allowed Bristol to develop a metallurgic industry on some scale, and when the City Council began to purchase muskets in 1642 there were at least six gunsmiths operating in the city.[6]

Prosperity encouraged physical growth with new suburbs spreading out beyond the old city walls as wealthy merchants built new homes and warehouses outside the congested city. To the east the area around Horsefair and Broadmead was already well established while Old Market had developed as far as Lawfords Gate. To the north the area between the river and what is now Park Row, Upper Maudlin Street and Marlborough Street was already a mass of small streets. Although map making was not a particularly precise art at this time an impression of the scale of this growth can be obtained by comparing Speed's map of 1610 with Millard's of 1671.[7] Although Bristol's population of 15,000 cannot be compared with the 250,000 people living in London on the eve of the war, it was very much the country's second city in terms of trade and manufacture.

This economic boom did not benefit all Bristolians to the same degree. Much of the city's trade was monopolized by the eighty or so members of the Society of Merchant Venturers.[8] The increased prosperity of this group stimulated social and political change, with this merchant community increasingly dominating local government. The city was controlled by an oligarchy of forty-three members, consisting of the mayor, twelve Aldermen and thirty common councillors. Sacks points out that of 123 members appointed to this body between 1605 and 1642, 56 (46.7 per cent) were described as merchants, 40 (33.3 per cent) were retailers of various kinds, 19 (15.8 per cent) were manufacturers but only 4 (3.2 per cent) claimed to be gentlemen or yeomen. The shift is even more marked during the two decades before the war when 75 per cent of those joining the Council were described as merchants.[9] Sacks suggests that this elite group was less united in political terms than in social origins, and that they were acting under economic rather than ideological pressures.[10] The need for royal support in the preservation of their monopolistic position may have secured the cooperation, if not the loyalty, of many merchant venturers but this uncomfortable alliance made those excluded resentful of both royal power and the city's ruling faction.

If relations between the crown and merchants of Bristol were sometimes strained they were at least based on mutual self-interest; it was the city's manufacturers who suffered as a result of royal policy during those years when Charles tried to govern without Parliament. One method of raising money adopted by the king was the creation of monopolies, and two Bristol industries, gunpowder and soap, illustrate the effects of such restrictions. The extraction of saltpetre and the manufacture of gunpowder had always been, for security reasons, a royal monopoly, in theory if not in fact. During the 1630s Saltpetre Commissioners controlled production of the critical raw material and supplied to a patentee who alone had the right to manufacture powder in England. All gunpowder produced had to be sold to the crown and unlicensed importation or manufacture was forbidden.[11] A substantial profit was made by charging an inflated price to the consumer. In late 1637 it was noted that gunpowder actually cost $7\frac{1}{2}d$ per lb to make but was being sold at $18d$ per lb, a profit margin of 140 per cent![12] In order to protect this profitable trade, competition was suppressed to ensure that 'market forces' did not bring down the price.

In December 1631 the Attorney General informed the Lords of the Admiralty that there were a number of unlicensed powder makers in Bristol, at least one of whom, William Barber, had been operating for twelve years.[13] In October 1633 it was reported from Sherston Magna in Wiltshire that several local people had been making saltpetre without permission and had sold it to unlicensed Bristol powder makers.[14] In February the next year the patentee demanded the names of the Bristol powder makers and in March a warrant was issued to bring four of the offenders – Randal Tombs, William Barber, Walter Parker and John Corsley – before the Lords of the Admiralty.[15] No action followed because no evidence was produced, but John Corsley subsequently petitioned the Admiralty in April requesting permission to make powder. He was promptly ordered to enter a bond of £500 not to make powder again without permission or face immediate arrest.[16] In February 1635 it was discovered that Corsley had been buying saltpetre in large quantities although he had now ceased to do so.[17] Finally, in December 1637 a report from John Dowell at the Bristol Custom House to Sir Henry Vane referred to widespread abuse of the regulations.

I find many merchants have great quantities of powder by them which never issued out of his majesty's stores, and that there are 46 retailers of powder in the city, and two or three mills going contrary to the proclamation.[18]

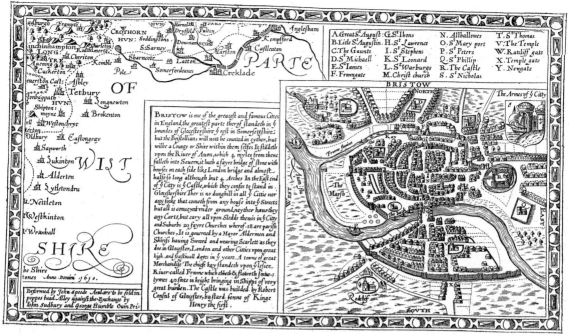

Although mapmaking was far from a precise art in the sixteenth and seventeenth centuries, these two representations of the city clearly show the extent of urban growth: (above) Speed's map of Bristol 1610 and (opposite) Millard's map of Bristol 1671. (Reproduced by kind permission of Bristol Central Library)

Two weeks later the Lords of the Admiralty wrote to the Mayor of Bristol ordering him to search for and close all mills in the city.[19] On 10 January the mayor reported that he had taken into custody the equipment belonging to two mills.[20] However, on 30 November John Dowell reported that gunpowder was still being produced in Bristol, and that William Barber was operating a mill in the suburbs producing two hundredweight a week, which was smuggled into the city for sale.[21] A week later the Gunpowder Commissioners wrote to the mayor demanding the suppression of Barber's mill and ordering a full investigation into how much powder had been produced and who had supplied the raw materials.[22] The Council were somewhat slow in complying with these orders and a second letter was sent on 26 April instructing the authorities in Bristol to imprison any powder maker still operating.[23]

The royal officials were never able to suppress fully the gunpowder industry in Bristol. At least two of the makers called before the Lords of the Admiralty in March 1634, William Barber and Randal Tombs, were still in business at the start of the civil war. However, the continual harassment by royal officials and the City

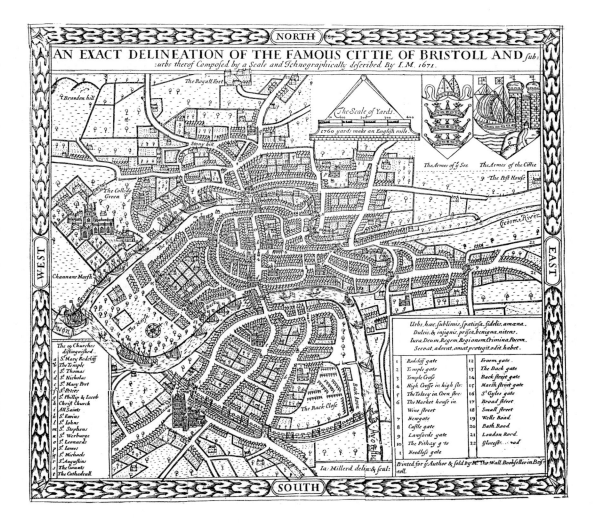

Council, combined with the risk of having stock and equipment seized, must have reduced their operations. The monopoly itself was a considerable source of resentment as it greatly increased the cost of this vital commodity; by 1638 the 'official' price of powder had increased to 2s 6d per lb, and the unlicensed makers enjoyed good profits and a ready market.

It is possible to argue that the manufacture and distribution of gunpowder had to be under royal control for security reasons but this was hardly the case with another Bristol industry. In December 1631 a patent was granted to the Society of Soap Makers of Westminster giving them the sole right to make soap from home-produced materials and empowering them to destroy the buildings and equipment of those who infringed their privilege. In July 1634 a proclamation was made in Bristol forbidding both the local manufacture of soap and its importation.[24] This was disastrous for the city's well-established soap industry; the Bristol Soap Makers Company was forced to reach a compromise with the patentees and agreed to reduce production to 600 tons a year. However, the Privy Council imposed further restrictions and a heavy tax on Bristol soap,[25] and so damaging were these additional restrictions that some members, in particular Thomas Longman, broke ranks and tried to ensure their survival by agreeing separate terms with the authorities.

> Petitioner being one of the soap-boilers of Bristol, and a young man governed by his Company, conceived he did well therein, but perceiving they have run into contempt, he disavows their proceedings and submits to pay his majesty what shall be ordered by the board. He has undertaken the house and trading of his master, who made 200 tons of soap by the year; 20 tons a year now allotted to him by his company on which he is not able to subsist. Prays the lords to settle his portion, he giving caution to pay duty for all he shall make hereafter.[26]

The patentees maintained spies in the city to ensure that their monopoly was fully protected and by May 1637 twelve Bristol soap-makers were in prison for non-payment of the tax levied by the crown. The Bristol Company was finally forced to submit to the king's terms, and the number of soap-houses in the city, as a result of the king's order in council, was reduced to four.[27]

The experience of the gunpowder and soap makers of Bristol was not unique. Few groups were not in some way adversely affected by attempts to extend royal power or raise money in these years. Latimer details a wide range of abuses and petty irritations which plagued merchants and manufacturers, and makes frequent complaints about the behaviour of royal officials in the city.[28] The king's determination to exploit every source of potential income is well demonstrated by the establishment of a Commission in Bristol during June 1631 to assess which citizens should, by virtue of their wealth, take the title of knight. Knighthood was a rather expensive privilege and it was common for individuals to pay a fine rather than accept the offered honour. Forty-four individuals qualified in Bristol, all of whom declined knighthood and paid fines of between £6 13s 4d and £41 6s 8d.[29] They included 14 merchants, 7 brewers, 4 mercers and 4 gentlemen, 2 soap makers, 2 drapers and 2 clothiers, with an innkeeper, a tanner, a grocer, a smith, a tailor, a mariner and a baker.[30]

The most infamous of Charles's attempts to raise funds during his personal rule was the imposition of ship money after 1634. In the first writ Bristol was included with the ports of Gloucester, Bridgwater and Minehead, as well as the counties of Gloucestershire and Somerset. They were ordered to provide a ship of 800 tons with a crew of 260, fully provisioned for six months' service; this demand was later commuted to a cash payment of £6,500, of which Bristol, after a great deal of complaining and internal wrangling, paid £2,166 13s 4d.[31] In August 1635 a second writ was issued and Bristol was informed that its contribution this time would be £2,000, although on appeal this was reduced to £1,200 which was paid in March.[32] In October 1636 a third writ was received, requiring a ship of 100 tons or £1,000, later reduced to £800, and the next year the demand was for a ship of 80 tons or £800. By now the strain of such levies was beginning to tell and the mayor found it difficult to collect the money. The king accepted no excuses and ordered the mayor to appear before the Privy Council to answer charges of negligence and disaffection. Suddenly, the money was found! A fifth writ was received in November 1638 requiring only £250 and a year later there was a final demand for £800, reduced to £640 on condition that payment was made promptly.[33] Between 1634 and 1639 Bristol was subjected to six ship money writs totalling £5,823 13s 4d, an unprecedented peacetime tax burden. In mitigation of this royal policy, it must be said that Bristol, unlike many areas, did receive something in return for its money, as small warships patrolled the Irish Sea to suppress piracy.

The king's policy in Scotland was no more subtle than in England and his attempts to enforce religious conformity there provoked a popular revolt against his authority. The king sought to use his English subjects to force the Scots to comply. In February 1639 Bristol was ordered to supply 50 men out of a total of 24,000 infantry levied from forty-one Welsh and southern English counties.[34] These men, drawn from the trained bands and clothed and equipped at the city's expense, represented about one-tenth of the city's militia soldiers.[35] A year later a larger contingent of 200 men and 2 drummers were sent to the army facing the Scots in the north at, it was claimed, a cost of £700 to the city.[36]

The king's policy of personal rule collapsed in October 1641 when rebellion erupted in Ireland. In Bristol, with its close trading links with Ireland, news of the rebellion and the subsequent massacres of settlers, combined with the rebels' claims that they were acting in the king's name, was received with alarm. Refugees from Ireland seemed to confirm the worst fears of the Bristolians.

> At Bristol there landed certain Irish merchants who coming before the Mayor declared very sad tidings, the sum of which was, that at Waterford the King of Spain hath set up his standard. Likewise declaring the great misery that kingdom is like to undergo if present aid be not sent over.[37]

By early February 1642 Bristol vessels were outfitting, by order of Parliament, to cruise off the Irish coast.[38] On the 26th a Bristol ship intercepted a Spanish vessel trying to reach Ireland with eighteen passengers 'all of them being Spanish or French commanders, only one Englishman amongst them'.[39] In June an appeal from Parliament for funds 'for the defence of the kingdom and support of the army in

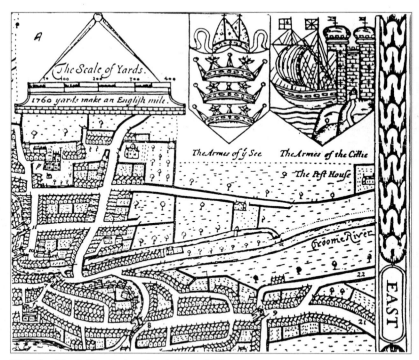

What did Bristol look like during the civil war? The streets were crowded with houses but hardly any of these building have survived the ravages of time, bombing and redevelopment. These illustrations show various buildings of the civil war era in various parts of the city. (Author's Collection) (a) Detail from Millard's Map

(b) The Fourteen Stars Inn, Counterslip

(c) A large house, Pithay Street

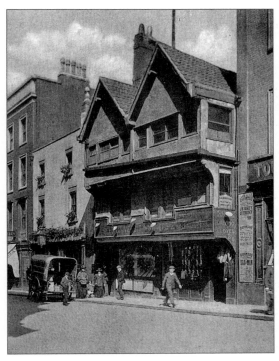

(d) House and shop, Small Street

(e) Brewer's Hall, Christmas Street

(f) House, Wine Street

(g) St Peter's Hospital

Ireland' raised the sum of £2,625 in Bristol by popular subscription; so emotive were the events in Ireland that future supporters of both the king and Parliament responded with equal generosity.[40] The level of popular support among Bristolians for the British settlers in Ireland can be gauged by the fact that two supply ships were financed and sent over to Ireland by the citizens in May 1643.[41] Their cargoes included over 43 tons of peas, beans and corn, plus more than 3,000 cheeses and 5 tons of bread in addition to large quantities of salted fish and meat, bacon and butter. It appears to have been a street collection to which everybody contributed whatever they had to hand.

The need for money to pay for the war with the Scots finally forced Charles to summon Parliament in April 1640. The two Bristol members were John Glanville, the Recorder of the City, and Alderman Humphrey Hook. Glanville was appointed Speaker to the Commons but was unable to control the more turbulent members. Under the leadership of John Pym Parliament refused either to confirm the duties being raised by the king on his own authority or to grant subsidies for the Scots war until their grievances had been addressed. On 5 May the frustrated king dissolved the Parliament which had not only refused to do his bidding but were increasingly critical of his personal rule.[42] However, renewed conflict in the north forced the king to call elections for a new Parliament; this met in November 1640 and was to became the 'Long Parliament' that opposed the king during the civil war. Glanville was replaced as a member for Bristol by Richard Long, but both he and Hook were later disqualified as members because they were 'beneficiaries in the project of wines'. They were replaced in June 1642 by John Glanville and John Taylor, two individuals who proved to have Royalist sympathies.[43]

On 4 January 1642 the king burst into the House of Commons in an ill–advised attempt to arrest his leading opponents. He was too late and his failure, exacerbated by the growing hostility of the London mob, forced him to flee Whitehall on the 10th. On that day Parliament claimed control of military forces by issuing the Militia Ordinance. The country was already slipping towards civil war. In February a letter from the king instructed the Mayor of Bristol not to admit troops of either party, but to defend the city for his majesty's use.[44] Although Charles did not raise his standard – calling those loyal to him to support him in arms against the Parliament – until 22 August, he was already preparing for conflict. From May onwards the Bristol corporation began stockpiling food and munitions and repairing the city's defences.[45] A week before Charles raised his standard at Nottingham, Bristol City Council, recognizing that a crisis was looming, resolved to make further repairs on the city walls and gates, provide artillery and gunners, and increase stocks of arms in the common store. They also spent £2,000 on building up stocks of foodstuffs.[46]

Parliament attempted to secure Bristol by appointing Denzill Hollis as Lieutenant of the City on 5 March 1642.[47] This was not an honorary title: Hollis and his fellow lieutenants were instructed to

. . . raise all the power and forces of their several counties, as well trained bands as others, and shall have power to conduct and lead the said forces of the said counties against traitors and their adherents, and with them fight, kill and slay all such as by force shall oppose them; and the persons of the said traitors and their adherents and accomplices to arrest and imprison them, to bring to Parliament to answer this their treacherous and rebellious attempts according to law.[48]

Hollis, a leading member of the parliamentary party, was one of those men the king had unsuccessfully tried to arrest in January. Clarendon thought highly of him and admitted that he had good reason to oppose the king, although Hollis was to become a supporter of the restoration.[49] Hollis came to Bristol and 'exercised the Militia there'; this, it was claimed, encouraged the 'disaffected' party within the city.[50] However, his services were required elsewhere and by late July he had returned to London to assume command of an infantry regiment being raised as part of the Earl of Essex's army.[51] His military career ended with the destruction of his unit at the Battle of Brentford in November and a leader who might have been of great advantage to the parliamentary cause in Bristol was lost. He refused to accept a further command and became a leading member of the peace faction in Parliament.[52]

In response to the Militia Ordinance the king issued Commissions of Array to local magnates, empowering them to muster trained bands and other troops in his name. Bristol fell within the area of south-western England and southern Wales, which was placed under the control of the Marquis of Hertford.[53] Hertford was effectively the regional military governor and as a reward for his support he was promised the income from customs duties paid at Bristol after the city was captured.[54] In July Hertford and his army approached Bristol. The City Council voted to provide suitable accommodation for the king's representative but to refuse admittance, in accordance with the king's order, to any troops that might accompany him.[55] The same policy had been adopted when Hollis visited the city for Parliament. There were certainly strong arguments in favour of the king's representative establishing his base in the city.

Some were of opinion, that Bristol would be the fittest place, being a great, rich, and populous City; of which being once possessed, they should be easily able to give the law to Somerset and Gloucestershire; and could not receive any affront by a sudden or tumultuary insurrection of the people. And if this advice had been followed it would, probably, have proved very prosperous.[56]

However, others argued that the city was of dubious loyalty and too far removed from the main areas of potential royal support in Somerset. Eventually, Hertford established his headquarters at Wells and began to assemble troops; the local parliamentary committee responded by summoning help from neighbouring areas to suppress the Royalists as common disturbers of the peace.

What role did Bristol play in the events developing just to the south? In the first of a series of reports to London, dated 1 August, the local committee informed Parliament of the action they had taken.

> We thought fit to give out warrants for the mustering two regiments, on Friday next at Chewton upon Mendip within three miles of Wells, and for the better enabling us to preserve the peace of the country we sent to Bristol (who have showed their good affections to us already in this service) for two field pieces of about six pound bullet, which we conceive very necessary for the present occasion which you see is dangerous.[57]

On 5 August John Proud wrote that five hundred men had left Bristol the previous day and had not yet returned; in addition, 'our well-affected people in the town' had sent three or four artillery pieces and a supply of arms to Sir Alexander Popham.[58] Two days later John Ash wrote to London describing the forces assembled at Chewton; he claimed they numbered some 40,000 men, drawn from as far away as Wales. Included in this host were 'about 300 lusty stout men of very good rank and quality of the city of Bristol, all of them on horseback with swords, pistols and carbines'.

> We had likewise two waynes loaden with powder, bullet and match and some arms sent us by the honest good men of Bristol, with two waynes more loaded with four small field pieces and their carriages and two gunners; although the Mayor and Sheriffs of Bristol by all means of the Lord Paulet and Master Smith (as we are informed) did hinder and oppose it with all their skill.[59]

Another printed relation, published in London the day after Ash's letter was received, quite specifically mentions 300 men from Bristol, although this detail could have come from the previous account.[60] It was not only Parliamentarian writers who remarked upon the presence of the Bristol contingent at Chewton Hill; Clarendon and Hopton in their accounts of these events both note that the local committee enjoyed support from Bristol.[61] Later, in a letter to Bristol, the king commented that he was 'little beholden' to them for opposing the Marquis of Hertford at Mendip.[62]

Heavily outnumbered, Hertford's small army withdrew to Sherborne Castle where they were besieged by local forces under the command of the Earls of Pembroke and Bedford.[63] Once again Parliament's supporters in Bristol responded generously:

> Bristow hath sent the Earl of Bedford both men and ordnance to batter down the outworks, so that they may have free recourse to the castle, the citizens being very ready to lend their aid and assistance, and disburse moneys and all

sorts of provisions that may further that service (namely) powder, match, and bullet and all things that can be thought necessary for such a design.[64]

Finally after the Royalists were forced to evacuate the castle and withdraw to Wales and Cornwall, the House of Commons passed a vote of thanks to the gentlemen of Somerset and instructed Taylor, the Bristol MP, to thank the city for having 'shown forward' in the affair.[65]

McGrath, in his history of Bristol in the civil war, dismisses these reports as 'highly improbable' as there was no reference to these events in the city's official records and such activities were 'highly unlikely in view of the city's cautious neutralism'.[66] However, there are a number of possible reasons for the omission of such activity from the city's records and, as McGrath himself points out, these records are far from complete for this period.[67] If such a body were raised, is it likely that the Council would record such a flagrant breach of the king's orders? It would probably have been easier to plead ignorance and make sure there was no evidence to the contrary in the city's records. McGrath presupposes that only

The Marquis of Hertford was the king's commander in the west of England and Wales during the early stages of the war. He was over-sensitive to his personal position and honour and quarrelled bitterly with Rupert after the capture of Bristol. (Reproduced by kind permission of Bristol Central Library)

the City Council would have had the resources to mount such a military operation; in fact, as Russell points out, volunteers had been mustered by supporters of Parliament in the city long before the king raised his standard.[68] If Parliament's supporters had gathered hundreds of well-armed 'lusty horsemen', could the city authorities actually have prevented them from joining their companions in Somerset?

Long before the outbreak of fighting at Mendip, another battle had been raging for the hearts and minds of the population as petitions were circulated urging king or Parliament to compromise. In May Bristol's Council resolved to send petitions urging reconciliation upon both parties, but after a committee spent two months arguing about the wording the whole project was dropped.[69] These petitions had little effect; neither side was particularly tolerant towards views that opposed their own, as can be seen by a Parliamentary reply to a fairly moderate Royalist petition from Somerset.

> There has come to my view a vagrant petition, which now travelleth the country, begging testimonial hands to pass it to the Parliament. It as far exceeds the Kentish petition in malignancy, as it is possible for one person to exceed another in venom, and is as far below that in wit and judgement as the least star in heaven is inferior to the sun in light and lustre. It is wholly without method and order and tends only to disorder and confuse.[70]

The Royalists were equally dismissive of what they saw as ill-informed advice, as the introduction to a pamphlet printed in York at this time shows.

> . . . so rare a gift have the illuminated fancies of the all-knowing age that old women without spectacles can discover popish plots, young men and prentices assume to regulate the rebellion in Ireland, seamen and mariners reform the House of Peers; poor men, porters and labourers spy out a malignant party and disciple them; the country clout-shoe renew the trade of the city, the cobbler patch up a religion and all these petition for a translation both of church and state, with so little fear of a halter, that they think themselves neglected if they had no thanks for their care of the republic.[71]

A petition from Bristol was finally sent to the king in January 1643 by four un-named aldermen calling for peace in what Latimer dismissed as 'absurdly bombastic language'.[72] The king was to publish this petition along with his own 'gracious answer' in the form of a propaganda tract.[73] The reasons given by the worthy citizens of Bristol for opposing the war were mainly economic rather than humanitarian or moralistic:

> Instead of the continual and gainful trade and commerce which all the maritime towns, in especially this city of Bristol, had into foreign parts; our ships lie now rotting in the harbour without any mariners or freight or trade into foreign parts, by reason of our home-bred distractions, being grown so contemptible and disprized there, that our credits are of no value. We being (through the misfortune of our nation) reputed abroad as men merely undone at home.[74]

Was Bristol adopting a policy of 'cautious neutralism'? The answer depends on how neutrality is defined and enforced. The city admitted Parliament's local commander and offered to entertain the king's representative in the same manner, but refused to admit troops, on the grounds that the king had expressly forbidden this. Bristol's interpretation of neutrality involved getting through a difficult time

without upsetting anyone; such a policy was not unique, as a letter from a
Parliamentary supporter in Dorchester shows:

> Our fears lye chiefly now at Weymouth (a considerable port town) which has in
> it nigh upon twenty demi-culverins and above forty sakers and minions. These
> townsmen are so malignant, that they will not admit any strength to be sent in
> out of the country: we offered them 150 men of the trained band near them,
> being men that were well known, and would have paid them 7s a week each
> man, but this offer was refused.[75]

The city of Bristol was divided on the issue of support for king or Parliament, a
division made all the more painful by the fact that all the protagonists knew each
other through business if not friendship. Neutrality in these circumstances was
not a positive policy decision but rather a pragmatic method of accommodating
competing loyalties within the community. The Council even attempted to
prevent supporters of the two factions wearing colours or badges that signified
their allegiance.[76] William Sanderson, writing in 1658, described these divisions:

> . . . Bristol, a town of great concernment by sea and land, and much distracted
> between both parties. The best and basest being for the king, the middle
> citizens for the other; and amongst them all, those of the religion intermixing
> distinguished (call them what you will) into two factions prelate for the king,
> presbyter for Parliament.[77]

John Ball complained of the behaviour of various Royalists, including merchants
and members of the clergy; however, he assured his friend, 'I conceive that the
major part of the city is the best part and stand firm to the Parliament.'[78]

Once the king had raised his standard at Nottingham, and especially after the
battle of Edgehill in October, neutrality could no longer be maintained. Bristol
represented a concentration of wealth and resources that could affect the outcome
of the war. Inevitably both sides came to the conclusion that if Bristol was not
with them it was against them. On the day after Edgehill, the City Council
discussed a letter received from representatives of the counties of
Gloucestershire, Somerset and Wiltshire which invited the city to join an
Association for 'the defence of the King and Kingdom against all forces sent into
the district without the consent of Parliament'.[79] The Council agreed to join but
did nothing to advance the project beyond continuing to improve the city's
defences. By the end of November its neighbours were suggesting that Bristol
should accept a garrison of troops from the Association; Bristol refused and
tempers became increasingly frayed.[80] The Council found itself under increasing
pressure from all sides to commit itself to one side or the other:

There came 3 letters to the city, one from the king, sent by Sir Baynam Throgmorton, the sum whereof was this, that the king said, he had been little beholden to them for their forwardness, to go against the Marquis at Sherborne and Mendip, but he would pass that by and that altogether he was brought to a low ebb by this war yet he had not hitherto taxed them, nor been burdensome to them, but did hope to find them loyal subjects in the conclusion. Charging them not to admit any Parliamentary forces into the city; which they observing, he said he would not trouble them with any of his forces (as he promised at Shrewsbury) but if they let any in, they would speedily hear from him. The second letter from the Parliament requiring them to admit of some forces for the securing of the city and their own safety. The third was from the Marquis of Hertford in Wales, sent by Prior his chaplain desiring them that if any garrison were to be set there he would send 1500 men. Upon these three letters the Common Council sat the most part of a day: but the answer they returned to each letter I know not.[81]

Of the prospective protectors, the most pressing was certainly the local Association which was determined that the city should be secured by parliamentary forces to ensure the safety of the whole region. Bristol's neutrality was about to end.

CHAPTER 3

Parliamentarian Bristol

The arrival of Parliamentary troops under the command of Colonel Thomas Essex marked the end of Bristol's attempt at neutrality. On 26 November, only two weeks after London had been saved from the king's forces by the stand-off at Turnham Green, a letter was read to the Commons from Edward Hungerford, a leading member of the Parliamentarian committee that had organized the resistance to Hertford in August. He claimed that three-quarters of Bristol's population favoured Parliament, but that a majority of the aldermen were Royalist sympathizers. Parliament issued instructions that a thousand local Association troops were to occupy the city immediately. While this was taking place a conference was held in Bath to try to resolve the differences, the Bristol delegates warning their neighbours that more time was needed before a garrison could be accepted.[1] Two of the Association's leaders went to Bristol to try to convince the city's council of the dangers they faced.

> There came to Bristol, that worthy and active gentleman Col. Popham and Sir John Seymer, a Stirling gentleman desiring to know of the city their resolution, whether they would admit any forces for the securing of that city being of consequence, and so near the Marquis his forces in Wales, and lying westward to Devonshire where Sir Ralph Hopton had an army; there was much agitation of the question some being for admitting the forces some against.[2]

This warning was backed by the threat of military force, as parliamentary troops were already gathering at Gloucester.[3] Bristol despatched the senior sheriff, Sheriff Jackson, Alderman Lock and Councillor James to meet Essex and, depending on which account you read, either to 'charge' or 'desire' the parliamentary commander not to advance on Bristol.[4] Jackson and Lock appear to have been Parliamentarians and James a Royalist.[5] The parliamentary commander, 'finding the malignancy of their message', arrested the messengers and marched towards Bristol.[6] The Parliamentarians issued a final demand for the admission of a garrison: 'There is news brought that unless a strength were admitted unto the city, the country would starve the city, keeping all manner of provisions by land and sea.'[7]

How did Bristol respond to the ill-treatment of its messengers and the threat of military force and blockade? Sanderson describes determined preparations to defend the city, gates being shut and manned and artillery positioned at those points where Essex's men were expected to arrive.[8] However, another account suggests that the determination of the City Council to resist was undermined by some of the city's leading women who burst in on the Council's meeting, arguing that the threat was too great and that Essex should be admitted.[9] Regardless of what had occurred in the Council Chamber, some of the king's supporters were determined to resist the occupation of the city by force of arms.

> The malignants had hopes to keep them out, and raised a mutiny and insurrection in the town, they hired some sea-men to go to Frome Gate (supposing it to be the place of entrance) and stand with their muskets and their swords drawn, and set two pieces of ordnance charged at the gate, an uproar and tumult they made, wounding one and hewing another.[10]

The Deputy-Lieutenants reported to Parliament that Essex met 'strong resistance' when he reached the city.[11] However, Essex was informed that only Frome Gate was held against him and he brought his troops in via New Gate and Pithay Gate which appear to have been opened by Parliamentarian sympathizers.[12] The Royalists found themselves outflanked and outnumbered as Essex advanced through the city streets, the captured messengers placed in front of his troops as a human shield.[13] The Royalists resistance melted away and Bristol become a Parliamentary garrison. As the Deputy-Lieutenants informed Westminster, this occurred only just in time:

> with the assistance of the good party in the city, they got entrance, which city and castle they have now secured for the king and parliament, and placing there a sufficient garrison, are gone into Somersetshire to join with the volunteers there to resist Sir Ralph Hopton in his march. The Marquis of Hertford was at Monmouth on his way to Bristol, expecting admittance thither; but understanding that Col. Essex was got in, he is again retreated into Wales.[14]

The new garrison was commanded by Col. Thomas Essex, who after Edgehill had assumed command of the regiment of Oliver St John, which remained in the west after the withdrawal of the Lord-General towards the Thames Valley and London. Essex had served as Governor of Worcester until December 1642 when he and his men were ordered to move south to Gloucester ready to move against Bristol.[15] The new governor was a colourful and controversial character, a professional soldier whose behaviour and attitudes were sometimes shocking to the civilian supporters of Parliament. His use of Bristol's messengers as a human shield indicated that his methods were rather brutal, an attitude that England was less willing to accept than other more war-accustomed countries in Europe.

On 25 January a party of about twenty troopers requested an audience with the governor to explain the problems that arrears of pay were causing. Essex came down to meet these men 'without his doublet on, having a firelock pistol in his hand'; in the ensuing discussion he shot and killed William Kendall.[16] For a soldier to demand his pay in this manner was technically an act of mutiny and thus the murder can be seen as a legitimate, if heavy-handed, example of contemporary methods of enforcing military discipline. However, this was not how it appeared to the citizens of Bristol and a serious rift opened up between the military and civilian authorities:

This view of the Pithay before it was demolished to make way for an extension to Fry's chocolate factory gives a good impression of the narrow crowded streets that formed the centre of old Bristol. When Essex was admitted at New Gate and Pithay Gate his troops moved through this street using arrested Bristol messengers as a human shield. Fighting in such narrow and easily blocked streets, dominated by overhanging houses, was to prove difficult and costly for attacking troops in the first siege. (Author's Collection)

From Bristol it was signified, that the citizens are not pleased with Colonell Essex, the governor of the city at this time for the two houses of Parliament, who having killed one of his men for demanding pay, and finding that the Citizens had sent their Coroner to take a view of the dead body and cause an inquest to pass upon him, beat them away, and not only would not suffer them to do it, but caused a proclamation to be forthwith made, which has much displeased them.[17]

To make matters worse, the Colonel's choice of friends raised questions. By 15 February it was reported to the Earl of Essex's Scoutmaster that 'the country generally cry out against Colonel Essex, and say that he will betray the towne of Bristol'.[18] Fiennes was later to justify his removal of Essex by claiming that a 'knight of good repute' had a son-in-law serving in the king's forces who had seen a letter from Essex stating that he supported the king. Fiennes also quoted William Walker who claimed that while imprisoned at Oxford he heard two Royalists discussing a promise made to Prince Rupert by Essex that he would 'never fire a shot against him and he would spend his life for him'. In addition William Aspley was said to know a groom of Prince Maurice's Chamber who had told him that the prince had received regular communications from Essex at Bristol.[19] He made serious accusations against his former commanding officer.

> I sent a letter long enough and full enough of particulars concerning Col. Essex, and which I think were sufficient to satisfy any man, that it was necessary he should be removed from hence before the town could be put in any possibility of security, although he had not been touched in the point of his fidelity: such was his excessive prodigality and profuseness in feasting, gaming and drinking whilst his soldiers were fasting and perishing for hunger; and such was his carelessness of the safety of the town, that he never went about strengthening the town by any works without, until two or three days before I came, nor to confirm it within by disarming and suppressing the malignants, but rather on the other side being himself familiar, and intimate with the chief malignants and siding with them against the good party.[20]

Essex appears to have done his best to ensure the safety of the city, which was recognized by the Royalists if not the Parliamentarians:

> This day by letters sent from Bristol, it is advertised that since the taking of Cirencester by His Majesties forces, the soldiers there are very fearful; and do not only fortify themselves continually against approaches from without, but begin to grow very jealous also of the inhabitants thereof within. For tying up whose hands, and the discovery of their hearts, there is a Protestation framed by Col Essex (the pretended governor thereof for the two houses of Parliament) to be taken by all the trained soldiers and other people of the city: though few of the inhabitants have took it hitherto. The Protestation is as followeth. *I do protest, that to the uttermost of my power, and to the hazard of my life and fortunes, I will defend the City of Bristol from and against all forces that shall or may attempt it, not having the consent of King and Parliament so to do.*[21]

However, the general distrust of Essex was so great that even Parliamentarians refused to take this oath, arguing that the wording might compel them to refuse access to parliamentary troops or even expel those already there as they did not have the king's approval.[22]

Fiennes and Essex clearly did not like each other. They may even have represented the two extremes of parliamentary support during the civil war; certainly Essex displayed a personal dislike of extreme Parliamentarians:

> even after I came to the town he imprisoned Capt. Birche (who is and always was the most active man in the town for Parliament) and swore that neither he or his men, nor any of the Bridgemen (who are known to be the honest men of the town, and who only appeared in arms for us, when Prince Rupert came before the town) should have any arms or command in the city, and this I can testify myself, for he swore it deeply in my presence: and after he swore he would commit Lieutenant Colonel White and so by degrees make approaches upon me, swearing that I should have nothing to do here, whereby I perceived, I washed a Blackmoor white, if I went about to do anything for the reclaiming of him, or the putting of the city in a posture of safety whilst he was there.[23]

Was this simply a personality clash or the resentment of a professional soldier towards a politically appointed amateur? Perhaps there was a real political division between the two senior officers at Bristol? Essex neither wrote a defence of his actions nor gave evidence at Fiennes's court martial, but a Royalist propaganda pamphlet may supply a vital clue.

> Sir John Hotham, Col. Essex with others (too many now to mention) have as amply been rewarded; the Colonel imprisoned because he was too fair a rebel, and not so vile an enemy as that bloody coward Nathaniel Fiennes.[24]

Hotham was the former Governor of Hull who was to be tried and executed for attempting to surrender the town to the king's forces. At the start of the war he had been a hero of Parliament's cause after his refusal to surrender Hull and its arsenal to the king. However, he was acting in what he saw as the best interests of the nation, 'the preserving that magazine from being processed by him [the king] would likewise prevent any possible rupture into arms'.[25] Did Essex also seek to prevent social chaos and civil war by controlling the more extreme elements within the parliamentary faction while retaining good relations with the king's supporters?

Whatever the truth of the matter, the evidence against Essex was too strong, if circumstantial, to be ignored and the military situation in the region was worsening for Parliament after Hopton's victory at Braddock Down. The hardening of attitudes, increasingly worrying to moderates on both sides, can be seen in the declaration issued by the two houses in the aftermath of this defeat.

Whereas his majesty by the advice and instigation of a wicked council about his person, hath raised forces against the Parliament, and hath actually made war against his great council and his good subjects of the kingdom, which forces raised by his majesty, for the most part are consisting of papists, notorious delinquents and other malignant persons, by whom the well affected of this kingdom are ruined in their estates & diverse outrages committed upon their persons; and for as much as Sir Ralph Hopton and his adherents, rebels and traitors combining together in pursuance of this most horrid, wicked and unnatural design, hath levied forces in the county of Cornwall and in a warlike manner already entered into the county of Devon and besieged, robbed, spoiled, plundered and pillaged diverse towns and places in the said county, and diverse rapes, murders and other misdemeanours, have acted and committed upon diverse of his majesties good subjects there, and many of them had been utterly destroyed and so as much as that now ruin and destruction is threatened not only by that hellish and accursed crew but also by the Welsh and other forces raised by his majesty.[26]

At the beginning of February Cirencester was captured by Prince Maurice and the Marquis of Hertford, marking a recovery in Royalist fortunes in the Bristol region. The city of Bristol was to be of critical importance in the emerging campaign in the south-west and along the Welsh borders. The Earl of Essex could not afford to risk treachery and dispatched Col. Nathaniel Fiennes with his regiment of horse and a company of dragoons to reinforce the garrison. Essex knew about the reinforcements, but not that Fiennes carried orders to replace the governor if he found reasonable cause. As an agent Fiennes was the ideal choice: a younger son of Lord Saye, he was a fanatical supporter of the parliamentary cause and, like his father, an adherent of the Independent rather than the Presbyterian faction.[27]

Fiennes arrived at Bristol on 14 February 1643, quickly discovering that the garrison was divided, little progress had been made in preparing the defences of the city, and the civilian population was discontented and worried by the behaviour of Essex who habitually consorted with known Royalists.[28] Although Fiennes was later to be accused of having displaced Essex to further his own ambition, in fairness – given the military situation at the time – there was certainly cause for concern.[29] On 27 February Essex was at the home of the Royalist sympathiser Captain Hall, beyond the city walls, where he was to be found 'feasting and revelling with diverse gentlemen and ladies after his accustomed manner'. Fiennes arrived at the head of a troop of horse, arrested Essex and immediately packed him off to the Lord-General's headquarters at Windsor by way of Berkeley Castle.[30] Fiennes returned to Bristol to find members of Essex's regiment furious at his treatment of their Colonel.

But it happened out well that Colonel Fiennes returned the night before to Bristol as he did; otherwise all might have been in combustion, by the insolence of an ensign in Col. Essex his regiment, which hurt a horse of Captain Long's troop to enter into the castle and there offered great affront to Lieutenant Colonel White whose company was then upon the relieving of that whereof he was ensign both by striking the said Lieutenant Colonel, As also by commanding his men to give fire on the other company: but Colonel Fiennes hearing of it hastened thither with a party of horse, and so the tumult was appeased, and the insolent ensign imprisoned.[31]

A volunteer infantryman. Several hundred citizens of Bristol served in volunteer units in defence of their city. This individual wears his ordinary civilian clothing to which military items such as a leather coat and a 'montero' cap have been added. He is equipped with a matchlock musket, a forked rest to support it while firing, a short infantry sword and a bandolier from which hang several small wooden bottles, each containing a measured charge of gunpowder. (With grateful thanks to Alan Turton)

Even before Fiennes arrived in Bristol Parliament had decided that the defence of the region needed to be more effectively organized, and on 11 February an Ordinance was passed naming Sir William Waller as General of the Western Association.[32] His commission covered the counties of Somerset, Wiltshire, Gloucester and Shropshire but not the city of Bristol. Waller brought his customary vigour to his new command, capturing Malmesbury and destroying a small Royalist field army under Lord Herbert in March before establishing garrisons at Monmouth and Chepstow to disrupt the king's recruiting. He then seized Wardour castle in April.[33] The following month Waller was operating in the west midlands, besieging Worcester, when news reached him of Hopton's success at Stratton on 16 May; this threatened Devon, Somerset and Bristol.[34] Waller moved to the Bristol area, establishing his headquarters at Bath and drawing men and supplies from Fiennes's garrison to assemble a field army to counter Hopton.[35] Although a drain, Fiennes was to admit in a letter to the Earl of Essex that a strong field army represented the best possible defence for the city of Bristol and extended his full cooperation.

Sr William Waller Major Gen: of Surry Suffex & Hampfhire

Sir William Waller, Parliament's commander in the west from early 1643. His defeat at Roundway Down allowed the Royalists to attack and capture Bristol. He resigned his military command as a result of the Self-denying Ordinance and became an outspoken critic of the army's political activities. He was later involved in Royalist plots to restore the monarchy. (With grateful thanks to Alan Turton)

How ready I have been to furnish Sir William Waller with men, arms, ammunition, money and all sorts of provision (that I may say nothing of the hundreds of his maimed soldiers that have been cast upon my care and charge).[36]

Fiennes was to claim he had supplied Waller with 1,200 infantry in addition to his regiment of horse for field operations,[37] and during his trial it was claimed he supplied Waller with sixty barrels of gunpowder.[38] A year later a pamphlet written by a supporter of the disgraced governor claimed Waller had received 2,000 infantry, 400 horse, 100 barrels of gunpowder and £8,000 in cash from Bristol.[39] Whatever the exact quantity of men and material supplied, Bristol certainly contributed heavily to Waller's army – perhaps too heavily.

As the military importance of Bristol increased, it was recognized that the city needed to be fortified, garrisoned and provisioned as a matter of the greatest urgency. Fiennes was not an experienced soldier, but rather a lawyer and politician who owed his rank and position to family and political influence rather than to any military ability. However, he was a good administrator and understood his limitations as a soldier, readily accepting the advice of more experienced officers.[40] However, his limitations were initially obscured by his enthusiasm; in April the Mayor of Bristol had fulsome praise for the governor:

Sir, having this opportunity, we heartily desire you to present to the House of Commons our thankful acknowledgement of their care of this city, in sending Colonel Fiennes to command the forces here: he is a gentleman of unwearied pains and watchfullness, not omitting anything which may conduce to our safety; our fortifications are in a good forwardness, and have cost us much money; Mr Fiennes is the sole director thereof, who in person followeth it daily, which being perfected (we hope unto God) may be the preservation of us and our neighbouring counties.[41]

The south coast ports had been refortified during the Tudor period against possible French or Spanish attack, but Bristol's fortifications still comprised medieval walls and a castle which was thoroughly outmoded by the mid-seventeenth century. A significant section of the walls had already been demolished to allow for the construction of new quays along the River Frome, while developments in artillery meant that the city was now vulnerable to bombardment from the high ground to the north and west. For a military engineer trying to design new defences for Bristol in the 1640s the city presented considerable problems. The new suburbs to the north and east of the medieval walled area had to be defended and the high ground which dominated the city had to be denied to enemy gunners; moreover, the city was built around two rivers, making the movement of troops from one sector of the defences to another difficult. Fiennes was to describe the city of Bristol, quite accurately, as the most difficult in the country to defend.

At the outbreak of hostilities the old city walls were repaired to as defensible a condition as possible. During August 1642, when the Marquis of Hertford was operating in Somerset, the Council ordered that the gates be repaired and supplied with chains and 'other necessaries' and artillery was to be mounted to defend the walls.[42] In November, as the city wrangled with its neighbours about accepting a garrison, it was ordered that a new floor should be fitted in the castle to allow cannon to be mounted and that earthworks should be constructed at various points.[43] Although Latimer claims that this was the origin of the new defensive line, these fortifications were not begun until February 1643. Ferdinando Atkins reported: 'They began 10 days since [14th February] to fortify one of three hills that command the town and make outworks without the town.'[44] This probably refers to the fort at Brandon Hill: in early March, when the Royalist plotters tried to open the city gates to Prince Rupert, his troops were fired on from that fort although the main defensive position appears to have been the medieval walls.[45] The old walls remained the primary defensive line on the southern side of the city; as Seyer noted, 'the old walls, ditches and gates were uncommonly strong'.[46] The wall was 2.45m thick, reinforced with towers along its length, and the ditch along its base was also a formidable barrier. Excavations have shown that during the early seventeenth century, the original medieval ditch had been recut to produce a barrier 7.7m wide and 3m deep with a near-vertical face next to the wall.[47] To support the line, the Church of St Mary Redcliff was converted into a fortified outwork mounting three guns.[48] The wall itself mounted twenty-five guns which would turn the ditch and the open ground beyond into a death-trap for any attacker.

Russell has suggested that an extensive defensive line was constructed beyond the walls to protect the Church of St Mary Redcliff and the suburb around it,[49] but as the medieval walls were exceptionally strong why was it necessary to construct a line in front of them? During the siege the Royalists were given specific orders to capture the Church of St Mary Redcliff, but there is no mention

St Mary Redcliff is the largest parish church in England and in the seventeenth century was just beyond the city walls. Its location and its massive construction made it an ideal outwork for the city's fortifications. Troops manning the building were able to fire into the flanks and rear of any force trying to attack the city walls from the south. Artillery was mounted on the roof of the church during the first siege. (Author's Collection)

of capturing or breaching a defensive line, which would have been the first objective of such an attack.[50] If this line had existed, the Royalist assault columns would have had half a dozen guns firing into their flank, and it is difficult to believe that this would not have been mentioned as an explanation of their failure if nothing else. Finally, as time and labour were both in short supply, why construct such defences when the southern suburbs were not extensive and were easily defended by guns positioned on the church and the walls?

The castle was to serve as the pivot of the defences, acting as headquarters, barracks, and storehouse for the city as a whole. Although de Gomme was dismissive of this fortification, other contemporary accounts suggest that the ancient building was still a formidable defensive position:

The castle was a very large stronghold, fortified with a very broad deep ditch, or graft, in part wet and dry, having a very good well in it: the castle stood upon a lofty steep mount, that was not mineable, as Lieut-Col Clifton informed me,

This early nineteenth-century print shows the old city walls and the River Frome which formed the inner defensive line on the northern side of the city. (Reproduced by kind permission of Bristol Central Library)

Bristol Castle. Begun in the twelfth century, this huge fortification occupied a narrow sandstone ridge between the rivers Frome and Avon, and it dominated the city. Although out-moded as a defensive work and poorly maintained the castle was pressed into service and equipped with artillery during the civil war. Although de Gomme dismissed it as a 'Large old castle; but weak still; notwithstanding the enemyes had something repayrd & fortified it', others, notably the Parliamentarian Maj. Wood, argued that its sheer bulk made it a strong defensive position. After the war the castle was demolished by the city council and new streets laid out on the site. (Author's Collection)

for he said the mount whereupon the castle stood was of an earthy substance for a certain depth, but below that strong rock, and that he had searched purposefully with an augur and found it so in all parts; the foot of the castle upon a mount or rampart was fortified with a gallant parapet well flanking, which with its well scarping must needs strengthen it from battering, the parapet at the base being as I would guess twelve feet thick, the walls of the castle were very high, well repaired, stored with strong flanking towers and galleries on the top, and if a little earth lined, I am sure had been past the power of cannon to batter.[51]

Although this description was certainly an exaggeration aimed at discrediting Fiennes, the castle *was* a considerable obstacle to any attack from the east, as there were six heavy guns mounted in the keep and another fourteen guns around the curtain walls.[52]

The most significant development was the line of earthworks to the north and east of the city, constructed at huge cost in both money and labour. Fiennes was to claim that this line was too extensive to be held although it seems he was the 'soul director' of their construction.[53] The accounts of Latimer and Seyer present these forts and lines as a formidable defensive system bristling with artillery.[54] However, descriptions by a Royalist engineer and an Ordnance officer not used by these two authors present a far more accurate picture of the defences built by Fiennes between February and July 1643.[55] The basic line stretched for almost 3 miles, running from Lime Kiln Dock in the west, along the high ground to the north of the city, turning south through Stokes Croft and Lawfords Gate and meeting the River Avon opposite Tower Harritz. It was completely excavated by hand, a considerable achievement in the time available. De Gomme described it:

> It's high, commonly, about a yard & halfe or 6 feete where highest. The thickness on the top, above a yard, usuallye. The Graff or ditch, commonly 2 yards broade, but somewhere a foote or twoe more. The depth scarcely considerable; as being hardly 5 foote, usually; & in many rockye places not so deepe.[56]

Although de Gomme could not resist an element of self-praise by remarking that the line was 'of mean strength & not comparable with those of Oxford', such an earthwork would nevertheless have presented a considerable obstacle to assaulting infantry. A soldier at the bottom of the ditch would have faced an earth embankment between 9 and 10 feet high!

Supporting this line were a series of forts mounting artillery, the strength of which has frequently been overstated; for example, Latimer described the fort at Priors Hill as mounting thirteen guns.[57] The reports of the two Royalist officers after the siege indicate a square fort, each side of which was 24 paces long, equipped with three medium guns and one light cannon.[58] Seyer presents the fort at Brandon Hill, the highest point on the line, as being 45 yards long and 30 wide, and armed with six cannon.[59] However, Royalists found a fort 'some 18 foot square, and as many high; its graff or mote but shallow and narrow, by reason of the rockiness of the ground'; this tiny enclosure contained four guns.[60] These forts were tiny, their main function being to provide secure artillery positions to support the infantry holding the line. They can be compared with the 'pill box' of later conflicts, strongpoints housing heavy weapons to support infantry in the trenches.

The building of this line represented a vast investment of money and labour but Fiennes and his engineers simply ran out of time. When the king's forces arrived in July the line had not been completed, as Fiennes himself admitted to Parliament.[61] Although Fiennes's account is highly inaccurate, and he would understandably have said almost anything to justify his surrender, de Gomme's description of the defences suggests that there was still considerable work to be done: 'These forts be all pallisadoed, but have no fauxbrays or fore-defences: nor on some sides, not so much as a barm, corridor or footbank.'[62] The fortifications of Bristol were well designed and constructed with great speed; they were far from complete but, as events would show, they were remarkably efficient. The cost of these works was astronomic. Fiennes reported to his father in mid-June that the cost of the garrison and the defences was 'sometimes at £1,300 sometimes at £1,200: seldom less than £1,000 a week.[63] In his report to the Lord-General after the loss of the city he stated that he had received only £4,000 from Parliament in a period of four or five months.[64] Clearly the bulk of the cost of both garrison and fortifications fell upon the city of Bristol; before the arrival of the parliamentary garrison the preparations for the defence of the city, being paid for by the Council, were recorded in detail in the mayor's Audit Books. These show work on the walls as well as considerable expenditure on weapons and ammunition prior to the outbreak of hostilities. On the day of his arrival Colonel Essex requested £1,000 in cash to meet the immediate needs of his troops; this was to be repaid by a bill of exchange in London.[65] Over the next two months Essex was to extract a further £2,400 'to furnish the present needs of the king and kingdom' while another £2,000 was lent to Gloucestershire and Somerset to further the Association's activities.[66] In the first week of March Fiennes received £1,000 in three payments from the city and a further £600 was sent to the Earl of Stamford. The following week £500 was paid to soldiers of Colonel Essex's regiment by the order of Sir William Waller to enable this unit to join his field army in operations in Gloucestershire and along the Welsh borders.[67] As a result of such payments the council's expenditure during the mayoral term of Richard Aldworth was £16,380 3s 11d while the average for the other nine mayors in the 1640s was £3,650.[68]

Prosperous as Bristol was it could not afford this scale of expenditure for long, and a more systematic method of collecting money had to be found. On 14 February 1643 Parliament passed an Ordinance to establish a system of local assessments. Each town or county was to have a committee who would be responsible for collecting money and passing it to the appropriate military authorities. In Bristol this committee consisted of Mayor Richard Aldworth, the Sheriffs Joseph Jackson and Hugh Brown, Alderman Richard Hallworthy and two common councillors, Luke Hodges and Henry Gibbs. This body was to raise an assessment of £55 15s a week by rates on households, and although they were all members of the City Council they were not answerable to that body.[69] A month later the committee's powers were extended and they were permitted to tax as obvious malignants those individuals who had refused to contribute to Parliament.[70]

By the use of local rates and sequestration of Royalist property this committee tried to meet Fiennes's demands for money. However, too much was required in too short a time and as the exactions increased, the council was obliged to warn citizens that their liability to payments for the garrison and defences did not cease if they moved outside the city boundaries.[71] Some assistance was received from the surrounding counties but, as Fiennes complained to the Earl of Essex in April, this stopped after Waller's arrival.

> I am utterly discouraged in the employment I have here, because I do not see a way of subsistance for the forces that are here, for I doubt I can expect little money from London, and all the ways whereby I got some heretofore out of Gloucestershire and Somersetshire, will be stopped up and diverted towards the maintenance of Sir William Waller's army, and I shall be left to feed upon the bare stones.[72]

Fiennes wrote to the Lord-General, his father and others in authority pleading for additional funds. However, his considerable success in building defences and stockpiling food and munitions was based mainly on money wrung from the city and on credit from the citizens.

When Essex occupied Bristol, the garrison consisted of his regiment and troop of horse reinforced by local units under the command of Hungerford and Popham.[73] In mid-February the garrison was joined by the six troops of horse under Nathaniel Fiennes and a company of twenty-five dragoons under Captain Mason.[74] A report to Luke suggests that before the arrival of these reinforcements there were 1,700 infantry in the garrison and three troops of horse.[75] On his arrival in the city Langrish noted that there were auxiliary units supporting the garrison in the form of a company of pro-parliamentary volunteers under Captain Birch and 500 men of the city's trained bands.[76] During the Royalist plot the garrison consisted of Fiennes's horse and the infantry regiments of Essex, Hungerford and Popham. The quality of these troops was very mixed:

> one regiment vis Col. Essex's something distempered by their Colonels removal especially the officers, although that did very good service with great diligence; and the other regiments being raw soldiers and hardly having one soldier for an officer amongst them all.[77]

Shortly after this Waller again requested that Essex's regiment join him along with most of the cavalry from Bristol.[78] At this time Fiennes raised a new infantry unit under his own command and another under his brother John, which was in the process of formation at the time of the siege.[79] Waller called half of Fiennes's infantry and six companies of Popham's out of the garrison, and these were probably the reinforcements from Bristol that Clarendon mentions after Lansdown.[80] Fiennes later claimed that these detachments left him with only 700

This cavalry officer is a particularly well-armed and well-equipped mounted soldier. He wears a thick buff leather coat with deep skirts over which is worn a pistol-proofed back- and breast-plate. During combat he wore a helmet of the type known as a 'lobster pot', but at other times this would have been replaced by a more comfortable felt hat. He wears heavy leather thigh boots to which are attached spurs with large star-shaped rowels. His weapons consist of a heavy straight-bladed broadsword, a pair of pistols carried in saddle holsters and a carbine slung from a shoulder belt. Such a complete outfit of arms and armour would have been uncommon during the civil war. (With grateful thanks to Alan Turton)

men in the city but Waller had reassured him that only a small guard was required in Bristol as the field army was operating in the immediate area.[81]

In the aftermath of Roundway the shattered remnants of Waller's army assembled at Bristol; of his 2,500 infantry and 2,000 cavalry, the Royalists claimed to have killed 600 and captured 800.[82] When he left the region Waller took with him between 500 and 600 cavalry but left 300 cavalry and some 300 to 400 infantry to reinforce the

Bristol garrison, the remainder of his forces having 'disbanded' themselves after the battle.[83] Fiennes quickly reinforced his garrison: 'I procured about one thousand or eleven hundred arms, and raised as many men in five days space.'[84] Exactly how many men he had commanded in the siege was to be hotly contested at his trial but even by his own figures his claim to have had only 1,500 infantry and 300 horse appears unlikely. In addition to the 700 men left in the garrison by Waller there were 1,100 newly armed troops which Fiennes claimed included 300 to 400 of Waller's men.[85] In addition there were the city volunteers and various small parties such as the garrison of Malmesbury which had made their way to Bristol before the siege.[86] He had at least 2,000 infantry, perhaps as many as 2,500, assembled in Bristol by the time Rupert arrived; they may have been poorly trained but they were substantially more numerous than Fiennes admitted to Parliament.[87]

Although Fiennes was able to raise troops in the city and the surrounding areas, they were helpless without weapons. How well armed were the defenders of Bristol in July 1643? The defences were designed around the use of artillery and infantry firearms. Was there a shortage of such weapons? Fiennes was accused of surrendering more than sixty pieces of artillery at his trial,[88] although both de Gomme and Fawcett agreed that there were more than ninety-eight guns in the city.[89] Bristol's defences represented an impressive concentration of heavy weapons in this period. Sprigg's *Anglia Rediviva* lists forty Royalist garrisons that surrendered to the New Model Army in the closing stages of the war (April 1645– August 1646), only ten of which contained more than twenty guns.[90] Artillery was a scarce and expensive commodity, and whereas no gentleman would feel dressed without a sword, or traveller safe without a brace of pistols, private individuals as a rule did not own artillery. There were exceptions, such as Lords Paulet, Mahun or Strange who owned a few light guns, but the very noteworthiness of this fact merely illustrates the rarity. There was one major exception to this rule: in this era of periodic conflict with France or Spain and endemic piracy, merchant vessels were armed for their own protection. In March 1629 a report covering forty-eight Bristol ships showed that forty-five of them were armed with a total of almost 500 guns.[91] Such a stock of artillery was a valuable military resource which the city and later the parliamentary authorities sought to exploit, ordering that guns and ammunition from the ships be landed in the city.[92] In addition Waller sent eleven guns taken from a ship he found in the harbour at Chepstow.[93] These would not have been beautifully cast bronze or brass weapons, but rather crude, functional iron guns, mainly of light calibre. To supplement this source Fiennes was able to 'borrow' brass guns from naval vessels in the area and a local blacksmith manufactured a number of 'hammered' guns.[94] There was certainly no shortage of artillery in the Bristol area: when the Royalists captured ten vessels in the Hungerode early in the siege they contained a hundred guns, and in addition there were other armed ships within the city.

Infantry firearms came from a number of sources and once again there appears to have been no shortage among the defenders of Bristol, in contrast to the attackers who lacked such weapons. The various parliamentary units transferred to the city to form the garrison were already armed, although it is possible that a degree of re-equipping was required. Before the war the city maintained a 'common store' of arms and armour for the use of citizens and this had been considerably expanded during the period of 'neutrality'.[95] In May 1642 Francis Ridges and William Jones received an order for thirty-seven muskets for the store at 17s each; the price was soon pushed up to 18s. By the end of November, 288 new firearms had been added to the city's stocks and older weapons had been repaired and cleaned.[96] Purchases continued after the arrival of the parliamentary garrison, with armour and swords being brought from London in addition to locally produced muskets and bandoliers.[97] Fiennes claimed that the trained bands were politically unreliable but that he used their arms to equip more selectively recruited units.[98]

The trained bands were not entirely armed from the common store; much of their equipment was supplied by the personal armouries of private citizens. On his death in 1639 it was noted that Richard Pley's goods included 'two corselets, a pike, muskets and two swords'.[99] Ten years earlier 'in the room at the head of the stairs', John Whitson had:[100]

Item five old corslets and a corslet for a horse and two new corslets.   iiiiL

Item three morrice pikes with heads and six staves all at   xiiis. iiiid.

Item two halberds, two partisans, two bills, a poleaxe, a bill, a leading staff, a rest, two darts, a walking staff, two swords, two daggers, a pistol, a flask, a touch box, two cross bows, a gath and racke   iiiL

Item one musket, six calviers   iiiL

Although not all Bristolians would have owned arms, an appeal for weapons among the loyal supporters of Parliament and the determined 'disarming' of the king's supporters which began in February 1643[101] would have produced a substantial quantity of arms and military equipment. There was no shortage of infantry weapons even in the crisis following the destruction of Waller's army at Roundway Down, as Fiennes himself admitted:

I was encouraged to try what strength of foot I could add to these I had already, and resolved to make use of the arms of the trained bands of the city, which I did, and by that means, and by ready money I procured about one thousand or eleven hundred arms.[102]

For artillery and infantry firearms to be effective supplies of gunpowder had to be adequate. Did Bristol's garrison suffer from a shortage of ammunition? To fill a musketeer's bandolier, containing twelve rounds, required ½lb of gunpowder; an English barrel of gunpowder contained 100lb or 2,400 rounds of small arms ammunition.[102] During the 'neutral' period this critical commodity was stockpiled and as early as August 1642 the city had at least fifty-one barrels.[104] The supplies acquired by the city before Essex's arrival came from London or from Randal Tombs, who had survived royal persecution and supplied forty-five barrels of powder by March 1643.[105] Clement Walker, who was an active parliamentary leader in the Bristol region at this time, claimed that when Fiennes assumed command at Bristol he had found a stock of forty-five barrels of powder in the magazines.

After Fiennes became governor the same basic pattern of supply continued. Walker was to claim that production in the city amounted to six or seven barrels a week; Fiennes did not deny that powder was being manufactured but said that production was only half that rate.[106] Bristol also received supplies of ammunition from London, and Walker suggested that thirty barrels had come from this source before the siege.[107] However, the main increase in the city's

A dragoon. Technically a mounted infantry man, the dragoon always thought himself a cut above the ordinary infantry soldier and indeed received higher pay. This individual is dressed in a 'soldier's coat' and civilian breeches. He wears shoes topped with buttoned riding leggings which are more suitable for fighting on foot than heavy cavalry boots. He is armed with a light fowling piece and an infantry sword. His ammunition is carried in a bandolier which in this instance has a leather cover to keep the powder dry in wet conditions. The dragoon's mounts varied in quality but were generally smaller and less costly than cavalry animals. (With grateful thanks to Alan Turton)

ammunition stocks consisted of 126 barrels imported from France, where a 'barrel' contained twice as much gunpowder as it did in England.[108] Fiennes was to admit having surrendered fifty barrels of gunpowder at Bristol, but at his trial the prosecution pointed out that his figures simply did not add up:

by his own printed relation there must have been at least 90 barrels left, for he therein confesseth (a) that he found 45 of powder in the town when he first entered upon the charge thereof: after which he received 30 barrels more from London,

126 barrels from France besides six or seven barrels weekly made in the city, all the powder taken out of shops, ships and the nine barrels from Malmesbury: all which (admit the barrels out of France single) amount to 210 barrels but to 336 barrels, if those from France were double, as they were: Of these he saith, Sir William Waller had 60 barrels, and that he spent 60 more in the siege: deduct 120 out of 210 there are left 90 barrels at least by his own confession, allowing him all that was made or found in the city and ships merely for waste and measure.[109]

Regardless of exactly how much powder Fiennes surrendered, there was clearly no shortage of gunpowder in Bristol in July 1643.

Bristol faced considerable problems during the spring and early summer of 1643, but did the parliamentary commanders in the region regard the city as seriously threatened? Waller certainly saw the city as secure enough during his operations in the region to send his Royalist prisoners there for safe-keeping.[110] However, the safety of the city was directly linked to the success of Sir William Waller and the field army under his command. The destruction of this force at Roundway Down on 13 July 1643 was to have serious consequences for the city, leaving it exposed to attack. As a naval commissary officer in the city wrote to a ship's captain the day after Waller's defeat: 'the troubles here are very high'.[111]

CHAPTER 4
The Royalist Plot

The occupation of the city was not welcomed by all Bristolians. Indeed, the resistance to Essex shows that some people were violently opposed to the city coming under the control of Parliament. There subsequently developed a Royalist resistance movement determined to deliver the city to the king's forces. The central figure was Robert Yoemans, a merchant who had served as a sheriff in 1641–2. Seyer suggests that he was commissioned by the king to raise a regiment of infantry in Bristol before Essex's arrival;[1] certainly one witness against Yoemans reported that he had been offered a commission as a captain at this time.[2] Yoemans claimed that his commission had been brought to Bristol at an early date but he did nothing with it for some time.[3] It was not, for example, until mid-March 1643 that he asked George Teague to become a captain in his regiment, although he had sent Walter Cowley to Oxford to invite Rupert to come to the city 'within three or four days after Col. Fiennes came to Bristol'.[4]

The appointment of Fiennes as governor, combined with disaffection among officers of Essex's regiment, finally encouraged Bristol's Royalists to begin plotting. The Royalist account naturally presents the conspirators as acting from loyalty to the crown and resentment against behaviour and extractions of Fiennes.[5] Certainly Fiennes was more active than his predecessor in harassing and disarming Royalists and enforcing oaths of loyalty on the city.[6] The behaviour of the city's Parliamentarians towards their Royalist neighbours was also provocative:

> The perpetual scorn and obloquie to which they [the Royalists] were exposed, reproached every day as they passed in the streets, with the names of Malignants and Papists; nay, as if they had been worse than Jews, they spit at them, and threatened to take a speedy course with them.[7]

The Bristol Royalists established contact with the Oxford authorities and the Royalist newssheet *Mercurius Aulicus* received regular reports of events in Bristol:

> But there's another thing which does more displease them [the citizens of Bristol] than the rough carriage of their pretended governor; which is, that those parts of Wales, which buy the most part of their commodities in that city,

Governor Nathaniel Fiennes, the parliamentary commander at Bristol during the first siege. Although a good administrator, he was an inexperienced soldier and proved weak and indecisive in combat. He was court-martialled for surrendering Bristol and sentenced to death, but was pardoned by the Earl of Essex. Cromwell was finally to exonerate him from any blame for the loss of the city and he was appointed to the Council of State in 1656. (By kind permission of Lord Saye and Sele)

and owe great sums of money to the merchants there, have published and declared, that none of them will be responsible for any debts which they owe in Bristol, unless the city do return to the king's obedience: a matter which concerns them much in case of profit, which in many times works more in some sorts of men, than a case of conscience.[8]

A propaganda coup arranged by the king's supporters in Bristol was a petition from four un-named aldermen which was sent to Oxford in January 1643 calling for peace.[9] However, information from Bristol went beyond propaganda, and the Royalists, it was claimed, enjoyed the benefit of 'a daily account' of conditions in Bristol.[10] The Bristol conspirators received detailed instructions from Rupert and other Royalist leaders and a number of agents visited the city to discuss the details of the plans and check on progress.[11]

> He [Robert Yoemans] saith that about a fortnight or three weeks before Prince Rupert came to this town Doctor Marks, came hither from Oxford and told this examinate that the king gave thanks to all his loyal subjects that were of his party in this city and wished them to keep themselves private, until he had occasion to send his forces to this city, and then they should have timely notice thereof.[12]

Who became involved in the plot? Seyer lists about one hundred individuals whose names appear in various contemporary pamphlets and proclamations.[13] These were most likely the 'big fish' who owned sufficient property to make it worth including them in the confiscation order of 28 March;[14] others escaped detection or were simply not considered worth naming. One description of the plotters by 'a most reverend Minister' said they consisted for 'the most part of sailors, butchers and hauliers and such like'.[15] Another described those assembled at Yoemans' house as being 'some merchants like himself, others seamen and all rogues' and stated that they were to be supported by 'a regiment of butchers and mechanics'.[16] John Tombes in his sermon of 14 March described the leaders of the plot as 'a malignant and treacherous party within this city' and their followers as sailors and hauliers.[17]

One notable feature was the frequent mention of seamen and ships' captains among the king's supporters in Bristol; for example, when the Royalists had tried to prevent Colonel Essex from entering the city, seamen with 'their muskets and swords drawn' were conspicuous.[18] In February one of his agents informed the Lord-General's Scoutmaster of 'all the seamen and watermen being wholly averse to the Parliaments proceedings' in Bristol.[19] Parliamentary accounts explain that Rupert brought no artillery with him as this was to be supplied by the conspirators.[20]

> Our grand Malignants to God and the country had combined with the forces aforesaid to draw near the city and had promised to assist them, with 16 pieces

of ordnance or more if occasion should serve, the guns were to be brought by 500 seamen from our Pill, where the ships lay and these men were to join with them for our confusion.[21]

According to Parliamentary accounts, seamen under Captain Boone were to set fire to the city in a number of places to spread confusion, while Captain Cole was to construct a bridge of boats across the River Frome.[22] The first Royalist account, published within a week of these events, also suggests that seamen were heavily involved:

> This day came news that Mr Nathaniell Fynes Commander of the forces of the two Houses of Parliament in the city of Bristol, had exercised a great deal of cruelty to many of the Principle Citizens and Merchants there, whom he suspected to hold any intelligence with His Majesty, or have any hand in practising to yield the town to the right owner. Which has so exasperated the mariners and seamen there (being men of courage and fidelity, and of as great experience in sea-fights as any subjects of this kingdom) that they have seized on 16 stout and lusty ships which had wintered there, furnished as with all things necessary, so with no fewer than 130 good pieces of ordnance; which they intended to keep for his majesties service.[23]

Another group in the conspiracy were a number of officers from Essex's former regiment who were resentful at the treatment of their former colonel and who, it was claimed, 'loathed and condemned themselves in their own employment'.[24] Indeed it appears to have been these men who finally convinced Yeomans to begin plotting:

> being in company with some of the commanders of Col. Essex forces, many of them declared themselves to be for the king, and that whensoever any of the king's forces came, they would deliver them the town; and the rather, for that they perceived that there were a great many of the town that would take their parts, by whose help they doubted not but easily to do it; Those that so declared themselves to me were Captain Hilsdon, Lieutenant Marshall, that commanded the Sergeant-Major's company; Lieutenant Cheyney, that commanded the Lieutenant-Col.'s company; and Lieutenant Moore, that commanded the company of a Captain that was in London.[25]

It has been suggested that these officers may have been acting as *agents provocateurs*;[26] however, reports mention the disloyal behaviour of Essex's officers while admitting the regiment 'did very good service'.[27] Recent research tends to support the view that some officers were passing on information about the plot; certainly Captain Hilserson (Hilsdon) not only survived the plot but was promoted to major of the regiment shortly afterwards.[28] However, a number of officers were sent under escort to Berkeley Castle to be imprisoned, and the lieutenant-colonel, the major and a captain all left the regiment at this time, although it is not clear if they were among those arrested. All later reappear in parliamentary service.[29] Was Fiennes simply using the plot as an excuse to purge the regiment of officers who disapproved of his treatment of their former commander?

The objective of the plot was to capture the city gates and secure access for Rupert's forces from Oxford. On Tuesday 7 March 1643 Rupert arrived on Durdham Down to the north of the city with a force described variously as 1,000 horse; 4,000 horse and foot; 4,000 horse and 2,000 foot; or 'A great party of horse and dragoons with some foot'.[30] In the town two of the renegades, Captain Hilsdon and Lieutenant Moore, were on duty at the guardhouse in Wine Street. At midnight Hilsdon was to leave to inspect the sentries with soldiers who were also involved in the plot, on arrival at Frome Gate they were to overpower the guards. Once the

The Illustrious & High-borne Prince Rupert, Count Palatine of yͤ Rhene & Knight of the most noble Order of the Garter, & Generall of the Horse to his Maiᵗⁱᵉ King Charles. Æ 1643.

The king's nephew Prince Rupert was perhaps his most capable and successful military commander. Although frustrated at Bristol by the discovery of the plot, he was appointed governor, at his own request, after the capture of the city. He spent little time there as his abilities were required elsewhere but he was responsible for Bristol's defence during the second siege. His surrender on this occasion resulted in his disgrace and the loss of the king's favour and support. (Reproduced by kind permission of Bristol Central Library)

gate was secured a large party of armed men would join Hilsdon under Mr Boucher, whose house in Christmas Street was an assembly point, and Mr Millard, who had collected a smaller group at his house in St Michael's. Simultaneously another group would capture the guard-house in Wine Street, having assembled in Yeomans' house which stood opposite. Once the gate and guard-house were secured the bells of St Michael's and St John's Churches were to be rung to inform Rupert that the city was now open.[31]

In order that the Prince's troops and those involved in the conspiracy should be able to recognize each other an elaborate system of field signs was adopted:

The better to distinguish themselves from those that were destined to destruction, those that were of their party had a word which was (Charles) and certain marks of white tape tied upon their breasts before and their hats behind and such as were to be spared within doors had certain marks set upon the inside of their doors.[32]

Once they had secured access to the city a proclamation prepared by the conspirators was to be read:

All inhabitants of Bridge – High Street and Corn Street keep within your doors upon pain of your lives, all other inhabitants of this city, that stand for the king, the Protestant religion and the liberty of the city let them forthwith appear at the High Cross with such armour as they have for the defence of their wives and children; and follow their leaders in the same defence for the same defence.[33]

Seyer claims that Rupert brought with him another proclamation printed in Oxford which promised pardon to all in Bristol, excluding Nathaniel Fiennes.[34] This was not to be the fate of the city according to parliamentary writers:

If we may believe the speeches of an officer amongst the enemy's forces one of them was heard to say that Prince Rupert had commanded to give no quarter to man, woman or child: that had not their marks upon their persons or houses.[35]

Despite all the careful planning, at 10 o'clock, as the conspirators assembled and collected their arms, Hilsdon and Moore sent word across the street to Yoemans that the plan had been discovered and telling him to disperse his men. Before he could, Captain Buck arrived with twenty musketeers supported by cavalry under Hercules Langrish.[36] Yoemans claimed he was alone in the house and that it was too late to open the door; when he was finally forced to open it, the searchers found twenty-three men in the house, several of whom put up a spirited resistance before submitting.[37] Although Seyer accuses Buck of brutality on other occasions, none of the conspirators was harmed but rather treated 'justly and kindly as prisoners'.

Langrish recorded that one of the prisoners taken with Yoemans tried to win favour with him by revealing the location of the party at Boucher's house. After delivering the prisoners to the castle he went there, but found Captain Goodier's soldiers already engaged in battering down the door.[38] What had happened? The captain who commanded the troops at Frome Gate ordered the inhabitants of Christmas Street to hang out lanterns to prevent Rupert's troops approaching under cover of darkness, but his men could get no answer at Boucher's house. Enquiries established that a number of men had entered the house and had not been seen leaving, and so the captain ordered his men to smash down the door.[39]

A watercolour sketch of the interior of George Boucher's house in Christmas Street shortly before it was demolished in 1821. In the notes with the picture the house was described as follows: 'The house was situated up a passage, on the west side of the street, nearly opposite to St John's Bridge, and consisted of a complete quadrangle.' It was here that large numbers of Royalist plotters were arrested in March 1643 during the attempt to surrender the city to Prince Rupert. (Reproduced by kind permission of Bristol Central Library)

The house contained sixty men and large quantities of arms and ammunition, although many of the conspirators were able to escape through the back door while the soldiers were battering their way in at the front.[40]

> They found about three score ready with their arms, of whom they apprehended 23 and the rest ran out at the water gate, on the backside of the house and went away through the water, it being low tide, and made an escape, and searching afterwards they found great store of arms, muskets ready charged some with seven and others with 10 bullets apiece with their pans primed with brimstone and powder mingled together that they would not misfire; their

linkes ready by them, their powder papered out, and all things ready for the design, which should have been put in execution within an hour after this time of their apprehension.[41]

Rupert was soon informed of these developments and recognized that he could not attack the city with the force he had. At daybreak his men came under artillery fire from the fort on Brandon Hill and as his position was clearly untenable he ordered his troops to withdraw. The whole operation proved profoundly embarrassing for the young Royalist general.

> I am informed Prince Rupert went away weeping. For certain he was so incensed against the parties that promised assistance and failed him, that he would speedily return with ordnance and would be revenged upon altogether. He is retreated to Cirencester: I pray God convert him (but not turn him).[42]

How had Fiennes discovered the plot? Seyer offers a number of explanations, notably that Clement Walker claimed that he had been told of the plot by one Dobbins.[43] He also mentions that Barret said it had been discovered by 'tattling females' of parliamentary sympathy but this could well have been simple tradition.[44] In his *Military Memoir* of John Birch, Roe offers a quite different account of these events:

> I cannot omit God's great goodness to you at Bristol, when Prince Rupert came before it, having with him 75,000 men, Anno 1642, he having assurance from Mr Yoemans, Mr Bowcher, and others in that city, that it would be delivered to him the guards surprised, with diverse principle persons; and I suppose you will never forget the message delivered to you on the bridge of that city that night about eight of the clock : that before the next morning you would be a dead man; and that instead of fear and flying as diverse others, whose presence was very necessary, and profession should have taught them otherwise, you addressed yourself presently to find out where those parties were gathered together, who within a few hours were to act upon that treachery; which endeavour the Lord was pleased to see to order, that before eleven a'clock, you had about one hundred chief men in your custody.[45]

Although contemporaries claim that the plot was only discovered at the last moment, it is likely that Fiennes knew of its existence and allowed the plot to run its course, thereby allowing as many Royalists as possible to implicate themselves. Too many people knew about the plot for it to remain a secret in seventeenth-century Bristol – security was not helped by the indiscreet nature of the leaders and their habit of holding meetings in a tavern.[46] The surprising thing is not that the plot was discovered but that the Royalists seriously thought it would not be; they also probably over-estimated the degree of popular support they enjoyed in the city of Bristol.

On 14 March a day of public thanksgiving was declared in Bristol, and two sermons were preached by John Tombes, a man whose recent personal experiences ensured that he shared the citizens' joy at their delivery.

Having by God's providence been driven hither for shelter against the unreasonable and impetuous violence of superstitious people enraged by the instigations of bloody minded papists, corrupt priests and loose libertines.[47]

Having given his audience a brief outline of the plot he then described the repulse of Rupert's troops.

Having shown themselves upon the Down the next morning after two or three shot of cannons made against them from our work upon Brandon Hill, they wheeled off, and so God put a hook into their nostrils, and turned them back again; for which great mercy of his in delivering us from a dangerous invasion of the enemy without, and a damnable conspiracy of some treacherous inhabitants within the city; both this town and the whole kingdom (so far as it is concerned in the preservation of this city) has great cause to give thanks unto almighty God, unto whom alone the glory thereof is due.[48]

As if this were not sufficient, one signing himself T.P. wrote a poem with almost McGonagall-like qualities:

> O thou who durst excel the highest praise;
> Though wonder-worker, life and length of days,
> Thou never-failer in the mount to thine,
> Only wise, present, in each place and time
> What brazen column, or what marble stone,
> Shall we engrave the noble feats upon?
> This act, thy strange act counterplotting those
> Blood-thirsty (Foreign and Domestic) foes?[49]

However, Fiennes and his supporters felt that the crisis had not passed, as Royalist newsheets reported:

There is conceived so deep a rancour, that it was moved by Master Martyn, that letters should be written to the Earl of Essex, for a commission of Martial Law to be issued out to Master Fines, for the quick dispatch of such malefactors.[50]

Two days later the Royalist pamphleteers were reporting the ill-treatment of Royalist sympathizers in Bristol and claiming that martial law would allow the confiscation of Royalist estates simply on the governor's orders.[51] By the end of the month there was disturbing news from London:

> It was signified by letters bearing date from London, March 26, that at last the Lords have yielded unto the proposition of the House of Commons, and passed an ordinance for enabling the Earl of Essex to grant commissions of Martiall law for the dispatch and execution of those loyal citizens of Bristol.[52]

The trials began in Bristol in May, although questioning of the prisoners and the collection of evidence predated them.[53] Fiennes had received a commission appointing him president and instructing him to use all severity and expedition in dealing with the conspirators.[54] The Council of War trying the prisoners was composed of sixteen officers drawn from the garrison.[55] In the role of prosecutor was Clement Walker, a trained lawyer, and also a garrison officer.[56] The prisoners could expect little mercy from their captors who argued:

> who could not be so ignorant, as to promise themselves any hope of entrance by sudden assault, but by surprise and treachery, confidently presuming on the malignant party within, that first invited them hither, a design more damnable than the powder treason and more barbarous and cruel than the massacres in France, being destroyers of their own liberties, and the supplanters and overthrowers of the same religion that they themselves pretend to profess.[57]

The case against Robert Yoemans was easily proven and the court quickly found him guilty and sentenced him to hang. George Boucher, William Yoemans and Edward Dacres also received death sentences. On 22 May it was reported in Royalist newssheets that the mayor and aldermen of Bristol had written to Parliament asking clemency for the condemned conspirators, but noted that extreme Parliamentarians in the city argued for execution.[58]

The authorities at Oxford were not ignoring events in Bristol. Patrick Leven, Lord-General of the king's forces, wrote to Fiennes on 16 May. The letter stated that if the Bristol authorities executed individuals 'for expressing their loyalty to his Majesty' then he would 'put Master George, Master Stevens, Captain Huntley and others taken in rebellion against his majesty at Cirencester, into the same condition'.[59] Fiennes's reply, dated the 18th, left little room for misunderstanding: Yoemans and his companions had not been taken in open war but in conspiracy and therefore had no right to treatment as captured soldiers:

> if by any inhumane, and unsoldier-like sentence you shall proceed to the

execution of the persons by you named, or any other of our friends in your custody, that have been taken in a faire and open way of war; Sir Walter Pye, Sir William Crofts, Colonel Connesby and diverse others taken in open rebellion and actual war against the king and kingdom, whom we have here in custody, must expect no favour or mercy. And by God's blessing upon our just cause, we have pawns enough for our friends security.[60]

Finally the king wrote directly to the Mayor and Council of Bristol ordering them to prevent the executions, and if necessary to 'kill and slay all such who shall attempt or endeavour to take away the lives of our said subjects'. The king warned the mayor, 'you may not fail at your utmost peril'.[61]

Even if the Council had wished to obey the king's orders they arrived too late. On 30 May Robert Yoemans and George Boucher were brought out of the castle and hanged in Wine Street.[62] There is a highly partisan description of these events, written shortly afterwards, which described the sufferings of the 'martyrs' to the king's cause:[63]

After sentence of death passed upon them, they pursue them with threats, and use no language to them but death and hanging, often menacing what they could but once inflict: so that each night they thought to die next morning: having some days languished under the insulting cruelty of these bloody butchers, and being frequently robbed of their necessary food by the sentinels (that stood at their prisons, not so much that they might not withdraw themselves from their intended death, as to intercept all comforts that were brought unto them) had they not hastened the execution, famine would have saved them that labour.[64]

Fiennes refused them access to clergy of their choice and sent 'Cradock and Fowler, two emissaries sent to that city, to poison it with schism and rebellion'.[65] Two officers were said to have abused the prisoners even as they addressed the crowd that had assembled to watch the execution.

Sergeant-Major Langridge and Clifton called upon the executioners to hasten the work: nay they did not stick to interrupt Master Yoemans in his discourse, and to goad him on the sides and thighs with their halberds, bidding him to contract and make an end.[66]

It is difficult to judge the accuracy of this account, but it is likely that the prisoners were roughly treated by their captors who considered their actions horrendous treachery.

The deaths were profoundly shocking to the king's supporters who presented Yoemans and Boucher as:

The two State

MARTYRS,

OR,

The Murther of Master ROBERT
YEOMANS, and Master GEORGE
BOWCHER Citizens of *Bristoll.*

Committed on them by *Nathaniel Fiennes*
(second Sonne to the Lord *Say*) the pretended
Governour of that City, and the rest of his
conspiracie, whom some call a
Councell of Warre.

PSAL. 94. 20. 21.

*Wilt thou have any thing to do with the stoole of
wickednesse which imagineth mischief as a Law?
They gather them together against the Soul of
the Righteous, and condemn the Innocent bloud.*

Printed in the Yeer *M. DC. XLIII.*

The Two State Martyrs. *This Royalist propaganda work was of great importance in shaping
the views of the king's supporters of events in Bristol. The city was to pay heavily for its
'crimes' in this case. (Reproduced by kind permission of Bristol Central Library)*

Most barbarously and inhumanely murdered by the hand of the publick hangman, upon Tuesday last, at the command of Master Fines (heir to his Fathers good affections, though not of his lands) whom nothing else would satisfy but the blood of the guiltless.[67]

On 5 June a spy told Samuel Luke of the response of the Royalists to the executions.

It is reported in Oxford that some of the chiefest townsmen in Bristol being put to death by our forces for adhering to the king, they threaten that many thousands of ours shall suffer in the like manner for their sakes. That the Prince Robert [Rupert] sent a trumpeter to Bristol to demand those men which were to suffer, and they detained him and imprisoned him, where he remains. That his majesty intends to send out a party of horse to Cirencester to fetch away some of the chief of the townsmen to Oxford, and that they shall be served as we used the townsmen of Bristol.[68]

Fiennes and the members of the Council of War who tried the Bristol conspirators were, to use a modern expression, classified as war criminals and specifically excluded from the pardon eventually granted to Bristol.[69] Members of the City Council, having failed to obey the royal command to rescue the condemned prisoners, found themselves under house arrest after the city fell into Royalist hands.[70] As none of the council actually faced charges, it seems that the king, if not his supporters, accepted that they could have done nothing to protect the unfortunate Royalists.

The effects of the execution and the subsequent 'terror' aimed at the king's supporters in Bristol are difficult to assess. The Royalist account suggests that Fiennes knew his actions would alienate the population of the city and had used troops 'to awe the citizens, and to suppress insurrections'.[71] Indeed the Parliamentarians are presented as being fearful that the last words of the prisoners might provoke a rebellion among the local population.

Langridge and Clifton, the chief hang-man under Fiennes their master, knowing how much his [Yeomans'] words might prevail with the people, and that one martyr falling quickly springs up into many converts, caused him instantly to be thrown off, hardly giving him so much time as in some short ejaculations to recommend his soul to God.[72]

In June *Mercurius Aulicus* reported that Fiennes had written to Parliament warning of the ill-feeling the executions had created within the city. Nevertheless, his political masters in London ordered further trials and executions to serve as an example to others.[73] However, the other two prisoners sentenced to death were not executed and although over a hundred Royalists were implicated in the plot no one else received a death sentence.[74]

If Fiennes was not hanging Royalists he was certainly making life extremely unpleasant for the king's supporters in Bristol. The Governor and his Council of War were to prove zealous in confiscating the property of those involved in the plot and they threatened serious repercussions for anyone caught trying to conceal the goods of the known Royalists.

> Bristol the 28th of March 1643
>
> It is this day ordered by a council of war with direction to be published.
>
> That whosoever in this city or county, have or shall have in their hands any goods or estates belonging to any of the late conspirators of Bristol, whose names are hitherto annexed, who endeavoured to cut off the garrison there and let in Prince Rupert's plundering forces, or shall know where any of their goods are, and conceal the same, or hath or shall help to carry any of them away, or whosoever hath, or oweth, any debts, rents, annuities or sums of money to any of the said conspirators and shall not in some convenient time after the publishing hereof make them know to the governor of the city of Bristol, shall undergo and suffer the same penalty and forfeit in their own goods, estates and persons as men adherent to them, which are or shall be inflicted upon the same conspirators, and whosoever servant or other that shall make known to the said governor any of the concealed goods, estates, rents, annuities or sums of money to or of the said conspirators belonging whereby the said goods, debts and sums of money shall come unto our possession for the service of King, Parliament and kingdom shall have a good reward.[75]

Fiennes was to claim that the goods seized from the plotters were worth only £3,000, a not inconsiderable sum in this period but rather a paltry amount considering the number of conspirators involved.[76] It is possible, as Seyer suggests, that Fiennes or his officers were lining their own pockets, but equally large-scale concealment of Royalist assets by sympathizers could have occurred.[77] However, Fiennes's repression, if severe, was by no means totally successful and a large number of Royalist sympathizers either avoided arrest altogether or were quickly released and soon active again. For example, both the merchants who brought ships over to the Royalists at the start of the siege in July were named in parliamentary newssheets as conspirators but released.[78]

The 'Royalist plot' can be seen as a farcical failure which allowed Fiennes to imprison and harass a large number of the king's supporters who were foolish enough to become involved. The success was so great it has been presented as a carefully arranged counter-intelligence operation intended to make Royalists betray their identities.[79] Was this an 'end-game' in which Yoemans and the rest of the king's supporters were the victims of a 'strange act counterplotting those blood-thirsty (foreign and domestic) foes'?[80] Charles Nichol, in his account of the death of Christopher Marlowe, shows that by the Elizabethan period English counter-intelligence methods were certainly sophisticated enough to create such a plot.[81] There are some very suspicious aspects to this whole story, not least of which was the comparative silence of parliamentary writers on the question of how exactly the plot was discovered. Was it really accidentally discovered at the last minute or was Fiennes protecting his 'mole', possibly Captain Hillsdon, within the Royalist organization?

Conspiracy theories, though attractive, do not explain how many of the Royalists escaped on the night and during the 'terror' that followed, if their organization had been infiltrated by parliamentary agents. It is possible that Fiennes and his officers were simply inefficient or unwilling to persecute their opponents to the extreme, but this seems unlikely if they had already committed the time and resources needed to successfully infiltrate the plot. The main long-term consequence of the Royalist plot to surrender Bristol and the execution of the two principal 'conspirators' was to exacerbate ill-feeling between the factions in the city. According to the Royalist account of the executions, Yoemans 'prayed for his persecutors, and adjured his friends not to harbour a thought of revenge'.[82] Sadly for Bristol neither side paid any attention to his dying wish.

CHAPTER 5

The First Siege of Bristol

In order to understand the events in Bristol in July 1643 it is necessary to examine in some detail the condition of the Royalist forces. Ian Roy's study of the Royalist ordnance papers illustrates the problems faced by the king's forces. In May the Oxford magazine contained only thirty guns of various sizes and four mortars to supply both the field army and the city's garrison. The outlying garrisons of Wallingford, Abingdon and Banbury contained only eighteen guns and a single mortar.[1] Stocks of gunpowder consisted of 130 barrels, over half of which had already been issued to the field army or the garrisons, leaving a reserve of only 57; stocks of bullets and match were also limited. The supply of weapons was equally depressing. The magazine contained no swords or pistols and only 100 muskets listed as 'at ye gonne smyths to bee fixed'. The only serviceable arms were pikes and bills, and such was the shortage of weapons among the king's infantry that these were being issued in large numbers.[2] When the field army was mustered at Abingdon at the end of May a convoy of arms was sent to make good the shortages after the Reading campaign; it contained only 250 muskets compared to 1,050 pikes and 600 bills.[3] Military theorists at this time usually recommended two muskets to every pike but in practice by the 1640s the actual ratio appears to have been as high as three firearms to each pike.[4] The Oxford infantry were poorly provided with firearms and oversupplied with cold steel, but it was the shortage of gunpowder that presented the most critical problem. An English barrel contained 100lb which would have been sufficient for 2,400 musket charges, 30–50 rounds for a light field piece or 7–10 rounds for a siege gun.[5] The Royalists simply did not have sufficient ammunition to continue the war.

The main supply route to Oxford ran from the Low Countries/Denmark via the Royalist-controlled ports of the north-east. However, as Clarendon noted, 'by the vigilance of the Parliament agents in those parts, and the power of their ships, too much of it was lost'.[6] When a Royalist vessel landed its cargo, the munitions were loaded on to wagons for a long overland journey through potentially hostile areas.[7] The result was a 'Catch 22' situation: in order to obtain supplies from the north the Royalists had to maintain field forces and garrisons to protect the long and exposed lines of communications, but the need to arm and supply these troops left little for Oxford. A week after the review of the magazine in May, a convoy arrived from the north containing 136 desperately needed barrels of powder and almost 5 tons of slowmatch, but only 345 muskets for the Oxford infantry.[8] A month later a huge convoy of almost 100 wagons arrived with the queen; although it looked impressive the material actually delivered to the general store included only 78 barrels of powder and 70 muskets.[9] The northern route was not a viable lifeline for the king's forces in the Oxford region.

Was it possible for the Royalists to replace imported arms with locally produced supplies? By the summer of 1643 efforts were being made to organize arms manufacture and by July a munitions plant established in the Schools at Oxford was supplying a range of military stores including gunpowder, slowmatch, bullets, pikes and bills. However, production was limited: in July 32 barrels of gunpowder were delivered and the following month a further 15 but it was not until November that a further 50 barrels were supplied.[10] As there were no natural deposits of saltpetre in the country, Oxford, like all other gunpowder mills in England, was dependent upon supplies manufactured by a slow and unpleasant process from human and animal waste. By one of those strange twists of fate the king's powdermakers in Oxford were William Barber and Randal Tombs of Bristol who had suffered persecution from Royal officials in the 1630s.[11] Iron guns and cannon balls were supplied from Worcester and the Forest of Dean via Evesham and Chipping Camden or Stow-on-the-Wold, although again troops had to be deployed to protect these areas.[12] In July a foundry began operation in Oxford re-casting old brass guns into modern three-pounder weapons; in the long term this was to improve significantly the quality of Royalist field artillery, but it did little to solve the immediate shortages.[13] Despite the best efforts of the king's ordnance officers at Oxford production in the city was not sufficient to meet the demand for arms and ammunition.

In contrast to the king's position, the strategic situation facing the parliamentary leaders at the beginning of 1643 was a source of justifiable optimism. They controlled not only the most populous regions but also the bulk of the military and economic resources of the country. Following the initial indecisive campaign in the Midlands and Thames Valley, Parliament fully exploited these advantages to reorganize and expand its armies.[14] By the 1643 campaign season regional armies such as Waller's in the West had been established in East Anglia and the Midlands while the Fairfax family waged a guerrilla war against the northern Royalists.[15] Parliamentary garrisons threatened Royalist supply routes and were disrupting recruitment and administration in areas under the king's control. At the start of the war the navy had sided with Parliament and in 1643 the 'Ship Money Fleet' was reinforced with hired merchant ships in a determined effort to cut Royalist arms supplies.[16] The main Parliamentarian field army under the Earl of Essex was encamped in the Thames

Valley, having been reinforced to a strength of 16,000 foot and 3,000 horse ready to strike at Oxford.[17] In the face of this the king's generals found themselves crippled by shortages of men and munitions. Help had been promised from the north – but would it arrive before Essex?

Essex began operations on 15 April. Thereby he gained the element of surprise, his contemporaries considering the weather too unpredictable for military movements. His army marched from Windsor to besiege the exposed Royalist outpost of Reading, trapping a Royalist garrison of 3,000 infantry and 300 cavalry before they could evacuate the inadequately fortified town. In Oxford it was recognized that these troops could not be abandoned and a relief force was assembled to try to extract them;[18] this attempt was frustrated by a decisive repulse at Caversham Bridge on 25 April.[19] Reading surrendered the following day, on terms that allowed the garrison to march out and join the king's main army. Despite assurances of honourable treatment the surrender was marked by indiscipline among Essex's men.

> But at their coming out of the town, and passing through the enemy's guards, the soldiers were not only reviled and reproachfully used, but many of them were disarmed, and most of the wagons plundered, in the presence of the Earl of Essex himself and the chief officers; who seemed to be offended at it, and not to be able to prevent it; the unruliness of the common men being so great.[20]

This irritating but apparently trivial incident was to have serious repercussions at Bristol three months later. The Royalists had been successful in their primary military objective of recovering the troops trapped at Reading, but this was forgotten in the storm of recriminations following the loss of the town.

Oxford was now directly under threat. Only 25 miles from Reading, it lay within three days' leisurely march of Essex's huge army. Plans were made to evacuate the Royalist capital and retreat to the northern counties, while the king's infantry were massed at Culham to try to block Essex's advance. However, the threatened move never came, the Parliamentarians remaining encamped around Reading.[21] Although this has frequently been attributed to lethargy, it was sickness rather than lack of enthusiasm which frustrated Essex's plans.

> When the season of the year grew ripe for taking the field, the Earl of Essex found that his too early march had nothing advanced his affairs; the soldiers having performed so strict duty, and lodging upon the ground, in frost and rain, before Reading, had produced great sickness and diseases in his army, which had wasted abundant of his men; so that he wanted rather another winter quarter to recover and recruit his men, than an opportunity to engage them in action.[22]

A messenger from Bristol in July noted. 'His Excellency had 2–300 men fall sick about this time in one day and 1000 or more in a week's space.' The army that had marched from Windsor was to be decimated by sickness: 'His Excellency had but 4000 foot able to march, many of his men being then sick and not in marching condition.'[23]

The infection that caused Essex's problems was called by contemporaries 'morbus campestris' and was probably typhus, the scourge of all armies during the sixteenth and seventeenth centuries. Transmitted by lice, the infection would have spread rapidly among Essex's troops, housed in crowded and insanitary conditions and huddled together for warmth in the chill of early spring. Typhus can kill in seven to fourteen days and death rates of up to 75 per cent have been recorded.[24] Doctors of this period were unaware of the actual cause of the disease, ascribing it to humours or vapours in the air. Although it was recognized that it was contagious there was no knowledge of the connection with infected clothing or bedding. Society in this period was not given to the practice of personal hygiene, and standards would have fallen still further in the crowded conditions of an army encampment. Lice and epidemics were viewed with a fatalistic acceptance; they were simply part of everyday life and as such could even be accepted as the will of God. Such attitudes, and the lack of basic knowledge, made prevention or control of infection difficult, if not impossible.

The two armies lay facing each other: the Royalists awaiting troops and supplies from the north, Essex waiting for the debilitating sickness in his ranks to abate. In mid–May the first Royalist reinforcements began to arrive and the strategic initiative began to pass to the king. Essex finally moved his army in early June, not against Oxford but to the north-east towards Thame and Aylesbury to protect Buckinghamshire from Royalist marauders. The king's commanders had sufficiently recovered their confidence to begin aggressive operations against Essex's thinly scattered troops.[25] The most memorable of these raids was led by Rupert and culminated in the death of John Hampden following a minor skirmish at Chalgrove Field on 18 June.[26] In early July Essex wrote to the Speaker of the House of Commons explaining the situation. The dispatch found its way into Royalist hands and was published to demonstrate the weakness of their opponents.

> The enemy being so strong in horse and this army being neither recruited with horses, arms or saddles, it is impossible to keep the counties from being plundered, nor to fight with them but where and when they list, we being forced when we move to march with the whole army, which can make but slow marches, so that the counties suffer much wrong, and the cries of the poor people are infinite.[27]

The threat to Oxford had evaporated and so serious was the situation that Essex even suggested that peace negotiations should be considered.

Sold by P Stent

The high borne Prince Maurice
3d Sonne to Fred: K: of Bohemia

Prince Maurice. The younger brother of Prince Rupert and effective commander of the western army at the first siege of Bristol following Hopton's injuries at Lansdown. He later commanded a Royalist field army in the south-west. After the surrender of Oxford, Maurice joined his brother in exile, finding employment in the Dutch army. He later returned to the service of the Stewarts as a naval officer but drowned when his ship was wrecked in 1652. (Reproduced by kind permission of Bristol Central Library)

On 16 May, as the first arms and reinforcements from the north were arriving in Oxford, the Royalist western army under Hopton, which numbered 2,400 foot and 500 horse, fought a parliamentary force of 5,400 infantry and 200 horse at Stratton. The Earl of Stamford, who had sent most of his mounted troops on a raid, suffered a crushing defeat with 300 dead and 1,700 captured; the Royalists also gained 13 guns, 70 barrels of powder and large stocks of food.[28] The local Parliamentarian leadership collapsed into recriminations and accusations, and effective resistance to Hopton's invasion of Devon proved impossible.[29] Both sides quickly recognized the significance of these events. The Royalists immediately sent reinforcements to the west, including a veteran cavalry brigade under the command of Prince Maurice.[30] Parliament had already dispatched Sir William Waller, a general with a reputation for efficiency and success, to reorganize the parliamentary forces in the region. He was reinforced by, among other units, 500 'prodigiously armed' cavalrymen, nicknamed 'lobsters', under the command of Sir Arthur Haselrig.[31] By mid-June Essex was struggling to protect Buckinghamshire from Royalist cavalry and the two armies in the west were locked in a bloody war of skirmish and manoeuvre.[32]

The Royalists advanced into Somerset, capturing the towns of Taunton, Bridgwater and Dunster and establishing garrisons at each to protect their lines of communication.[33] Waller and other local parliamentary commanders were collecting troops:

> Though Sir William Waller himself continued still at Bath, yet the remainder of those horse and dragoons that escaped out of Cornwall, after the battle of Stratton, and such others as were sent out of Exeter for their ease, when they apprehended a siege, and those soldiers who fled out of Taunton and Bridgwater, and the other regiments of the country, were by Alexander Popham, Strode and the other Deputy-Lieutenants of the Militia for Somerset rallied; and with the trained bands and volunteer regiments of the country, drawn together.[34]

The Royalists faced stronger and better organized resistance as they advanced through Somerset and fought a substantial skirmish with Waller's troops near Wells on 12 June. Two weeks later a parliamentary correspondent reported that Waller was holding over seventy Royalist prisoners.[35] Shortly after this, in a night raid on Royalist quarters, the cavalry regiment of Sir James Hamilton was virtually destroyed.[36]

Waller appeared to be winning this campaign of manoeuvre which by early July centred on his headquarters at Bath. Time and resources favoured him and he refused to attack but rather kept his army in strong defensive positions.[37] On 5 July the Royalists finally attacked Waller's army on Lansdown Hill west of Bath; both sides claimed the victory.

Thus the battle continued for the space of nine hours at least, until all the enemy's horse left their foot naked, and night being come on, hindered us from completing our victory. Our horse being in continual service for three days, without meat or water for 24 hours, and our foot much scattered; it was held fit by a council of war, that we should return to Bath for refreshment [for] our horse and men, and rallying our foot, well knowing we might easily recover the hill, and so fall upon the enemy again to prosecute our victory. Our retreat was so orderly performed, that the enemy durst not follow us, having learnt by experience, that our giving ground hath been much to their disadvantage. The next morning, whilst we were preparing for a march, we were informed that the enemy was retreated to their old quarters at Marshfield.[38]

The king's army found themselves possessed entirely of the field, and the dead, and all other ensigns of victory; Sir William Waller being marched to Bath, in so much disorder and apprehension, that he left a great store of arms and ten barrels of powder behind him; which was a very seasonable supply to the other side, who had spent in that day's service, no less than fourscore barrels, and had no safe proportion left.[39]

Although both armies had suffered losses, Waller was in a far stronger position and appeared keen to re-engage, but the Royalists decided to retreat towards Oxford and join the main army rather than 'stay and attend the enemy, who were so near his supplies'.[40] Waller pursued the withdrawing Royalists with great vigour, constantly harrying the rear and flanks of their army.[41] Finally Hopton, who had been seriously injured in an ammunition explosion after Lansdown, sent his cavalry on to Oxford and waited with his infantry and guns in the town of Devizes for help to arrive.[42] Waller surrounded the town, and seemed confident that Hopton's army would fall as easily as Lord Herbert's had in March.[43] As a result Waller was caught off guard on 13 July by the arrival from Oxford of a fast-moving column consisting of 1,500 horsemen and a couple of light field guns. Seeing the small size of the relief force, he divided his army, leaving the infantry to contain Hopton while leading his 2,000 cavalry against the relief column. There followed one of the most dramatic victories of the war: the Royalists scattered Waller's horse with a single charge, inflicting a crushing defeat on the main parliamentary army in the west of England.[44]

This glorious day, for it was a day of triumph, redeemed for that time the king's whole affairs, so that all clouds that shadowed them seemed dispelled and a bright light of success to shine over the whole kingdom. There were in this battle slain on the enemy's part, about six hundred on the place; nine hundred prisoners taken, besides two or three hundred retaken and redeemed whom they had gathered up in the skirmishes, and pursuit; with their cannon, being eight pieces of brass ordnance; all their arms, ammunition, wagons, baggage and victual; eight and twenty foot ensigns and nine cornets; all this by a party of fifteen hundred horse with two small field-pieces (for the victory was perfect, upon the matter, before the Cornish came up; though the enemy's foot were suffered to stand in a body uncharged, out of ceremony, till they came; that they might be refreshed with a share in the conquest) against a body of full two thousand horse, five hundred dragoons and near three thousand foot and an excellent train of artillery.[45]

News of Waller's defeat and the massacre of his army reached Essex as he was disengaging his troops and withdrawing towards Uxbridge to rebuild his depleted regiments with recruits from London.[46] The strategic position had been transformed and the Royalists now moved quickly to exploit the situation. As the king left Oxford to meet his queen and the 3,000 reinforcements she was bringing from the north, Rupert assembled the field army to march west. Two days after Roundway the ordnance officers were ordered to prepare two demi-cannon siege guns, the heaviest the king possessed, to march the next day. These were followed two days later by six other guns prepared 'for his Majesties present service under the command of Prince Rupert'.[47] On the 18th, Rupert marched from Oxford with the main body of the field army towards Gloucester to open communications between Oxford and the vital recruiting grounds in Wales.[48] On the 20th, Rupert learned that Waller had arrived before him with a force of 500–600 cavalry; despite the small size of his force and his recent defeat at Roundway, Waller's reputation was such that his presence could not be ignored. Misjudging his opponent's intentions, Rupert placed his army between Gloucester and Bristol in an attempt to trap Waller and his cavalry, but Waller took advantage of Rupert's movement to withdraw to London. With his main antagonist in full retreat Rupert decided to postpone operations against Gloucester and to try instead to capture the far greater prize of Bristol. They halted

till they might receive new orders from the king; who, upon full advice, and consideration of the state he was in, and the broken condition of the enemy, resolved to make an attempt upon the city of Bristol; to which Prince Rupert was most inclined, for his being disappointed in a former design; and where there were many well affected to the king's service from the beginning and more since the execution of two eminent citizens. And the disesteem generally had of the courage of Nathaniel Fiennes the Governor, made the design to be thought the more reasonable.[49]

How strong was the Royalist force now moving against Bristol? It represented a combination of the 'Oxford Army' under Rupert's personal command and the

'Western Army' in theory under Hertford but in effect commanded by Maurice. The exact number of men this force contained has been the subject of considerable debate.

> The king's army consisted of about 14,000 men according to Lord Clarendon, others (Barrett) say 20,000; well-informed men in the city computed them at only 8,000, mostly horse; Fiennes says they were 15 regiments of foot and 12 regiments of horse.[50]

The Oxford Army was the main Royalist field force. It had been in existence for ten months and was composed of battle-hardened units, but what was its strength? The king had begun the war with about 10,000 infantry; these formed the core of the Oxford Army, although reduced by battle losses and desertion to about 8,000 by the end of the 1642 campaign.[51] Attempts to increase the strength of the infantry arm by recruiting existing units up to strength or drafting in new regiments were only partly successful: desertion continued and many units had to be detached from the field army to protect outlying areas or man the increasing number of garrisons.[52] Had the Oxford Army not been successful in rescuing the Reading garrison, they would have been unable to muster a balanced field force, but even with these units the Oxford infantry consisted only of fourteen weak infantry units when it marched westward.[53]

This weakness was not untypical of Royalist infantry units (or indeed parliamentary ones) throughout the war: some of the king's 'regiments' in the Cornish campaign of 1644 contained fewer than 200 men. None of the regiments forming the Oxford foot at Bristol was particularly prestigious and most were a long way from their original recruiting grounds in Wales, the Midlands and northern England.[54] As recruiting was difficult if not impossible for these regiments, they lost still more strength during the winter of 1642/3 and as pay began to fall increasingly into arrears disillusionment set in for many. This process of wastage is illustrated by the Reading garrison. Its six regiments contained 3,000 men while a seventh unit sent to reinforce them had 500.[55] These regiments, Stradling's, Bellasyse's, Fielding's, Salusbury's, Fitton's, Bowle's, and Lunsford's, had had a strength of almost 4,000 in November 1642.[56] Thus these units suffered an average loss of 12 per cent between them owing to sickness and desertion during the winter months.

If the fourteen regiments had been fully up to strength they would have contained 17,000 men but in fact only 6,000 were mustered at the start of the campaign season in 1643.[57] From Reading the poorly fed and clothed infantry moved to Culham, where they were housed in mud huts in cold wet weather.[58] Inevitably they began to fall sick: with the garrison from Reading had come typhus. The sick were evacuated to hastily prepared hospitals near Oxford, where the hard-pressed Royalist medical staff were stretched to the limit trying to care for them.[59] The drain on Royalist manpower can be assessed from the numbers of weapons of sick soldiers returned to the ordnance stores.[60] Thirteen regiments returned 913 pikes and muskets in the period up until mid-June, but only 196 were reissued, a recovery rate of only 21.5 per cent. This, however, is not the complete story as the schedule lists only pikes and muskets. Other weapons were also returned. For example, Col. Herbert's regiment is listed as returning twenty-five muskets but a receipt to the regiment shows they also handed in nine Welsh hooks and halberds.[61] Typhus epidemics do not pass quickly, and the infection would have lingered throughout the six weeks from mid-June until the siege of Bristol. Given the limited medical care, and the poor standard of food, clothing and accommodation, recovery would have been slow. Consequently it is unlikely that the Oxford Army would have been able to field more than 4,500 effective infantry at the time of the siege of Bristol.

How strong was the mounted arm of the Oxford Army? Fiennes reported to Parliament that his attackers included twelve regiments of horse.[62] If these units had been fully up to strength this would have meant some 6,000 men. Fiennes's use of the word regiments rather than actual numbers appears to have been intended to make the attackers appear more numerous, although a Royalist source provides confirmation:

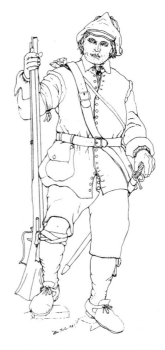

An 'Oxford' infantryman. This individual wears a suit of clothing consisting of coat, breeches and cap which were supplied in red, blue or white to units stationed in the Oxford area. The Royalist army at this stage of the war was desperately short of firearms but this individual is equipped with an up-to-date firelock musket and a straight sword called a 'tuck'. He carries rations and spare clothing in a snapsack slung across his shoulders. A clear indication of the shortage of equipment is the leather bag (rather than a bandolier) used to carry ammunition. (With grateful thanks to Alan Turton)

> The great number of the king's horse; which was so brave a body, that when that part of it, which joined the Cornish was away, he could march with at least six thousand horse, which were as many as would be able to live on any country within a due distance of quartering.[63]

This time at least, Fiennes was telling the truth. However, few Royalist mounted units were at full strength and the king's 6,000 cavalrymen were organized into more than twelve regiments. Fiennes's claim of twelve full-strength cavalry units may have been intended to suggest that the fifteen infantry units were also at full

A Royalist cavalryman, 1643. Compared to his fully equipped parliamentary rival (see page 40) this Royalist horseman is lightly armed and poorly protected. He wears a buff coat with a wrap-around skirt but no armour. He is armed with a heavy basket-hilted sword and a pair of pistols in saddle holsters. (With grateful thanks to Alan Turton)

strength. It appears unlikely that the Royalist horse would outnumber the infantry, although as the cavalry were largely recruited from the lesser gentry, squires and yeomen they were less likely to desert and would have been better fed and clothed than their infantry comrades. There was also only a limited role for cavalry in garrisons, and thus the bulk of the mounted arm remained available for field service. In addition mounted troops were deployed in outposts and could travel further looking for quarters, thereby reducing overcrowding and helping to reduce the prevalence of infectious disease. The king had 3,000 horse at Edgehill; this force was augmented by the arrival of new units over the winter, the latest and most substantial reinforcement being those sent from the north by the Earl of Newcastle in June. Even allowing for a large detachment serving with Hopton's Western Army and some cavalry in garrisons, Clarendon's figure of 6,000 remains plausible.

The final element of the army Rupert led into the west in July 1643 was the artillery with its accompanying engineers and specialist troops. The artillery train was supplied with guns, ammunition, transport and other equipment from the main ordnance stores in Oxford. The actual force which marched was very modest, consisting of only 8 guns supported by 59 carts and requiring a total of 393 horses.[64] Why so little artillery with an army intended to attack a fortified town? The relief force for Reading, according to the ordnance office, had required an artillery train of 19 guns supported by 76 carts loaded with ammunition and equipment. This hardware was available in the storehouses, but what was lacking was the motive power – 524 draught horses. Shortage of transport animals plagued both sides throughout the war, and limited the artillery available to Royalist field armies. The horse has a gestation period of one year, and during much of this time a mare cannot be used for heavy draught work without great risk to both foal and dam. The young horse is not ready for training until it reaches the age of three and is not fully mature until the age of four or five. Well cared for and properly fed, a horse will give twenty years' work; however, overworked and undernourished horses will quickly lose condition and could be worn out in as little as three years. Horses were clearly not a flexible commodity and studs were unable to respond quickly to meet sudden increases in demand.[65]

The guns sent with Rupert's army also appear a strange choice. Four were heavy siege weapons – two 27-pounder demi-cannon and two 15-pounder culverins. In addition there were two dual-purpose 12-pounders and a couple of 6-pounder field guns.[66] The four heavy guns were too cumbersome for use as field artillery, while the smallest pair were useless for siege work. The value of the heavy guns against a fortified town was severely limited by the amount of ammunition supplied to the train. The demi-cannon had only forty-two rounds of solid shot each and the culverins fifty, with anti-personnel case-shot being issued at a rate of ten and twenty rounds per gun respectively.[67] At the siege of Gloucester the guns fired seventeen rounds a day at the city's walls; this was considered insufficient to reduce the town,[68] and thus any attempt at an effective bombardment would soon exhaust the Royalists' meagre ammunition supply.

With the gunners marched various specialists. These included a young Walloon named Bernard de Gomme, an experienced and gifted military engineer, who had been in the service of the Prince of Orange before coming to England with Rupert in 1642. He had already planned and supervised the construction of defences around Oxford, and his highly detailed description of the defences of Bristol may indicate that he was responsible for the pre-assault reconnaissance to locate suitable points of attack.[69] Another specialist in Rupert's retinue was the Frenchman M. de la Roche, who manufactured explosives and incendiary weapons, known as fireworks, in a small factory established in buildings close to Magdalen College. Having recently been granted the somewhat cumbersome title of 'Captain General of all Masters of Artificial Fires and Fireworks', he left Oxford with four carts loaded with grenades, petards, firepikes and other weapons of his own manufacture.[70] His subordinate, the fireworker Samuel Fawcett, was responsible for a mortar sent with the army and was to attempt to break open Lawfords Gate with a petard during the siege.[71] After the siege it was Fawcett who inspected the city's defences and listed the artillery captured.[72]

The Western Army that fought at Bristol had been formed only a month before by the amalgamation of the Cornish forces of Sir Ralph Hopton and reinforcements brought to the west by Prince Maurice. When these two forces joined at Chard, Hopton had 500 horse, 300 dragoons and 3,000 infantry supported by four or five guns, while Maurice brought 1,600 cavalry, 1,000 newly raised infantry and seven or eight artillery pieces.[73] The hard core of this new army was the Cornish infantry; tough, hardened troops with a magnificent fighting record, they were also notoriously ill-disciplined: 'These were the very best foot I ever saw for marching or fighting but were so mutinous withal that nothing but an alarm could keep them from falling upon their officers.'[74] It was fortunate that the officers leading these troops were as singular as their men, as one contemporary noted.

> Men remarkable for their conduct in keeping their counsels, in disguising their actions and fore-seeing the designs and courses of the enemy. Being well acquainted with the passes of the country, and strangely dextrous in gaining intelligence, scouring the enemy before Bristol, as the grey-soap of that place doth cloths.[75]

The Cornishmen, many of whom spoke no English, saw themselves as serving in a foreign land and had little liking for foreigners. They took great exception to being placed under the command of Maurice's officers and had a particular dislike of the cavalry: 'the Cornish foot could not well brook our horse (especially, when we were drawn up on corn) but they would many times let fly at us'.[76] Maurice had 1,000 foot, 250 of them belonging to the regiment of Col. Bamfield which had escorted the artillery from Oxford,[77] the rest consisting of newly recruited troops assembled on the march. However, Maurice contributed the mounted strength of the new army. The bulk of the 1,600 horse he brought to Chard belonged to three veteran regiments which were reinforced by new units and Hopton's 800 experienced horse and dragoons.[78]

On 4 June the new army at Chard had a strength of 6,300 foot, horse and dragoons. Were they able to maintain this strength in the weeks before the siege of Bristol? This was unlikely, although there is no evidence of disease in the Western Army and desertion would have been a minor problem as long as the Cornish remained near their homes. However, the garrisons established at Taunton under Sir John Stawell, Bridgwater under Edmund Wyndham and Dunster under Francis Wyndham all required at least some men.[79] Sir James Hamilton had been left in Devon with a regiment of horse and dragoons but these troops were so poorly behaved that, as Clarendon noted, they 'weakened the king's party'. A detachment, including one of the veteran cavalry regiments, had to be sent to relieve Hamilton, who was ordered to join the field army with his men.[80] According to Col. Bamfield, whose regiment was one of those detached, this represented a considerable reduction in the Western Army.

A Cornish infantryman of the 'western' army, this unarmoured pikeman wears civilian clothing typical of the 1630/40s. He wears a knitted Monmouth cap to which has been fixed a bunch of ribbons signifying his company. He has been issued with a snapsack which he wears slung from his shoulder and has a shepherd's purse fixed to his belt. (With grateful thanks to Alan Turton)

Taunton and Bridgwater being taken, and garrisons placed in them; the body of the army marched, towards General Waller, having dispatched my Lord Berkeley, with four regiments of foot and some few troops of horse, to block up Exeter, to prevent the Earl of Stanford raising of forces in Devonshire.[81]

A parliamentary account of the fighting between Waller's forces and the advancing Royalists gives detailed information on Maurice's losses prior to Lansdown.[82] The first casualties occurred in a skirmish near Wells on 12 June and two weeks later Waller was said to be holding 70 prisoners including 3 captains,

2 ensigns and a quartermaster. Shortly after this the Royalists suffered a major loss when Hamilton's regiment, which had just arrived from Devon, was surprised and almost destroyed during a raid on their quarters.[83]

Richard Atkyns states that the Royalists had only 6,000 men at the battle of Lansdown so it would appear that recruiting and reinforcements had not been sufficient to keep pace with detachments and battle losses.[84] Although the Royalists were to claim this battle as a victory, it was a costly one, with one parliamentary account claiming Royalist losses of 500 men killed or wounded and a similar number deserting.[85] Another account claims that the Royalist horse suffered 600 losses out of the 2,000 engaged that day.[86] The Lord Mayor of Bristol was to report that losses were particularly heavy among the Royalist officers:

> they lost Sir Beville Grenville, Lieutenant Col Ward, Sargent Major Lower, Captain Basset, Captain Cornishan, Captain James and five other Captains and two Captains more in the powder, of ordinary men we know not the number, seven cart loads of dead men were carried from the place, diverse wounded 20 in a house and not one like to live and more in other places, they want surgeons much.[87]

After Lansdown the Royalists made a fighting retreat to Devizes, sustaining still further losses in skirmishing and rear-guard actions.[88] Although two or three hundred prisoners taken by Waller were released after his defeat, these could only partly have compensated for the battle losses.[89] After such losses and detachments I would suggest the Western Army at Bristol comprised 3,000 infantry and 1,500 horse. The Royalists were certainly not fielding 20,000 men. A more realistic figure would be 15,000, with about two-thirds of these being troops of the Oxford Army. An unusual feature of this army was the equal numbers of mounted troops and infantry – a far from ideal mixture for an army seeking to attack a fortified city.

As Rupert's army began to march towards Bristol Maurice arrived. His troops had occupied Bath after the battle of Roundway and he had now received orders to cooperate with his brother.[90] It was agreed that the Oxford Army would invest the city from the north and the Western troops from the south. On 23 July Rupert established his headquarters at Westbury, and carried out a reconnaissance of the northern defences. Clifton Church was occupied at this stage by Royalist dragoons under Col. Washington, as a counter to the fort at Brandon Hill. That evening, after the bulk of the king's troops withdrew, there was considerable skirmishing between the detachments in the fort and church. This was the beginning of the siege.[91]

The following day, Monday 24 July, the Western troops crossed the Avon at Keynsham and drove back the garrison's outposts south of the river. Maurice established his artillery on a small hill facing Temple Gate and his infantry camped around the village of Bedminster. Bristol's defenders, whose land communications were already cut by a cordon of cavalry, suffered a major blow when Royalist

This early panoramic view of Bristol was taken from the site of the civil war fort on Brandon Hill. This was the highest point on the defensive line and would have dominated the city. (Author's Collection)

sympathizers secured the ships in the Kingsrood, thus hampering sea communications.[92] Rupert held a general review of his army, drawing up the units in shallow formations so that they looked larger than they were.[93] To make the parade even more impressive it was claimed that the parliamentary standards captured at Roundway were displayed by his troops.[94] After this theatrical exhibition Rupert sent his trumpeter, Richard Deane, to demand the surrender of the city. Fiennes replied that 'being instructed to keep the town for King and Parliament he could not yet relinquish that trust till he were brought to more extremity'.[95] Thus the siege formally began. The rest of the day was spent in probing attacks and the construction of gun positions around the city; by evening the Royalist infantry had occupied advanced positions surrounding Bristol.[96] Skirmishing continued after nightfall in the area between Water Fort and Brandon Hill, while after midnight an unsuccessful attack was mounted in the area of Prior's Hill Fort.

The next day saw heavy fighting on the northern side of the city. Rupert crossed the river to meet his brother and his officers, and it was agreed that the two armies should mount a synchronized assault the next day rather than undertaking a formal siege.[97] Clarendon offers a number of reasons for this decision but omits to mention factors such as the shortage of ammunition and continuing disease among Rupert's troops which must have influenced the decision.[98] Rupert would

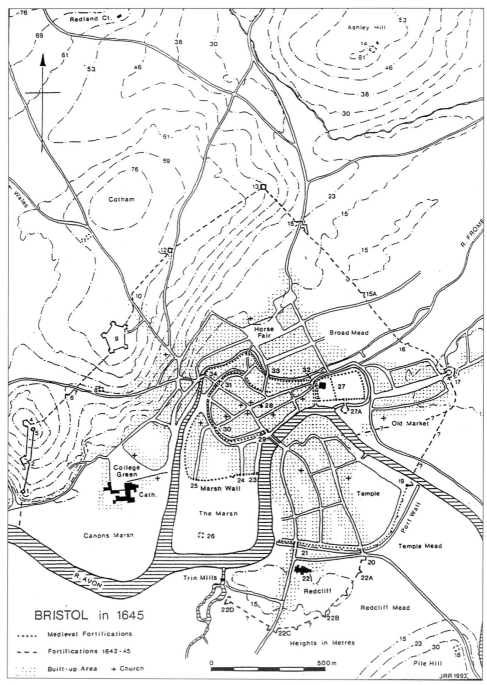

General plan of Bristol during the civil war. (Reproduced by kind permission of James Russell) (See page 77 for key.)

Key to map:

The numbered sites are graded as follows:

*** Proven civil war feature, the location of which is precisely known from archaeological or cartographic evidence.

** Documented civil war feature, the location of which is only approximately known.

* Possible civil war feature identified from cartographic sources.

***	(1)	Water Fort	**	(18)	Siege Battery (1643 and 1645)
***	(2)	Spur	***	(19)	Tower Harratz
***	(3)	Outwork	***	(20)	Temple Gate
***	(4)	Bastion of Brandon Hill Fort	***	(21)	Redcliff Gate
***	(5)	Brandon Hill Fort	***	(22)	St Mary Redcliff Church
**	(6)	Spur enclosing Stone Barn	**	(22A)	Spur next to Temple Gate
***	(7)	Washington's Breach (1643)	**	(22B)	Platform behind Redcliff Church
***	(8)	Essex Work (1643)	**	(22C)	Bedminster Gate
***	(9)	Royal or Great Fort on site of Windmill Fort	**	(22D)	Demi-Bastion by Trin Mills
**	(10)	St Michael's Hill Battery	***	(23)	Marsh Gate
*	(11)	Bewell's Tump (possibly Royalist redoubt, 1645)	***	(24)	Back Street Gate
			***	(25)	Marsh Street Gate
***	(12)	Colston's Fort or Redoubt	**	(26)	Battery on site of Bowling Green
***	(13)	Priors Hill Fort	***	(27)	Castle
**	(14)	Parliamentarian Siege Battery and HQ (1645)	**	(27A)	Redoubt to south of Castle
			***	(28)	Guard House, Wine Street
**	(15)	Stokes Croft Gate and Outworks	***	(29)	St Nicholas Gate
**	(15A)	Spur by Newfoundland House	***	(30)	St Leonard's Gate
*	(16)	possible Spur (from Rocque's map of 1743)	***	(31)	St John's Gate
			***	(32)	Newgate
			***	(33)	Nether-Pithay Gate
***	(17)	Lawford's Gate and Outworks	***	(34)	Frome Gate and Bridge

undoubtedly have noted Fiennes's faint-hearted reply to his summons and perhaps in view of 'the disesteem generally held of the courage of Nathaniel Fiennes's he suspected that prompt action might break the governor's will to resist.

Orders were issued for a general attack by both armies at dawn. The password, to allow Royalist troops to identify each other in the darkness and confusion, was 'Oxford' and everyone was ordered to wear a white band or handkerchief at his neck.[99] These precautions were vital in the coming battle as both defenders and attackers wore uniforms in a similar range of colours.[100] The general order for the attack laid special emphasis on capturing Mary Redcliff Church and instructed the assaulting troops to break down the defences to allow access to cavalry.[101] The Royalist gunners concentrated their fire on Prior's Hill Fort until nightfall while Rupert assembled his officers for a final briefing at Capt. Hill's house, where Essex had been arrested by Fiennes in February. He ordered that the defenders should be kept awake that night by continuous skirmishing and that the two demi-cannon should fire the signal for the general assault at dawn.[102]

Such attacks did not consist of massed troops rushing blindly forward. Assault tactics were sophisticated and there were foreign-trained veterans among the king's officers able to direct such operations. Col. Bamfield's account of the attack at Exeter (4 September 1643) shows how assaults were undertaken:

> At the place where we intended to fall on; the enemy had two out guards advanced from the southgate the distance of a musket shot, of about 3 or 400 men; with a line of communication from the port, to the outworks, which we could perceive was but slightly manned; we resolved with firelocks, and pikemen, with pistols by their sides; that lighted matches should not discover our design; to march silently an hour before break of day, to assault the line jointly by way of surprise. He [Col. Chudley] on the left hand near the outguard, I on the right, near the port; hoping thereby (if successful) to cut the retreat of the enemy which we did.[103]

The account of Bernard de Gomme suggests that similar tactics were employed by at least some of the Royalist units at Bristol. The assault was ordered 'just at the break of day', presumably to allow troops to concentrate and move forward to their assault positions under cover of darkness.[104] Grandison's attack was spearheaded by groups of musketeers attempting to cut the lines of communication above and below Prior's Hill Fort.[105] In the fighting at Stokes Croft the Royalists are described as coming to 'pistol and push of pike with the defenders'.[106] Bellasyse's attack was led by a forlorn hope (skirmish line) of 30 musketeers, 6 fire pikes and as many hand grenades.[107]

The plan went horribly wrong. The Western Army attacked prematurely at about 3.00 a.m. owing, it was claimed, to the enthusiasm of the Cornish and the inability of their officers to control them.[108] Not only were the attacks thrown out of synchronization, but the assault equipment had not yet reached Rupert's units. Despite this, the Royalists in the north attacked in support of the Cornish. What Rupert could not know, as he hurriedly committed his units, was that the southern assault was already faltering. The Western Army had attacked in three columns: the central one commanded by Sir Nicholas Slanning, with Col. Buck on his right and Col. Basset to the left.[109] They planned to cross the ditch using wagons as assault bridges, but the ditch proved too deep and fascines had to be used to build paths for those bringing forward the assault ladders.

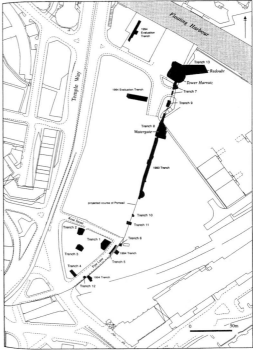

The southern defences of the city consisted mainly of the massive medieval wall and ditch (left). Recent excavations on the site of the former Great Western Railway goods yard at Temple Meads have uncovered substantial remains of these defences, as can be seen in the trench location plan (right). The sheer size of the wall can be gauged by the 2-metre measuring rod used to provide a scale. (Copyright Bristol Museum and Art Gallery)

These three divisions fell on together with that courage and resolution, as nothing but death could control; and though the middle division got into the gaff, and so near filled it that some mounted the wall, yet by the prodigious disadvantage of the ground and the full defence the besieged made within, they were driven back with a great slaughter; the common soldiers, after their chief officers were killed, or desperately wounded, finding it a bootless attempt.[110]

The commanders of all three assault columns and two regimental commanders were killed or wounded almost immediately and after half an hour the attack began to collapse, with the Cornish withdrawing to the cover of nearby hedges. Maurice moved from unit to unit rallying and encouraging his men, saying he was sure his brother had broken through;[111] somehow he managed to keep his men in battle, thus tying down the defenders on the southern walls until finally news arrived that the line was broken in the north and reinforcements were urgently needed there.[112]

The Oxford Army attacked at three points using a weak infantry brigade in each assault. The units under Lord Grandison spent the first hour and a half in a futile attempt to force the defences on the Gloucester Road at Stokes Croft, before attacking Prior's Hill Fort which had been the target of much of the Royalist artillery the previous day. The bombardment had not weakened the fort and the attackers were again repulsed, in part at least because they lacked ladders to scale the walls. At this point, as Grandison rallied his men for a third attack, he was shot in the leg, a wound that led to his death shortly afterwards. His successor Col. Owen was almost immediately wounded in the face and the brigade began to disintegrate.[113] The units under the command of Bellasyse attacked the line around Windmill Hill Fort, but again the attack was frustrated by the lack of ladders and materials to fill the ditch. Having suffered serious losses the brigade fell back under heavy fire to the cover of a stone wall to reorganize.[114] By six o'clock two of the three brigades in the north and all those in the south had disengaged; despite suffering heavy losses, they had achieved nothing. The two Oxford brigades were badly shaken and probably unwilling to fight on, but at this point they began to receive orders to support a breakthrough by the third column.

Col. Wentworth's four infantry regiments, reinforced by dragoons under the command of Col. Washington, who had previously held Clifton Church,[115] attacked the defences around Brandon Hill, concentrating on a weak point in the line not covered by the defenders' guns.[116] Fiennes had been warned about the weakness of the line at this point and had placed a body of cavalry to cover it[117] but his choice of an officer to command this detachment was unfortunate. Hercules Langrish, although a loyal supporter of Fiennes, had a reputation for cowardice.[118]

At first the attack appeared to be doomed to failure. The rough ground disorganized the attacking troops so that only a small body of men successfully crossed the wall, due in no small part to de la Roche's fireworks.[119] It was later agreed that the Royalists could have been dislodged by a prompt counter-attack and they recognized that their position was desperate;[120] however, to the relief and amazement of the Royalists, Langrish and his troopers did not attack until reinforcements arrived.

> But the horse did not charge (sayth he) as they were commanded and by others entreated. But whoever it was that did charge, most sure it is that by that time 200 or 300 of ours had gotten over, ere ever they could well rank themselves into order; charged they were by a troop of horse; which governor Fiennes says were his troop. Our pikes staggered at the charge: but some 50 or 60 musketeers from a hedge giving them a round salvoe, they retreated with some loss. By (the time) that we had ranked the men already gotten over the line, the enemy's

horse rallied again: so that wheeling on the side of Windmill Hill they gave us another charge. Our pikes (which should have stived them off) could not yet make a stand: but some 6 of our dragoons firing on them & other musketeers first discharging & then laying at them with their musket stocks; they again retreated. But the truth is, Capt. Clark, Ancient Hodgekinson (and some others) running upon them with firepikes neither man nor horse was able to endure it. These firepikes did the feat.[121]

If a single troop of horse could so nearly turn the battle after the Royalists had been in possession of the breach for almost two hours and received reinforcements, what would have been the effect if Langrish's 100 troopers had attacked all at once?

Having breached the city's defences, the Royalists attempted to consolidate and exploit their initial success while the Parliamentarians struggled to contain the breakthrough. Fiennes ordered the troops holding the northern line, but not those holding the forts, to retire into the city; several officers tried to persuade him to reconsider his orders and to launch a counter-attack using reserves rather than abandoning the line. Fiennes insisted that the withdrawal should continue and accused his critics of mutiny, threatening to execute anyone who disobeyed him.[122] After the siege Fiennes explained that he feared that the defenders would be cut off and destroyed in small groups by the advancing Royalists and that the men in the city could do little to support them. While the withdrawal proceeded, panic seems to have set in.

A heap of them [Royalist Infantry] now newly gotten over the line and being there charged by the enemy's horse, before they could range themselves into order: made up all together with such good speed into a lane towards the town, the enemy retreating still before them and here (all unknown to ours) the enemy had a strong work: and they in it suspecting our men's running haste, to be the courage of such as pursued the victory, and were resolved to carry all before them with as much haste ran out of it.[123]

The 'strong work' was Essex's fort at the top of what is now Park Street, and, its capture opened the way for attacks on the area around College Green and the Quay, as additional troops – infantry under Bellasyse and cavalry under Thomas Aston – were becoming available.

Wentworth moved to occupy College Green, his forces suffering casualties from artillery fire from Brandon Hill and Water Fort, and from guns positioned on the opposite bank of the river. The houses surrounding the Green were manned by infantry supported by light artillery which kept up a damaging fire on the exposed Royalists.[124] These light guns may have been some of the 'hammered'

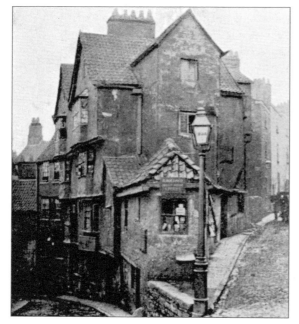

These early images show the areas through which the Royalists had to fight after they breached the outer line. These suburbs were defended with great vigour by the garrison and the attackers suffered heavy losses. (above left) Christmas Steps; (above right) Christmas Street; (left) Steep Street. (Author's Collection)

guns produced by the order of Sir Edward Hungerford:

Diverse small iron hammered pieces before the castle and in the forts and streets mounted upon little carriages about a yard and three quarters long of the bore of double rabinetts or double hacques. They were made by a country smith and shot a pound or more of musket balls or one pound iron balls.[125]

Although these weapons may sound appallingly primitive they are best considered in similar terms to modern weapons such as heavy machine-guns or mortars: they provided the infantry with additional firepower.[126] The Royalist advance was becoming bogged down in house-to-house fighting and some commanders requested permission to set fire to ships in the harbour to divert the defenders' attention and relieve the pressure on their men. Rupert refused, fearing that if the fires got out of control they would destroy both his reputation and the city which had already cost the Royalists so much.[127]

Meanwhile, the infantry under Bellasyse and Aston's cavalry were fighting their way through the heavily built-up suburbs towards Frome Gate in another house-to-house battle:

Marched up to Froomegate losing many men, and some very good officers, by shot from the walls and windows; insomuch as all men were much cast down to see so little gained with so great a loss; for they had still a more difficult entrance into the town, than they had yet passed, and where their horse could be of no use to them.[128]

It was at Frome Gate that one of the strangest events of this siege occurred:

When the news came into the said city on the Wednesday morning, that some of the enemies were entered within the line, this despondent and divers other women, and maids, with the help of some men, did with wool sacks and earth, stop up Froome Gate to keep out the enemy from entering the said city, being the only passage by which the enemy must enter.[129]

According to witnesses at Fiennes's trial, this barricade was a massive structure 16 feet thick constructed under the supervision of the garrison's engineers.[130] Whatever the role of the city's women, the sealing of the main gate nearest to the Royalist line of advance was a logical military precaution.

By nine o'clock the brigades of Wentworth and Bellasyse were bogged down in street fighting and their advance was faltering; although a recent account of the siege suggests that Royalist troops captured Frome Gate and were about to launch at attack across the quays this was not the case.[131] After six hours of heavy fighting the king's supporters had been repulsed completely in the south and made only one breach in the north; their advance was bogged down in the suburbs and the inner line of defence had not been seriously threatened. They had no reserve troops, except cavalry, whose effectiveness in street fighting was limited and the initial breach had to be expanded using units already repulsed at other points whose morale had been shaken by serious casualties. At Fiennes's trial it was claimed that the Royalists had suffered 700–1,000 fatalities and another 700 wounded: this represents between 9 and 11 per cent of their total force.[132] These figures are deceptive; the majority of identifiable casualties of field rank (major and above) were infantrymen, the cavalry of necessity taking a secondary role during the assault and subsequent street fighting. Five out of six Royalist brigade

This is the only gate of the old city defences to survive to the present day. St John's Gate/ Frome Gate formed the main access to the city from the north and was to feature in both the Royalist conspiracy and the first siege. It was through this gate that Rupert and his troops were to be admitted by the plotters, while the crypt of the church was to be used to imprison captured Parliamentarians. It was here that the women of Bristol constructed a huge barricade of earth and woolsacks to deny access to the Royalists in the first siege. (Author's Collection)

commanders were killed or wounded, and if regimental commanders are included, 39 per cent of the army's senior officers were now *hors de combat*. Such losses in the upper echelon of any army would be serious, but where regiments were raised by commanders from among friends and tenants by virtue of personal influence such losses were potentially catastrophic. De Gomme states that the Cornish lost 100 men killed or wounded although Slingsby suggests a higher figure.[133] Allowing 300 casualties for the Western infantry and the cavalry, the remaining 1,100–1,400 would have fallen among the infantry units of the Oxford Army, giving a casualty rate of 23–31 per cent. In the face of such losses the surprising thing is not that the attack began to lose its impetus but that it did not degenerate into a rout.

As for the defenders, the line had been breached but they still held the forts on the high ground whose guns dominated those areas captured by the Royalists.[134] The importance of these forts can be seen by Rupert's decision to send the Western troops (when they finally arrived) to attack them rather than supporting the units fighting in the suburbs.[135] The inner line of defences based on the River Frome was intact and would have proved a considerable obstacle to attackers.[136] Resistance by the garrison and elements of the civilian population showed little sign of weakening and there were considerable reserves of manpower in the city and castle which as yet had not been committed.[137] More surprisingly the defenders' losses were very light, amounting, according to some accounts, to fewer than ten men.[138] Although such figures seem too low, the casualties suffered by the Parliamentarians were certainly far lower than those among the king's supporters.

However, despite these advantages, the defenders' morale was crumbling and the inexperienced Fiennes failed to restore confidence. His order to withdraw from the line, although logical, created widespread dissatisfaction among his troops, as did his heavy-handed treatment of those who questioned the order.

The said Langrish afterwards coming back to Froom Gate; his troop came along with him whom he had brought from the lime-kilns or thereabouts, and upon the sound of the trumpet he was let in at Froom Gate. All men then crying shame that the soldiers were called off the line, and complaining they were betrayed; I further say, that one of the soldiers drawn off the line then reported, they were commanded to retreat into the city upon pain of death, for that city was like to be lost.[139]

Although better known as a naval officer, Robert Blake commanded the troops defending Brandon Hill Fort during the first siege of Bristol. His garrison was cut off from the city after the Royalists breached the line and Fiennes failed to inform him of the surrender. As a result Blake had to face accusations from an angry Rupert of breaking the truce. He was finally allowed to march away with his men. (With grateful thanks to Alan Turton)

This discontent might have been countered if Fiennes had acted in a positive manner, issuing clear orders to the troops and giving them something to do to take their minds off resentment. Instead they were left waiting in the streets for almost two hours while the battle raged in the suburbs. Understandably many came to the conclusion that orders were not going to arrive and wandered off to find food or a quiet place to sleep.[140] When Fiennes finally ordered a general assembly of the garrison, offering food and money to those who attended, only 200 of the 1,000–1,200 men he expected appeared;[141] a significant number of the 'missing' men were still manning the forts or fighting the Royalists in the suburbs but the small numbers who assembled in the Marsh seem to have reduced Fiennes to blind panic. As the Royalist advance slowly ground to a halt through exhaustion and determined Parliamentarian resistance Fiennes sent out a drummer to request a parley.[142]

He returned without success, for the Royalists simply could not believe that Fiennes would consider surrender and suspected a trick. At about 11.00 a.m. Fiennes finally ordered the garrison to make a sally against the Royalist troops in the suburbs; after eight hours of fighting, the condition of the king's supporters can be gauged by the fact that a number attempted to surrender to the garrison.[143] This sally lasted about an hour and a half and disrupted the Royalist advance at a cost of a single fatality[144] yet, as the troops returned to the city from this sortie, Fiennes once again ordered a drummer to go to the Royalists and offer negotiations. This time they were only too happy to accept the proposal.

> Which the Prince willingly embracing and getting their hostages into his hands sent Colonel Gerard and another officer to the governor to treat. The treaty began at 2 o'clock in the afternoon and before 10 at night these articles were agreed upon and signed.[145]

To describe Fiennes's actions as unpopular among the garrison and elements of the population of Bristol would be an understatement. He had great difficulty enforcing the cease-fire[146] and afterwards found himself accused of treachery and cowardice by his own side[147] and ridiculed by the Royalists.[148] The conditions granted to the Bristol garrison were notably harsher than those granted to the defenders of Reading. Fiennes's men were not only stripped of their arms but also

Following the capture of Bristol the Royalists struck a commemorative medal. This sketch and description come from the original notes for Barlett's History of Bristol. *(Reproduced by kind permission of Bristol Central Library)*

denied the courtesy of marching out of the city with the honours of war.[149] In view of the military situation it seems amazing that Fiennes could not have obtained better conditions, also that he accepted them without calling a full Council of War to discuss them.[150]

Thus ended the first siege of Bristol. Like all battles it was a mixture of courage, incompetence, cowardice and confusion. Both sides made mistakes which were to affect the tide of battle but on balance only Parliament seems to have been particularly poorly served by its commander. The final word should go to one who fought there:

That day I came over the river and viewed that side where I found very many of our men slain especially in those places where my Lord Grandison and my Lord Henry Bellasis fell on: they were commanded to assault Brandon and Prior's Hill forts, which is not to be taken by a storm; they were both wounded and left the grafts full of dead bodies.

This is all I can remember of the siege of Bristol; but this much I can say is perfectly true.[151]

CHAPTER 6

Repercussions

The capture of Bristol shattered Parliamentarian hopes of an easy victory.

> The direful news of the surrender of Bristol, which was brought to the two houses on the 31st of July, struck them to the heart, and came upon them as a sentence of death, after a vast consumption of money, and confident promises of destroying all the King's forces by a day, every tax and imposition being declared the last; and for finishing the work, the Earl of Essex was at the same time returned to Kingston, within ten miles of them, with his broken and dismayed troops, which himself would not endure should have the title of an army.[1]

For the first time there were public demands for a negotiated peace and criticism of those who had opposed such a move when Parliament held a stronger position.[2] In the west the supporters of Parliament were equally disillusioned, and local leaders who had surrendered at Bristol frequently visited friends and local communities on their way to London, spreading gloom and despondency.[3] William Stroode visited Dorchester and was asked to give his opinion as to the town's defences, but his reply did little to improve morale: 'these works might keep the Cavaliers about half an hour'.[4] Not surprisingly, the town surrendered as soon as a force of Royalist cavalry appeared.

Among the king's supporters the capture of Bristol raised hopes of victory and encouraged many people to adopt a harder line on the question of negotiations. The king published a pamphlet stating his war aims and objectives, the very title of which included the capture of Bristol among his triumphs.[5] The army at Bristol now divided, with the Oxford forces marching to besiege Gloucester, an action which finally galvanized a dispirited Parliament to reinforce the Earl of Essex's army. The Western Army under Maurice and Hopton launched an offensive which the surviving Parliamentarian forces were initially unable or unwilling to resist effectively. 'Five garrisons by assault and seven by surrender, with 3000 prisoners, five thousand arms, six ships and sixty-four pieces of ordnance in a fortnight's time.'[6] Discipline among the king's forces was not strict enough to prevent looting and destruction of civilian property. The Earl of Carnarvon, commander of the western horse, was so disgusted by the behaviour of his troops that he resigned and joined the king at Gloucester. Clarendon argued that such disorders did much to alienate the population in the western counties and finally provoked effective resistance to the Royalists at Lyme and Poole.[7]

The success of the king's forces was so great that it began to worry those who supported his cause but believed that negotiation was the only hope for peace. Even Prince Rupert, himself accused by Parliamentarians of being a major cause of the war, began to have serious doubts.[8] John Butler was foolish enough to write to Sir William Waller saying that Prince Rupert favoured peace and would use his influence to promote it, but he requested that 'nothing might be put in print concerning the delivery of Bristol, which might reflect upon the Prince's honour'. The messenger, a servant of Butler's, had a pass signed by Rupert. He was waylaid at Bostal House by the Royalist garrison, who plied him with drink; they then read the private dispatches he was carrying. In view of their contents, the dispatches were copied and forwarded to Oxford.[9]

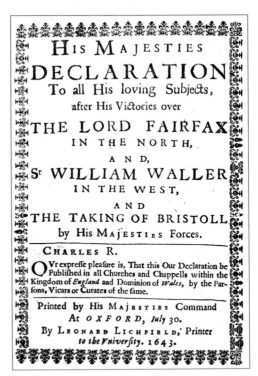

His Majesties Declaration . . . *The significance of the capture of Bristol to the Royalist cause is well illustrated by the title page of this pamphlet. In this tract, published at the peak of his success in the war, the king outlined his war objectives. (Reproduced by kind permission of Bristol Central Library)*

Bristol was coming to terms with Royalist rule. Although the conditions on which Fiennes surrendered were harsh to the point of humiliation, they contained guarantees as to the treatment of both the garrison and the civilian population. These proved worthless: both the Parliamentarians who evacuated the city and those who chose to remain suffered at the hands of the victorious troops. Bristol, it was argued, had brought such treatment upon itself by supporting Parliament and by its failure to prevent the execution of the Royalist conspirators.

I wish I could excuse those swerving from justice and right, which were too frequently practised against contracts, upon the notion, that they, with whom they are made, were rebels, and could not be too ill used.[10]

The first article stated that the garrison should have 'safe convoy to Warminster; and after not to be molested in their march, by any of the King's forces, for the space of three days'. The fifth article allowed any civilian who wanted to do so to 'travel with the governor and forces' or 'have three days liberty to reside here, or depart with their goods, which they please'.[11] When the time came for the garrison and those who chose to accompany them to leave there was confusion about time and route and the Royalists failed to supply the promised escort. This may have been a deliberate act but many supporters of Parliament blamed Fiennes's failure to observe the conditions for their subsequent ill-treatment.[12] Certainly many Royalist troops were unwilling to allow the garrison to leave unmolested.

> Here the ill example of Reading in the breach of the articles, was remembered and unhappily followed; for all that garrison was now here. So that they, with some colour of right, or retaliation, and the rest by their example, used great license to the soldiers, who should have been safely conducted; which reflected much upon the Prince, though he used his utmost power to suppress it; and charged Colonel Fiennes to be accessory to his own wrong, by marching out of the town an hour before his appointment; and thereby his convoy was not ready; and at another gate than was appointed and agreed on.[13]

A Parliamentarian pamphleteer catalogued the humiliations suffered by the refugees at the hands of the Royalist leaders and the troops who 'escorted' them.[14] Fiennes publicly stated that Rupert and Maurice had used their swords on their own men to try to prevent the disorders.[15] The Royalists blamed Fiennes for creating chaos by leaving the city at the wrong time,[16] as did many of the witnesses at his trial.[17]

> The governor broke the conditions with the enemy, in not soldier like delivering up the town and arms according to the Articles agreed on, for which the enemy (as they told me themselves) had no reason to perform their conditions to us, when the governor in the first place broke his conditions with them. I know no greater cause why the officers, soldiers and others were so plundered, miserably abused and many seduced to forsake us and take entertainment of the enemy, than the miscarriage of the governor, whom (so far as I could discern) wholly put every man to shift for himself; and neglected performing conditions.[18]

Other Royalists felt that the treatment of the departing garrison was justified by other abuses of the surrender terms:

> Diverse of them also, offered to carry away their pistols in their cloakbags: others had sold their swords and muskets, and broken their pikes, and spoiled

their ammunition in the castle; driven iron slugs to close some of their greater ordnance and lastly, carried away diverse of their colours: and all this contrary to Articles.[19]

If those who left with Fiennes received rough treatment, those who chose to stay also suffered and Parliamentarian accounts describe the horrors of the 'sack of Bristol':

> When they came in they ran like a company of savage wolves into men's houses, and fell to plundering all sorts without distinction, as well malignants as others. But at last through the instigation of base and ill affected persons, they were directed in special to fall upon such in every street as were well affected to Parliament especially in the High Street and Bridge.[20]

Clarendon makes no attempt to conceal the fact that there was looting:

> As the articles were thus unhappily violated to those who went away, so they were not enough observed to those who stayed, and to the city itself: for many of Col Fiennes's soldiers taking conditions, and entering with the King's army, instructed their new friends, who were most disaffected; so that one whole street upon the Bridge, the inhabitants whereof lay under some brand of malignancy, though, no doubt, there were many honest men among them, was most totally plundered; which because there was but little justice done upon the transgressors, was believed done by connivance from the officers.[21]

It was probably this behaviour that John Butler referred to in his letter to Sir William Waller. Rupert certainly seemed genuinely outraged by the behaviour of his troops, but the propaganda potential was too great to allow his opponents to maintain a gentlemanly silence about the matter.

The troops, with their pay in arrears, used this opportunity to gain immediate rewards for their services.

> Some men had given money for protections to some of the officers, yet were plundered notwithstanding. Others paid fines for their goods taken away and having regained them they were plundered again of the same goods: yea the Cavaliers take up commodities of some men who had protections, promising payment when his majesty paid them, and when they show them their protection they answered that this was no plundering.[22]

The very wording of the 'protections' issued by Rupert would seem to indicate that he expected many of his men to behave in this manner.

By virtue of ye authority and power given to me from our Sovereign Lord King Charles under ye great seal of England. As General under his Majesty of all his Majesty's forces of horse. I do hereby strictly charge and command you and every of you whom it may or shall concern that immediately after sight or knowledge hereof you shall do no manner of violence, injurie, harm or detriment by unlawfully plundering to Thomas Lloyd of Whitminster in ye county of Gloucester, Gent, in his person, families, houses, goods and chattels whatsoever directly or indirectly by yourselves or others. As you will answer ye consequences at your utmost peril. Given at Bristol under my hand and seal at arms this 30th day of July 1643.[23]

There was nothing particularly unusual in the treatment of Bristol after its capture. Accounts of the behaviour of John Stewell after he became governor of Taunton show that such events were marked by extortion, ransom, malicious damage and persecution of former opponents.[24] A Bridgwater resident informed a friend in London that he had been fined a hundred pounds when the Royalists arrived and afterwards was assessed at 15s 6d weekly, besides having to provide accommodation for five soldiers: 'a lamentable thing to consider; but yet it is not only my case but hundreds of my fellows'.[25] The misconduct of Royalist troops was of course exaggerated for propaganda reasons:

Whereas we are informed of many monstrous outrages in several towns and parishes, in this county, by the French papists of the Queen's regiment, and others who are put amongst us by some ill-affected gentlemen, to assist them in raising forces, and amongst the rest a most horrid act, most execrable and abominable in the sight of God and man, committed by six of those French troopers, who forced a woman in the most beastly manner, one after another three days after her delivery from childbed, to the hazard of her life, and have also committed diverse other rapes, murders and other actions unfit to be named by us, in sundry places of this country.[26]

The behaviour of the Royalist troops quartered on civilians after the capture of Bristol did nothing to improve relations, at least according to Parliamentarian sources.

They fill the ears of the inhabitants with their blasphemous, filthy and ungodly language, which no chaste ear or honest heart can endure, yea so desperately wicked are they, that those that billet them dare not perform any act of religion neither to give thanks at meals, nor yet to pray, read or sing psalms: But instead thereof they fill their houses with swearing and cursing insomuch that they corrupt men's servants and children, that those who were once civil have learned to curse and swear almost as bad as they: and on the Sabbath these guests or rather these beasts spend their time in dicing, drinking, carding and other such abominations.[27]

As for those charged with looking after the moral well-being of the king's troops:

> Whereas the chaplains that go with them should teach them better, some of them swear as bad as the soldiers; as namely one of the Prince's chaplains swore 'By the flesh of God' and 'God Damn him' with many other horrible oaths, and in a tavern the Friday after they came to the city, a lords chaplain wished 'the devil might roast his soul in hell if he did not preach such a sermon next Sunday as was never preached in Bristol' some part of which sermon was a railing against the doctrine of predestination calling it a damned doctrine of the Roundheads and in his very sermon from the pulpit burst out into a fearful oath.[28]

The religion of the king's followers may have been judged to be bad, but their taste in music appears to have been truly scandalous.

> They had certain fiddlers who sung blasphemous songs not fit to be mentioned calling them the 4 and 12 psalms and making music on their instruments and standing in the street and praying in a mocking manner saying 'O Lord thou wast with us at Edgehill and Brentford, but where wast thou at Runaway Hill and where art thou now O Lord?' speaking through their noses and looking up to heaven: and when their fellow Cavaliers were beaten and killed before Gloucester those in Bristol swore that God had turned Roundhead.[29]

Although exaggerated, these accounts were based on real events. The need to accommodate large numbers of troops, many of them wounded or sick, created serious overcrowding in Bristol after the siege.

> They quartered soldiers upon all sorts as well malignants as others and all upon free quarter; placing 20 and 30 soldiers in a house upon men of but reasonable estates, which puts them to an unreasonable charge, and the more because diverse of the Cavaliers will have a variety of victuals at each meal, and will not be content to feed upon good beef, but must have mutton and veal and chickens with wine and tobacco etc. and much ado to please them all; causing also men women and children to lay upon boards, or as they make shift, while the Cavaliers possess their beds, which they fill with lice.[30]

Lice and overcrowding created ideal conditions for the spread of typhus and other diseases. By September Luke's agents reported that 'there dye 100 a weeke of the new disease at Bristol'.[31] Parliamentary newssheets had little sympathy for the Bristolians:

> It is credibly informed, that at this present, there are about a thousand men sick in the city of Bristol, whereof the most (as is supposed) are Cavaliers, who by

their stench and nastiness infest every place wheresoever they come, witness Reading, Abingdon, and Oxford from which last town (it is conceived) they have brought that infection. And it is observed, that God's hand hath of late followed them with mortality wheresoever they come, and that justly for their execrable oaths, cursing and imprecations. And if Bristol now suffer with them, they may thank their cowardly admittance of them, and withal take notice of God's judgement upon them for it.[32]

Sickness was to feature throughout the Royalist occupation of Bristol but it peaked during the autumn of 1644 when a plague broke out that was to continue until the end of

Although considered indecisive by Clarendon, Ralph Hopton was one of the king's most capable officers. He was recovering from wounds at the time of the first siege but was subsequently made lieutenant-governor of Bristol. He acted as garrison commander and spent much of his time in the city supervising recruiting and constructing defences. In 1645 he was appointed to the Council of the Prince of Wales and accompanied him to Bristol and afterwards in his withdrawal westward. (Reproduced by kind permission of Bristol Central Library)

1645. In October 1644 the Council and the military authorities in the city agreed that infected persons should be removed to accommodation beyond the defences, and that the city be cleared of 'strangers and straggling poor people' to reduce infection.[33] In June 1645 orders were issued that infected persons were to be held in the Pest House for thirty days and then remain in their own homes for a further fifteen, during which time 'they are to wash their clothes, and houses for avoiding of future infection'.[34]

There was a furious row as to who should be the governor of the city, a position that promised both status and profit. The origin of the dispute lay in the divided command structure of the army. Hertford was irritated by Rupert's lack of respect for his position as commander in the region and he had appointed Hopton governor without consulting the Prince.[35] Rupert regarded the victory and the spoils as his, as it was his army not Hertford's that had captured the city and therefore he felt the governorship was within his patronage. He was, however, unwilling to offend Hopton and so asked the king for the post for himself.[36] The king was happy to grant his nephew's request, and his reply was delivered by the same messenger who brought the first report of the capture of the city. Shortly afterwards a messenger from Hertford arrived informing the king that he had used his authority to appoint Hopton. Charles realized that this apparently trivial clash of personalities could create serious problems as many of his supporters saw his over-mighty German nephew trying to bully Hertford, creating friction within the army.[37]

The king decided to go to the west to settle this dispute between two principal supporters in person, but first he wrote to Hopton assuring him that no offence had been intended.[38] The king confirmed Rupert as governor but instructed him to offer Hopton the lieutenant-governorship. This he did, promising to leave Hopton in complete control of the city 'as if the original commission had been granted to him'.[39] Hopton accepted this compromise which allowed both sides to claim victory.[40]

> But Sir Ralph Hopton, abhorring very much that his Majesties affairs should be disturbed by any concernment of his, disposed all his endeavours to the composing of the business between the two great lords, and for himself wholly submitted to his Majesty's pleasure.[41]

Sadly not all those who had supported Hopton were so generous and antagonisms resurfaced later among the garrison of Bristol.

> But yet the face of affairs within the garrison wore a very unpromising aspect. Some unhappy breaches having happened amongst the officers, the private men at length interested themselves in the quarrels, and animosities ran so high in the army as nearly to destroy all order and discipline.[42]

The king's visit to Bristol also served to rally support. A Royalist newssheet described scenes in the streets:

> His Majesty was brought into the town with great joy and triumph, the Acclamations of the multitude being so lowd and general, as if they never knew till now the happinesse of being under the command of a gracious Soverigne; and that the Bonfires in the night were so great and many, that the towne seemed to be on fire, and folke could hardly passe the Streets for the throngs of people.[43]

Shortly after the siege a gift of wine and sugar was sent to the injured Hopton and over £150 was distributed among wounded Royalist soldiers by the City Council.[44] Some councillors suggested that the king's visit should be marked by a gift of £20,000 but it was agreed that a more modest £10,000 should be raised by public subscription. If the Council hoped that that such generosity would satisfy the Royalists they were soon disillusioned. Rupert let it be known that he expected a similar 'gift' and the Council had to appoint a committee to raise £20,000.[45] The siege had cost the Royalists heavy casualties and Bristol's support of Parliament and its failure to prevent the execution of Yoemans and Boucher meant the city could expect little mercy.[46] However, early reports that the Royalists had hanged the mayor were soon proved false.[47]

If Bristol experienced a period of rough treatment after its capture, so too did the man who surrendered the city. Military commanders who lose battles and survive are never popular: it is better to die a hero on the field of defeat than return home a failure amid excuses and recriminations. Early reports indicated that Fiennes had been captured and executed; from Parliament's point of view this would probably have been preferable to his return to London.[48] Fiennes made a verbal report to the House of Commons justifying his actions and a similar written one to the Earl of Essex, both of which he published.[49] He was risking disgrace and possible death in an effort to salvage his personal reputation and his family's honour. Although quick to point out his personal reluctance to accept the post of governor, he emphasized his diligence in fortifying, provisioning and garrisoning the city;[50] anything less would certainly not have impressed the Lord-General or his political masters.[51] He had made considerable efforts to prepare the town for defence, proving himself a capable and determined administrator.[52] His surrender was, he claimed, unavoidable, largely because of the actions of Sir William Waller who had stripped his garrison of men and, having lost everything at Roundway Down, fled to the west leaving Fiennes and his city to their fate.[53] This accusation was coloured by more than mere professional disagreement or jealousy. Waller was a leading member of the Presbyterian faction in Parliament while the Fiennes family were Independents; Nathaniel was seeking both to save himself and to harm a rival. However, at his trial it emerged that Waller had been *asked* to leave by

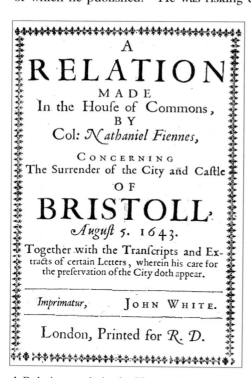

A Relation made in the House of Commons . . . *This report of events at Bristol in July 1643 was to shape views of these events long after the war. Although highly inaccurate, this was the accepted version for most historians. (Reproduced by kind permission of Bristol Central Library)*

Fiennes, who feared that the presence of the general commanding the Western Association would undermine his authority in the city.[54]

Fiennes's accusations against Waller were undermined by his own admission of how easily he had been able to raise and arm men after Roundway[55] and his deliberate understating of the size of the garrison which he claimed had only 1,700 to 1,800 men rather than over 2,500.[56] Conversely, he greatly exaggerated the strength of the Royalist forces and claimed that the king's commanders had expected him to surrender as soon as they arrived at Bristol and were amazed when this did not happen.[57] This is clearly inconsistent with the evidence of hostile witnesses at his trial and is hardly supported by the events of the siege.[58] His contention that the garrison was exhausted by continuous assaults and bombardments has more truth and certainly Rupert ordered skirmishing to be used to keep the defenders awake before the final assault.[59] However, the main assaults were quickly repulsed and the Royalists lacked sufficient guns or ammunition to maintain an effective cannonade.[60] In fact the king's forces had just completed a long forced march and were living in the open without adequate supplies, clothing and shelter – it was the attackers rather than the defenders who might have complained of exhaustion.

Fiennes's account of the actual fighting is highly suspect. He claimed, for example, that he launched a sally as soon as the troops were withdrawn from the line,[61] but officers of the garrison stated that there had been a delay of almost two hours before the sally and there is no reference to such a movement in Royalist accounts.[62] Even more damaging for Fiennes, he failed to mention that before ordering the sally he unsuccessfully requested a parley with the attackers.[63] His claim that the Royalists were able to commit fresh reserve troops to the battle ignores the fact that Rupert was so short of men that he had been unable to keep any units in reserve.[64] The only troops the king's army could call up to support their breakthrough were either cavalry, who were of limited use in street fighting, or infantry who had already been repulsed at other points around the city. As these reinforcements had already been in action for several hours they can hardly be described as 'fresh'.[65]

Fiennes informed the Commons that the surrender of the city was discussed and agreed by a full Council of War.[66] However, two of the three men he named as being present categorically denied attending such a meeting, and others complained that the Council had not been consulted about surrendering the city.[67] Fiennes also claimed that he was forced to surrender the castle as it was unable to contain the whole garrison and the loyal population, whom he was unwilling to leave to the mercy of the Royalists.[68] Yet Fiennes was never reduced to the point where he had to evacuate the city into the castle: although the outer line was lost, the inner, which protected most of the city, remained intact, resisting all the Royalist attacks.[69] Fiennes even claimed that the Avon could be forded at low tide and thus did not form a tenable defensive barrier.[70] This was refuted at his trial and must appear absurd to anyone who has ever seen the mud banks in a large tidal river. The former governor claimed he was desperately short of ammunition by the time he surrendered, believing there were only ten barrels of powder left;[71] however, there were at least another fifty barrels in the castle's magazine, with more in forts and magazines around the town.[72] His critics pointed out that many garrisons had withstood sieges with far lower stocks of ammunition – in particular, the garrison of Gloucester had only thirty barrels at the start of their siege.[73] Rupert's army had begun the campaign with only seventy barrels of powder and the defenders certainly had more ammunition than the attackers by the time of the surrender.[74]

Although Fiennes claimed the defences were too extensive to be easily manned, the fact that the Royalists did not alter the basic system of defence laid out by the Parliamentarian engineers in 1643 suggests they were reasonably well designed. He tried to cast doubt on the ability of the castle to withstand siege guns, claiming that the effectiveness of the Royalist guns against the earthen forts on the line had convinced him that its medieval walls would not survive.[75] In fact the bombardment of the northern forts had been almost totally ineffective and the fire of the heaviest Royalist guns had been directed against Prior's Hill Fort which had subsequently easily repulsed Grandison's assault.[76] If the king's gunners had failed to weaken a small hastily built earthen fort, how much hope did they have against the castle which was massively built and, it was claimed, had been strengthened against artillery.[77] Another product of Fiennes's imagination were the protected assault boats and siege engines that he claimed were available to attack the castle.[78] There were none in the artillery trains sent with Rupert and his engineers certainly did not have the time or resources to manufacture them on site.[79]

Fiennes lied to Parliament. This is understandable: he had surrendered the second most important city in England to the king's forces with almost indecent haste after suffering insignificant casualties, and the Royalists were now besieging Gloucester and rampaging through the western counties as a consequence. Fiennes desperately tried to create an acceptable version of events to save his honour, and perhaps his life, as criticism of his actions mounted. He asked the Earl of Essex to allow him to explain his actions before a military court: he was anxious to avoid facing his family's political rivals in a trial before the House of Commons.

Many in Parliament, including the Earl of Essex, were inclined to accept Fiennes's account, simply to allow the memory of an embarrassing defeat to fade away. However, his version of events was so riddled with contradictions and inaccuracies that others, among them a particularly vocal group of refugees from Bristol, were demanding that the truth be uncovered and the guilty punished. The former governor generated further popular antagonism by attacking William Waller, a popular figure in London and a leading member of the Presbyterian faction in Parliament.[80] Fiennes's account of the events at Bristol was challenged in a pamphlet by the lawyer Clement Walker, who was a member of the Parliamentary

Committee for Somerset. He had acted as advocate during the trial of Yoemans and Boucher and was now in London.[81] One part of his pamphlet could be interpreted as an attack on Fiennes's father, Lord Saye and Sele, who complained to the House of Lords. Always sensitive to their dignity, the Lords fined Walker £100 and ordered him to pay £500 damages. Walker not only refused to submit to this judgment but questioned the right of the House to try him, at which the Lords ordered the fractious lawyer to be committed to the Tower of London. The high-handed behaviour of the Fiennes family created resentment against both father and son, but Nathaniel might still have survived but for one final indiscretion.

After taking Bristol the Oxford Army besieged the city of Gloucester. The king, appalled by the losses at Bristol, ordered that the city should be taken by the slower but less bloody method of investment. The city was less defensible than Bristol but it was held by Col. Massey with such determination that it became a beacon of parliamentary hope in a sea of failure. London was alive with talk of a relief expedition and Fiennes was foolish enough to state in public his opinion.[83]

> Colonel Fiennes soon after his coming from Bristol having a conference with him concerning the surrender thereof, and likewise concerning Gloucester, told him, that he verily believed, or was certain, that Gloucester could not hold out many days (as he remembered he said not 3 or 4 days) if the kings forces came before it.[84]

On 5 September the Earl of Essex arrived at Gloucester after a ten-day march from London and found the Royalists had abandoned the siege. This news was catastrophic for Fiennes.

> The brave defence of Gloucester, and the great success that attended it, made the loss of Bristol the more felt by the Parliament; and consequently the delivery, and yielding it up, the more liberally spoken of and censured. The which Colonel Fiennes having no patience to bear, he desired, being a member of the House of Commons, and of a swaying interest there, 'That he might be put to give an account of it, at a Court of War, which was the proper judicature upon trespasses of that nature' and in the mean time, he was powerful enough upon some collateral, and circumstantial passages, to procure some of the chief who inveighed against him, to be imprisoned and reprehended. This begot greater passion and animosity in the persons that thought they suffered unjustly and only by the authority and interest of the Colonel and his father; which by degrees brought fraction into the House of Commons and the army.[85]

It is possible to detect a hint of desperation in a letter Fiennes sent to Rupert after the news of the relief of Gloucester reached London:

Sir

When I parted from you at Bristol, you expressed a great dislike of the disorders then committed by your soldiers, contrary to the articles agreed upon and were pleased to tell myself in case of anything of seriousness should be done contrary to the agreement if I should write unto you if you needed to seek satisfaction should be given to us wherein agreeable to honour and justice . . .

I have represented unto your Highness the complaints that are brought to me and can expect no less but that according to the agreement and past soldierly promise, your Highness will cause right to be done to these persons, who are so unjustly detained contrary to the agreement made on their behalf, whose the interest but your honour is most concerned in doing them right you shall do yourself more right than either to them or him that is,

Your Highnesses Humble Servant
Nathaniel Fiennes
London Sept. 16 1643[86]

Even if Rupert had been interested in assisting Fiennes he had other concerns, as the Royalist cavalry under his command was then manoeuvring to intercept Essex as he marched back to London from Gloucester. It seems he did nothing to help Fiennes.

Another potentially more dangerous opponent now joined the dispute. William Prynne was a lawyer, propagandist, political extremist and religious reformer. Clarendon commented that 'he became involved out of activity and restlessness of his nature and was afterwards sharpened by contempt'.[87] Indeed opinion had turned so far against Fiennes that on 26 October the House of Lords issued an order to the Lieutenant of the Tower of London that Walker should be 'permitted to go abroad to prepare himself for the hearing'.[88]

On 15 November the charges drafted by Walker and Prynne were read to the House of Commons. 'The Articles of Impeachment' accused Fiennes of cowardice, incompetence and treachery, and compared his defence of Bristol with that of Gloucester. In a particularly vicious dig it was pointed out that Fiennes had executed Yoemans and Boucher merely for planning to surrender the city.[89] In the face of such detailed and extensive charges, the Commons had no choice but to pass them to the Lord-General with a request that there should be a fair and equal trial.[90] The element of personal animosity between Fiennes and his accusers can be seen in Prynne's reply to a letter delivered by Fiennes's footboy:

If you be really as confident of your own innocence and valour, as you are querulous of our pretend calumnies of them (who believe we have written far more truth of you than yourself have done) I conceive you will cordially second our petitions for such a fair public hearing as we desire, and the world expects.[91]

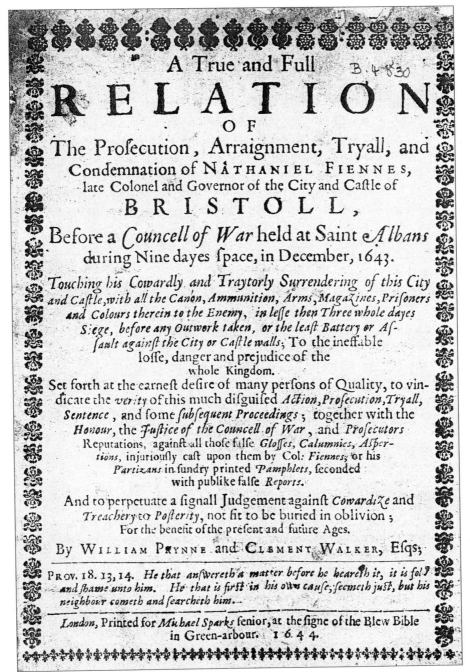

A True and Full Relation . . . *Although the authorities tried to make Fiennes's trial a private matter the prosecution published their own account of the proceedings. Although highly partisan, this account of the events of July 1643 contains a vast amount of detail. (Reproduced by kind permission of Bristol Central Library)*

Although Prynne and Walker wanted the trial to be held in London or Westminster before a General Council of War, it opened on 14 December at Essex's headquarters in St Albans, a choice of venue that appeared yet another act of favouritism to Fiennes. There was more evidence of partiality at the opening of the trial when a prosecution request that the hearing be open to the public was contested and referred to the Lord-General who ruled against an open trial on the grounds that such proceedings might be seen as implying distrust of the court's honesty or competence. The prosecutors were obliged to accept this ruling, but afterwards published an extensive, if highly biased, account of the trial.[92]

One after another the various charges were discussed and disputed, a process that at times degenerated into vicious clashes of personality. For example, Fiennes argued that his surrender was not cowardly because

> When he sent to the enemy for a parley and their hostages came to Frome Gate which was barricaded up, they swore 'God damn us, we will come in at Frome Gate (which was the nearest by) or have no parley at all'; Whereupon he sent them this resolute answer, that they should not come in there, but at Newgate, which they were enforced to do after much contest: ergo the surrender was not cowardly.[93]

In reply Prynne pointed out that the gate was blocked by 15 or 16 feet of woolsacks and earth, the removal of which would not only have been difficult but would also have left the city open to attack if fighting were renewed. If the gate had been cleared, as the Royalists demanded, it would have been:

> an indiscreet and cowardly act, as was not only below the spirit of a governor, or soldier, but of a sucking child, and would have argued the defendant (if consented to) a man utterly destitute, not only of courage but common discretion.[94]

It soon became apparent that the case would be decided on the evidence of witnesses to the events at Bristol. Both sides were to accuse the other of bribing, threatening and intimidating witnesses, with some justification. Fiennes objected to a number of prosecution witnesses on the grounds that they were either women (and thus not competent to give an opinion) or Royalists who would readily slander him. Prynne replied:

> Some of the witnesses only were women and those seconded by men. Secondly that they declare not their own weak opinions but the judgements of men yea of the enemy's own commanders in private serious conference amongst themselves, as well as open discussion with others. Thirdly that these women witnesses and other females of the city showed more true courage and undauntedness than the defendant and some of his officers.[95]

It was in this case the best and strongest of any other [the evidence of Royalists] it being the natural disposition of every soldier that takes any strong fort or city to extoll the enemy's valour and difficulties in winning it as much as possible the more to advance their own prowess. It's no great honour in any man's judgement to conquer a coward, or a place not tenable; therefore those who detract from their enemy's valour or strength, degrogate their own honour, conquest, prowess and as much disparage themselves as their enemies thereby: Since then the enemies both in private discourses among themselves and in conference with others so frequently censure this surrender as cowardly, taxed the defendant for a coward and confessed that they could not have taken the town nor all the devils in hell the castle, had the defendant held them valiantly out against them and not cowardly surrendered them beyond their expectations. Their testimonies backed with the premises must be the most convincing evidence in this particular.[96]

The attacking of witnesses was by no means confined to Fiennes. Prynne was to dismiss most of those called by the defence as,

Either his own kindred, officers, servants, who were parties involved in the same crime and had pay due from him; some young beardless soldiers, never in arms before, who refused to charge the enemy, or citizens to whom he owed money and so scarce competent witnesses in law, in such a case as this.[97]

There was a near riot in the court room when Robert Bagnall, one of the officers who had signed the original letter from Fiennes to the Earl of Essex, 'changed sides' and offered damaging testimony on the behalf of the prosecution.

Capt. Bagnall thus cleared in all particulars; was basted unsufferably by the defendant himself before the Council, and by his witnesses as soon as the Council was risen, some of them giving the lie in the Council Chamber, others challenging him, others menacing him in such sort, that Mr Prynne complaining of these insufferable abuses to the Council, it was ordered to exhibit Articles of Complaint in Capt. Bagnall's name against those who challenged him and gave him the lie, which he did accordingly.[98]

Disputing of witnesses took on an almost farcical quality, as in the case of Maj. Edward Wood, whom Fiennes, not unreasonably, claimed was biased against him because his brother John had cut off Wood's finger during an argument. The court took the view that as the argument had been with John rather than Nathaniel Fiennes, Wood's evidence was admissible.[99]

After nine days of bitter disputation, Fiennes could not convince the court of his innocence. His 'Relation' was shown to be inaccurate to the point of dishonesty and many of the charges against him were proven. The court pronounced the former governor guilty and sentenced him to death for 'not having defended Bristol so well or so long as he ought to have done'.[100] To the fury of the prosecution he was not convicted of either cowardice or treason, probably out of consideration for his family rather than for Fiennes himself. However, the hapless governor did not face the axe or firing squad. The Earl of Essex granted him a pardon, although he was forbidden further military command, and he retained his seat in Parliament despite his conviction.[101] He went abroad to nurse his wounded pride but controversy about the trial continued[102] as it had touched some very significant issues in the 'English Revolution'.

Many looked upon this example, as a foundation of great awe, and reverence in the army, that the officers might see that no titles or relations should be able to break through the strict discipline of war. For this gentleman was a person of singular merit, and fidelity to the party that he served and of extraordinary use to them in those councils that required the best understanding. Others thought it an act of unadvised severity to expose so eminent a person, who knew all their intrigues upon the importunity of useless and inconsiderable persons to infamy; whilst others considered it a judgement from heaven upon a man who had been so forward in promoting public calamities, and no doubt it increased much the factions and animosities both in Parliament and in the army, and might have done them further mischief, if it had not fallen on a man so thoroughly engaged that no provocations could make him less of their party, or less concerned in their confederacy.[103]

CHAPTER 7

Bristol and the Royalist Armies

Following the capture of Bristol, the Royalist army faced a critical manpower shortage; already weakened by disease and desertion, they had suffered 1,200–1,400 casualties. On 9 August the first report reached Samuel Luke of conditions in the newly captured city:

> The King's party confess that they lost near 2000 men and that the soldiers mutinied that so many gallant men should be lost and the town not pillaged and they would not be satisfied till Prince Robert [Rupert] had given the foot 5s a man and promised the horse liberty to plunder any man wheresoever they came of any money, goods or cattle that had done anything for the Parliament.[1]

The first source of recruits were the officers and men of the Parliamentary garrison and it was reported that some were being forced to join the king's army.[2] However, the thousand or so men of the garrison who changed sides[3] were not sufficient to fill the Royalists' depleted ranks. At Fiennes's trial a Mr Saviage, a veteran of the Irish wars, told the court about a muster of Royalist troops at Bristol where 42 or 52 companies paraded only 1400 men rather than 4–5000. When he asked one of the officers why they were so under strength he was told that it was due to losses during the siege.[4] The brigade of John Bellasie had suffered such heavy casualties during the fighting around Frome Gate that it was broken up before the field army marched to Gloucester.[5] It has been suggested that Bellasie was temporarily appointed governor of Bristol but, as both Hopton and Rupert were in the city this seems unlikely; more probably, as was reported to Luke, he was temporarily appointed governor of the castle.[6] It was units from his brigade that formed the bulk of the initial garrison. To judge by ammunition issues and de Gomme's account the six regiments of infantry included Hopton's, Rupert's, Maurice's, Bellasie's, Stradling's and Washington's dragoons or foot.[7] These infantry units had a total strength of only 1,200 men and were supported by Maurice's regiment of horse which numbered only 200.[8]

However, recruits were now 'coming in freely to the new government' and the ranks of these regiments were quickly filled. By the beginning of September, when Hopton was ordered to draw out troops from the city to reinforce the field army at Newbury, the garrison contained 2,000 infantry and 4–500 horse and Hopton had already dispatched 2,500 infantry and 400 cavalry to the king.[9] In a period of five weeks 4,000 infantry and cavalry recruits passed through units based in Bristol. Parliamentarian information on the garrison was confused. On 9 September it was reported that there were only 200 Royalist soldiers in the city and they were threatening to burn the city 'if they be not supplied with necessaries'. Three days later another agent returned from the city and told Luke that there were a thousand men in the garrison, and that the citizens had offered to 'provide 4000 men at any time'.[10]

Bristol provided a secure area well removed from the front line where newly arrived recruits from Wales, Ireland or the West of England could be organized and equipped. The city's central position relative to the main recruiting areas, combined with plentiful accommodation and large magazines, made it an ideal assembly point for field armies. Hopton, who was acting as governor of the city after its capture, noted that there were large number of recruits coming in but that they expected 'reasonable means of subsistence, which expectation, if the lord Hopton had been able to continue to them, it would certainly have proved a garrison able to have recruited most of the king's armies'.[11] Clarendon described Hopton's new garrison as 'a magazine for men, arms, ammunition and all that was wanted'.[12] In December 1643 John Ravenscroft returned from Oxford to report that men had arrived in the city from Bristol and were being used to bring other companies up to strength.[13] Bristol seems to have acted as a replacement depot for the king's armies, as the author of *Mercurius Aulicus* boasted to the king's enemies in May 1644:

> the west hath such plenty that 500 muskets, 2 tunne of match, with abundance of Powder, came to Oxford from Bristol, conducted by 500 lusty western soldiers, who will spend it to some purpose on the rebels army.[14]

In late October 1643 a parliamentary newssheet reported 'there are ten or twelve ships at Bristol ready rigged and going out to fetch over rebels from Ireland'.[15] Parliamentarian propagandists left their readers in no doubt as to the consequences of this:

> His majesty's late sending of at least 30 sail of ships from Bristol (a sad effect of its unhappy surrender) besides other ships elsewhere, to bring over Irish rebels, to ruin our kingdom and cut our throats, many of which are already arrived, and have committed great murders and insolencies at Bristol and elsewhere without restraint or punishment.[16]

Troops from Ireland had begun to arrive at western ports. In Minehead such reinforcement was said to have provoked serious unrest among Royalist troops.

On Monday night last, Noah Rendall came from Minehead and brought certain news that there were landed in that place about a thousand Irish rebels, which so amazed the poor soldiers that they all with a unanimous voice cried 'away to Minehead, let us cut those papist throats' . . . one of the soldiers swore with a great oath saying 'we have brought our hogs to a fair market; what be there not Protestants enough in England to fight for our religion but that the king must send for the Irish papists? (I see I must not call them rebels.) I'll never hold with papists so long as I breathe' and presently all the soldiers cried no papists should join with them. So there was a terrible mutiny till the master of the town came and appeased them.[17]

The author of this account also claimed that 2,000 Irishmen had landed at Bristol, but this was certainly an exaggeration.

During this period two regiments joined Hopton at Bristol from Ireland although they represented a somewhat mixed blessing:

bold, hardy men, and excellently well officered, but the common men very mutinous and shrewdly infected with the rebellious humour of England, being brought over merely by the virtue and loyalty of their officers, and large promises, which there were then but small means to perform.[18]

The landings at Bristol and the behaviour of the 'Irish' there formed part of William Prynne's vicious attack on the king's policy towards Catholics.[19]

some of the Irish rebels lately landed at Bristol (where they murdered two vintners and a tapster, beating out their brains, upon no just occasion at all, and yet were suffered to go Scot-free and march up in Sir Ralph Hopton's army against Parliament, as I am certainly informed by some lately come from hence) have openly blamed the Cavaliers, for that when Bristol was surrendered, they did not put man, woman and child therein to the sword, notwithstanding their articles; though punctually observed in no particular, but violated in everything.[20]

These accounts are inaccurate. Most of the 'Irish Papists' were 'English Protestants', previously engaged in trying to suppress the rebellion in Ireland; however, the anti-Irish and anti-Catholic sentiment prevalent in England at this time ensured that such horror stories were widely accepted. There may have been problems in Bristol: it is claimed that the arrival of Irish troops provoked a strike among pilots and a near mutiny in the trained bands of the city.[21] Certainly Hopton quickly moved these regiments out of the city to Bath and thence to Wiltshire.[22] However, other contingents were to arrive in Bristol over the next few months: 1,800 foot and 300 horse arrived in November, followed by 700 infantry in

February 1644 and finally 400 infantry in April.[23] The parliamentary intelligence network frequently described the arrival of Irish troops but tended to exaggerate the numbers involved. Henry Cunington reported the November group as being 3,000 strong and in March 1644 reported another 2,000 had landed.[24]

These 'Irish' troops formed part of a new Royalist army assembling in the Bristol region in October 1643 under Hopton. The intention was to clear Dorset, Wiltshire and Hampshire before moving against London.[25]

> The Lord Hopton was appointed to command an army apart to be levied out of the garrison of Bristol, and those western counties adjacent newly reduced; where his reputation and interest was very great; and by it he had in a short time raised a pretty body of foot and horse; to which receiving an addition of two very good regiments (though not many in number) out of Munster, under the command of Sir Charles Vavasour and Sir John Paulet and a good troop of horse under the command of Captain Bridges, all which had been transported, according to former orders out of Ireland to Bristol.[26]

The army was to include units from Oxford, Wales, Dorset, Somerset, Gloucestershire and Ireland by the time it took the field.[27]

In late October Hopton's army left Bristol and began operating in Wiltshire and Hampshire.[28] The Bristol garrison now contained only one Oxford unit (Rupert's), and one Western regiment (Hopton's).[29] As these officers were respectively the honorary and *de facto* governors of the garrison the presence of these regiments was only to be expected.[30] The other four regiments in the city at this time, Hawley's, Stadwell's, Veal's and Bridge's, were new units recruited in the city and surrounding areas. These six regiments contained 200 officers and 2,236 common soldiers; 590 of them were Bristolians, mostly serving in Hawley's and Hopton's regiments.[31] Hawley's remained in the city, and their colonel was appointed deputy governor at Hopton's request. Most of the 450 unarmed men of the 904 listed as belonging to Hopton and Hawley were probably in the latter regiment.[32] Hopton had drawn 300 men of his regiment out of the garrison for field service in October, so many of those in the city were probably newly raised unarmed recruits.[33] Sir John Stewell was governor of Taunton, although his regiment was in Bristol, and only 100 of his 278 men had weapons.[34] Thomas Veal came from Alverston in Gloucestershire and the bulk of his regiment was raised in that county, but only 54 of his 294 men were armed.[35] Thomas Bridges from Keynsham raised his regiment in Somerset, and only half of his 250 soldiers had arms.[36] The only fully armed soldiers in the garrison were the 504 men of Rupert's regiment.[37]

It was not until 1 January 1644 that 900 muskets were issued from the Bristol magazine to complete the arming of these regiments.[38] Bridges was appointed Governor of Bath and appears to have taken his regiment with him; Veal and his men were ordered to Gloucestershire in February; and Stewell's men probably moved to Taunton.[39] The 'city' regiment under Hawley appears to have become the hard core of the Bristol garrison. This process of bringing newly raised units to be trained and equipped at Bristol prior to dispatch to other garrisons or the field armies was probably typical of the rest of the occupation.

Following his defeat at Cheriton on 28 March 1644, Hopton's troops were absorbed into the king's main army, and he returned to Bristol to supervise improvements in the defences and to organize recruiting.[40] He was in Bristol when the king defeated Waller at Cropredy Bridge and turned his army westward in pursuit of the Earl of Essex.

> His majesty had no sooner taken this resolution, than he gave notice of it to the Lords of the Council at Oxford; and sent an express into the west, to inform the Queen of it; who by the way, carried the orders to Lord Hopton, 'To draw what men he could out of Monmouth-Shire and south Wales into Bristol; that himself might meet his majesty with as many as he could possibly draw out of that garrison.'[41]

Hopton obeyed his orders with his customary efficiency and met the king on 11 August with 2,000 men.[42]

On 26 August Prince Rupert returned to Bristol, five days before the final surrender of Essex's infantry in Cornwall. He was in poor spirits: eight weeks earlier he had fought and lost a major battle at Marston Moor outside York, and his defeat cost the Royalists control of the north. He had come to Bristol with the hope of recruiting fresh troops in Wales to launch a fresh campaign in the north-west.[43] Reports of his movements and activities flew between London and local commanders throughout September, although it was reported that he had only 300 men in Bristol.[44] However, by mid-September a new force was entering the Bristol region and Massey reported to the Committee of Both Kingdoms that he had clashed with Royalist cavalry. 'Their number is computed to be about 2,500 horse, ill armed. There are diverse brigades of horse and near 50 colours when they are all together.'[45]

These were the 'northern horse', survivors of the army defeated at Marston Moor, moving towards Bristol to join Rupert. On 6 October Massey reported that the northerners would not be able to combine with Rupert as his forces were too weak to march out to meet them.[46] Following a meeting with the king at South Parrot on 30 September Rupert and Hopton had returned to Bristol to, as Waller reported, 'draw out the garrison'.[47] Their objective was to draw together as many troops as possible to create a new field army, thereby forcing the Parliamentarians to divide their forces. If this failed the troops under Hopton and Rupert would be able to reinforce the king's army which was then marching back to Oxford.[48] Bristol was to act as the pivot of a movement allowing dispersed units to be assembled on the march. Kitson explains the difficulty and risks involved:

In essence Rupert had to arrange for the movement of 2,000 foot soldiers recruited by Gerrard in South Wales for a distance of about sixty miles to a crossing of the River Severn, picking up the Northern Horse in Monmouthshire on the way. These troops then had to get across the river in the face of such interference as the Parliamentary garrison at Gloucester could arrange: this turned out to be slight although the lines of communication of the force with South Wales were cut after it crossed the river. The force next had to march south for about thirty miles towards Bath where they would join Rupert and the troops he was bringing with him from Bristol.[49]

Although unable to reinforce the king before the second battle of Newbury (27 October 1644), it was reported that Rupert had arrived at Bath on that day with 4,500 infantry, 3,000 cavalry and a train of artillery.[50] If these figures are correct the 'Bristol contingent' brought by Rupert and Hopton numbered 2,500 infantry and 500 horse plus artillery. Waller and Hesilrige wrote to the Committee of Both Kingdoms warning them of this new danger:

> The king's army is exceedingly dispersed, and if ever victory might be followed with advantage this is one. We all know the activeness of the enemy to rally, especially Prince Rupert having so good a foundation for an army at Bath and the king in person with him [he had brought 500 cavalry with him]. We conceive if you suffer your forces to disperse before they either scatter Prince Rupert's or drive them to their winter quarters, the enemy will continue masters of the west.[51]

In November 1644, after the two armies had settled into winter quarters, an establishment was issued for Bristol and its subsidiary garrisons.[52] In view of the large area to be defended the number of troops allowed was modest: 3,600 infantry and 620 horse. The cost was to be met from the customs dues, plus weekly contributions from Somerset, Wiltshire, Gloucestershire and the city of Bristol, which it was hoped would raise £2,000 a week. The table opposite provides a detailed description of the organization and pay rates of a major Royalist garrison.

The garrison commanders were generously paid for their services. Rupert did not draw anything as governor, but Hopton received £21 as his lieutenant, and Hawley £10 as deputy. The governors of Bath and Berkeley each received £7 and those at Portishead, Nunny and Farley were allowed £5. In addition a number of 'staff' officers and military civil servants were included in the garrison's establishment.

| | Weekly Pay Rate | | | | | | Number in Garrison | |
| | Infantry | | | Cavalry | | | Infantry | Cavalry |
	£	s	d	£	s	d		
Colonel	5	–	–	7	–	–	3	1
Lieutenant Colonel	4	3	4	6	–	–	3	1
Major	3	16	8	5	10	–	3	1
Captain	2	10	–	5	–	–	21	5*
Lieutenant	1	8	–	3	–	–	30	8
Ensign/Cornet	–	18	–	2	5	–	30	8
Gentleman at Arms	–	8	–		n/a		30	
Sergeant		not given			n/a		63	
Drum Major	–	8	–		n/a		3	
Corporal	–	5	–	1	1	–	90	24
Drummer/Trumpeter	–	5	–	–	17	6	60	16
Quartermaster	1	–	–	1	10	–	3	8
Chaplain	1	–	–	1	8	–	3	1
Chirurgeon	2	–	–	–	17	–	3	1
Provost Marshall	1	–	–		n/a		3	
Carriage Master	–	18	–		n/a		3	
Common Soldiers	–	3	6	–	10	–	3252	546

| Artillery Men | Weekly Payment | | | Number in Garrison |
	£	s	d	
Master Gunner of the City	2	6	8	1
Master Gunner	–	17	6	9
Masters Mate	–	14	–	11
Gunners	–	10	–	42

Staff Officers: Weekly Pay Rate

	£	s	d
The Commissary General or Muster Master	3	10	–
The Quartermaster General	2	6	8
Petardier or Engineer for Fireworks	5	–	–
The Provost Marshall	2	6	8
The Proviant Master	1	–	–
The Treasurer	4	13	4
Eight Collectors of Contribution	1	18	–
Two Deputy Treasurers	1	15	–
Two Clerks to the Treasurer	–	17	6
Three Keepers of the Magazine of Vituals	1	3	4
Commissary of Vituals (Royal Fort and Castle)	–	15	–

Standard-bearer of the Bristol Trained Bands. The ensign was the junior officer of an infantry company whose main task was the defence and display of the company's colour. The two-metre square taffeta flag was the rallying point of the company or regiment on the smoky battlefields of the civil war and was always a target for enemy attack. To lose one's colours to the enemy or surrender them was a great disgrace and a unit that had lost its flag was forbidden to carry another until they had captured one of the enemy's. Ensigns were usually young men but not always, as in this case. He wears a sleeveless buff-coat over a rather old-fashioned slashed doublet. Around his waist is a sash or scarf which indicates that he is an officer and his allegiance. He wears bucket-topped boots as he would have been mounted while on the march, the colour being carried by a trusted pikeman. Only on parade or in battle did the ensign actually carry the colours. He is holding the standard in a posture known as 'Marching in state'. (With grateful thanks to Alan Turton)

A vital element of the Royalist garrison was the 'home guard' formed by trained bands and auxiliary units of the city. The trained bands were, in theory, the elite of the militia in each county or borough and during the 1630s it was reported that those in Bristol consisted of 'three companies each consisting of 100 private men and six officers'.[53] In February 1638 George Clarke reported that the city had increased its trained bands from the official strength of 300 to 500 organized in four companies, and that the city was 'very careful' of these troops.[54] These companies formed the basis of the forces with which Bristol attempted to maintain its independence early in the war and they were expected to serve one night in four.[55] Although pro-parliamentary officers were appointed to command them Fiennes distrusted the Bristol bands and after Roundway Down may have disarmed them and used their weapons to equip more reliable units.[56] After the capture of the city, the citizens promised to supply 4,000 men when needed and it was noted by a parliamentary agent that 'soldiers and townsmen keep watch by turns'. Like many promises made at this time it is doubtful if these men could have been fielded.[57] Efforts were made to reorganize the trained bands, and in February 1643 the Royalist ordnance officer in the city informed his superiors that the city was establishing a magazine of 600 muskets for its defence.[58] In June it was recorded that the city had purchased eighteen barrels of French gunpowder and two barrels of pistol powder for its stores at a cost of £102 13s 2d.[59] It was later decided to expand the trained bands to 1,000 men although it is doubtful that this strength was ever achieved.[60]

The Bristol 'home guard' was further expanded in March 1644 when an auxiliary band or regiment was formed to reinforce the existing body. Such units were common in the civil war with the best known being the London auxiliary regiments. The Royalists raised a number of similar units in garrisons such as Oxford, Reading and Chester.[61] In June 1644 the sum of £155 3s 10d was paid by the city of Bristol for 'ensigns, drums and other things for the auxiliary band'.[62] All able-bodied townsmen were expected to enlist in the new body but desertion was a serious problem and by November Hawley was complaining that many of the auxiliary troops had 'run away' and requested permission to impress another 1,000 men.[63] By 1645 the auxiliary regiment was composed of 'townsmen' and consisted of six colours (companies) which, depending on the organization adopted, would have meant the unit was, in theory, 6-800 strong.[64] These troops were under the control of the city rather than the military authorities, and on at least one occasion the mayor refused to release the auxiliary for field service under Rupert.[65]

Although often grouped together the trained bands and auxiliaries were distinct units. The trained bands were commanded by Thomas Colston, a merchant of the city,[66] the auxiliaries by John Taylor, one of the Bristol MPs who died during the second siege of Bristol.[67] When Rupert arrived in Bristol to organize its defence following Naseby, he complained that the trained bands and auxiliaries had been reduced to only 800 men rather than the 1600–1800 men on their establishments.[68] Nevertheless, this was not an inconsiderable force at this stage of the war.

When the Prince of Wales moved to Bristol in March 1645 it had been arranged that suitable foot and horse guards were to be raised and waiting for him in Bristol.[69] However, as Clarendon noted on his arrival, 'of his guards of horse and foot . . . not

The colours of the auxiliary regiment of Bristol, formed to reinforce the garrison in 1644. Richard Symonds, a member of the King's Lifeguard of Horse, recorded details of the standards in July 1645. They were white with red hearts to signify the company, with the cross of St George in the top corner. They all carried the motto 'For God and King' in Latin. (With grateful thanks to Alan Turton)

one man or horse [was] provided'.[70] The prince and his Council met the Royalist Commissioners for the western counties at Bridgwater and it was agreed to raise a new army:

> those Counties, according to their several known proportions, would in a very short time (as I remember a month was the utmost) raise, and arm six thousand foot, besides the Prince's guards, which would be full two thousand more.[71]

Such numbers of troops were not recruited and those that were assembled at points all over the west country. However, the prince's guards were mustered at Bristol and by the time he left the city in May he was able to leave a detachment of 500 men to garrison the Royal Fort at Bristol.[72] This was necessary because many of the regular garrison had been drawn out for service at the siege of Taunton.

How strong was the garrison of Bristol that faced Fairfax and his New Model Army in August 1645? Some pro-Parliamentarian authors have suggested that Rupert had 4,000 men available,[73] while at the other extreme a recent biographer of Rupert claims he had only 800 horse and 700 foot.[74] Rupert himself admitted that there were 500–600 effective infantry out of the 3,600 on the Bristol establishment and 800 trained bands and auxiliaries.[75] To this can possibly be added 500 men of the Prince of Wales Guards and the troops that Rupert brought with him as personal escort, say 150 horse and 500–600 foot.[76] Reinforcements came from Worcester in July, in the form of three veteran cavalry regiments (Rupert's, Maurice's and Vaughan's) containing 700–800 men.[77] After the battle of Langport on 10 July, Clarendon noted that 'very many ran away to Bristol':

Many of the troops brought to Bristol by the Royalists (and indeed by all armies of the civil war era) would have been accompanied by their wives and families. They performed a range of functions in support of the troops, such as cooking, washing and repairing clothing, and nursing the sick and wounded. The behaviour of women in the army was governed by strict regulations and there were severe punishments for those found guilty of criminal or immoral behaviour. (With grateful thanks to Alan Turton) these may have been soldiers detached for field service from the garrison or simply troops weary of Goring's erratic leadership.[78] In addition a large number of Welsh troops were drawn into the garrison: 'Prince Rupert sent for all those foot which were levied towards a new army, and part of those which belonged to General Gerrard.'[79] Even allowing for sickness in the city, Rupert had at least 1,000 horse, 2,500 infantry and 800–1,000 auxiliaries to defend Bristol in August 1645.

BRISTOL AS A NAVAL BASE

The exact number of ships captured at Bristol is uncertain. Seyer states that twenty-two vessels fell into the king's hands, and this seems reasonable if, as Powell suggests, eight ships were captured in the city itself in addition to the eight which went over to the king in the Kingsroode and a number of prizes taken there.[80] Included among the prizes was one of the small 5th rate 'whelps' of the pre-war fleet and two armed merchantmen of the Parliamentarian navy, *Fellowship* (28 guns) and *Hart* (12 guns). The ships were quickly placed under the command of Sir John Pennington, the most able of the king's naval officers, who set about creating a Royalist rather than a Royal navy. On 2 August a spy newly returned from Oxford informed Luke that Pennington had seized thirty ships at Bristol.[81] John Berkenhead, the Royalist author of the newssheet *Mercurius Aulicus*, visited Bristol with the king at this time and reported that Pennington had eighteen ships ready for sea, and further vessels were promised:

> The Citizens were so desirous to give His Majesty all possible content herein, that they resolved to trim and fit as many serviceable ships as belonged unto them, till they raised His Majesty a fleet of fifty sayle.[82]

However, while the king was visiting Bristol his naval forces suffered their first reverse. *Fellowship* and *Hart* were sent to Milford Haven to secure that anchorage and to inform the local gentry of the fall of Bristol, and suggest that they should offer the king their services.[83] Unfortunately a parliamentary squadron arrived while they were inside the harbour and both vessels were quickly captured, and subsequently reincorporated in the Parliament's fleet. The senior naval officer present, Capt. Smith of the *Swallow* (34 guns) refused to recognize the Royalists' commissions and threatened to treat his captives as common pirates.[84] Despite this inauspicious start, the Royalist naval forces, based at Bristol, soon developed into a serious problem for the Parliament. When the king marched against Gloucester it was reported that ammunition was sent with the army in '2 or 3 great barkes', and during the siege the Royalists evacuated their sick and wounded to Bristol by water.[85] By early September it was reported that Capt. Slingsby had sailed with a squadron of six ships 'to take what prizes he can light on'.[86] In October a report stated that a large number of ships were being prepared at Bristol to transport

John Pennington. The most senior and able of the naval officers to join the king's side at the outbreak of the civil war, Pennington organized a Royalist (as opposed to a Royal) navy, using ships and resources captured at Bristol. (Reproduced by kind permission of Bristol Central Library)

troops from Ireland.[87] In fact, seven vessels were prepared under the command of Baldwin Wake.[88] These ships were to transport a large number of troops from the English army in Ireland to North Wales and Cheshire.[89] At his trial the hapless Fiennes found himself being blamed for the successful arrival of these reinforcements, on the grounds that Wake's ships were provisioned from the food stocks that he had assembled for the use of his garrison.[90]

The Royalist squadron at Bristol received occasional reinforcements as ships deserted to the king's service. As early as March 1642 the king had issued a proclamation instructing seamen to refuse to serve under the Earl of Warwick in Parliament's fleet, a proclamation that Fiennes's had publicly burnt in Bristol.[91] In November 1643 the king went further and published a proclamation to 'seamen, sailors, mariners and other watermen', offering his Majesty's pardon to any who surrendered their vessels and entered royal service.[92] Even before this, ships were joining the king's navy in considerable numbers following the capture of the south-western ports.

Certain news is now brought hither, that the ship called *Charles* of Gloucester, is safely come into Bristol well laded with tobacco etc. from the West Indies. So as the ships come into his Majesty almost as thick as Sir William Waller's troopers have done all this week.[93]

Perhaps the most spectacular addition to the Bristol fleet was the 600-ton East India Company ship *John* (26 guns) commanded by John Mucknell, which arrived in June 1645:

The vessel had 36 peeces of brass and iron ordnance (whereof 26 peeces were mounted, and two brass cuts for her longboats, besides eight peeces more in the hold) which were better bestowed in his majesties service, with all her lading (Gold, Silver, Coral etc.) whereof his Majesty will give ample reward to the Captain, not only with present moneys, with other marks of Honour, but by a settled pension also for his life: there were in this vessel 78 English Mariners and 12 Black Moores, not one whereof but shall be bountifully rewarded for his loyalty ...[94]

After being knighted by the Prince of Wales for his services Mucknell set out on a privateering expedition. After out-manoeuvring and out-fighting a squadron of three parliamentary ships off Land's End, his ship was wrecked in the Scillies.[95]

What were these Bristol ships like? In view of the diverse trade carried on from Bristol the city's shipping would have varied from large ships suitable for the transatlantic trade to barks and trows used for coastal work. Green noted that most Bristol ships were small, the largest being a modest 400 tons and the majority less than 100,[96] but these small ships were very seaworthy and traded over great distances. A listing of Bristol ships lost after 1610 shows 40-ton ships lost in Portugal and Rome, 60-tonners in the Canaries and Gibraltar, and vessels of 80 tons in Genoa and Cadiz. Out of the forty-four Bristol ships listed as having being wrecked or taken by pirates only six were of 100 tons or more.[97] Two surveys of the shipping of the port of Bristol taken in 1626 and 1629[98] show that the average size of ships had increased in this period and that they were increasingly armed for their own defence owing to the wars with France.[99]

What type of ships did Pennington choose in assembling his new fleet? In all probability he selected a mixture of large heavily armed ships and smaller vessels, whose sailing qualities were superior. Judging by the data provided by Damer-Powell, a 'typical' Bristol merchant vessel armed for its own defence displaced between 50 and 150 tons and carried between 6 and 16 guns.[100] In some cases ships carried far heavier armaments: these may have been vessels employed on particularly hazardous voyages or early examples of the private warship which was to become a Bristol speciality during the eighteenth century.[101] The *Sampson*, which was part of a convoy carrying supplies to Ireland in 1643, was described as 'a ship of good defence and goeth convoy unto what we send'.[102] Could Bristol ships be compared with parliamentary warships of similar size? The *Reformation*, a 200-ton ship mounting 20 guns and owned by Richard Lock of Bristol, may be typical of the more heavily armed ships available to Pennington. The ship was commandeered by Fiennes to act as a guard vessel in the Kingsroode in February and July 1643 and subsequently formed part of the fleet under Wake bringing troops from Ireland.[103] To judge by the guns captured on the Bristol defences, which had mainly come from merchant ships, her armament would have been iron guns of fairly small calibre.[104] A merchant vessel of this size would have had a separate gundeck, on which may have been mounted a couple of demi-culverins and ten or twelve sakers and minnions. On the upper deck there might be another pair of minnions but more likely a mixture of falcons, falconnets and murderers. A purpose-built warship of similar size would carry the same number of guns but the gundeck would carry demi-culverins or sakers and the upper deck minnions.[105] The major difference was that the armament of a warship, even the smallest, was offensive while a merchant vessel's was primarily defensive.

The Bristol ships with their lighter construction and weaker armament were no match for the parliamentary navy but they made excellent blockade runners and commerce raiders. The shipping of Bristol may never have challenged the opposition's naval supremacy but they were an invaluable addition to the Royalist cause.

THE DEFENCES

Almost as soon as the city was occupied by the Royalists they began to repair and extend the defensive lines around the city. On 9 August a parliamentary agent reported that the Royalists at Bristol were 'making a blockhouse 6 miles from the town to examine all ships that pass that way'. This was the fort at Portishead which became an important sub-garrison of Bristol.[106] In the city itself the main efforts were devoted to reconstructing the small forts along the high ground to the north, making them into substantial defensive positions. To judge by the reports written by de Gomme there was little improvement in the line itself, which remained about 3 ft thick and 5–6 ft high, with a 6–7 ft wide ditch 4–5 ft deep.[107] However, this may be an understatement to justify Rupert's surrender. Russell suggests that the surviving section of the line between Water Fort and Brandon Hill at least was extensively remodelled and strengthened during this period.[108] The line to the east of the town was certainly not rebuilt and was particularly criticized by de Gomme as being only 5 ft high and the ditch 5 ft deep.[109] However, the defences around Lawfords Gate were substantially enlarged to produce a fortified position supporting the line.[110]

The fort at Brandon Hill was converted from a tiny 18 ft square enclosure into a huge bastion 45 yd long and 30 yd wide which was equipped with six guns by December 1644.[111] The tiny fort on Windmill Hill which had mounted three guns in July 1643 was reconstructed into a huge pentagonal bastion fortress mounting twenty-two guns and acting as a citadel to both defend the city and overawe it.[112] Prior's Hill Fort was rebuilt with two levels of firing slits mounting thirteen guns.[113] The five forts between the river and Prior's Hill had mounted fifteen guns at the time of the first siege but were rebuilt to mount fifty-five guns by November 1644.[114]

These improvements were carried out under the supervision of Bernard de Gomme, one of the best military engineers available to the Royalists, on the orders of Prince

A gunner. The defences of Bristol were designed around artillery during both sieges. As far as is known gunners did not receive any form of uniform and wore whatever was practical for their strenuous and grimy job. This particular individual has removed his doublet to reveal a heavy linen shirt. He wears a brimmed, knitted Monmouth cap. His woollen breeches are held up by a laced waistband and he wears two pairs of stockings, the outer pair of coarse linen or leather. Suspended by a cord about his neck is a large horn flask containing fine priming powder. In his hand he has a circular shot gauge used to ensure that the cast-iron shot would fit the bore of his gun. For personal defence gunners were usually issued with infantry swords and sometimes, as in this case, with a pole arm known as a 'bill'. (With grateful thanks to Alan Turton)

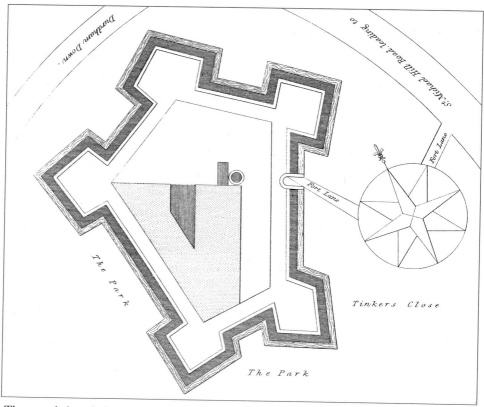

The ground plan of the Royal Fort built by the Royalists during their occupation of the city. By November 1644 the fort mounted twenty-two guns and contained store-houses and magazines separate from those of the rest of the city. On its surrender Cromwell noted that it contained enough food for 120 men to survive for 320 days. (Reproduced by kind permission of Bristol Central Library)

Rupert.[115] The city was responsible for supplying the necessary labour needed to carry out these improvements in the same way as it had built the original lines. By March 1644 it was ordered that two councillors should ride round the works each afternoon to encourage the workers.[116] Bristol could not supply enough labour to complete the works on time and so labourers were conscripted from the surrounding areas.

> By direction of Lord Hopton we therefore require you to grant warrants to all your petty officers to bring into the garrison at Bristol, unto the Fort Royal, near Brandon Hill, three score labourers out of your hundred next Tuesday by 7 o'clock in the morning with good and serviceable spades and pickaxes, and that you return the names of all such as are warned in writing unto one of us, and assure them from

Lord Hopton that none of them shall be pressed to be soldiers, and that they shall have their wages paid out of the monthly contribution money of the hundred, and shall be held at their work but a few days.[117]

It is sometimes suggested that the improvements were completed by December 1644 and the detail given in the Garrison Establishment certainly seems to support this.[118] However, as Parker points out, there remained a great deal to do to complete the Royal Fort at that date and de Gomme, writing to justify Rupert's surrender, listed many defects in the defences.

The ditch of the Great Fort on the right hand gate beyond the face of the Bulwark was not four feet deep and eighteen feet broad, so that horses did go up and down into it. The highest work in the fort was not twelve feet high, the curtain but ten. Within 100 foot of the fort there was a deep hollow way where the enemy might lodge what numbers he pleased and might be in the graff the first night and in that part the fort was minable.[119]

It seems strange that such basic structural faults were not recognized by de Gomme while he was supervising the construction of this fort. Was he trying to help his patron explain his surrender by criticizing his own work? The fortifications of Bristol were certainly greatly strengthened and improved during the Royalist occupation. They were not perfect but in view of their scale this is not surprising, as there was a continuing process of strengthening and improvement. In November 1644 the city's defences mounted 109 guns, yet by the time the city was attacked in the following August there were 151.[120]

CHAPTER 8
Manufacturing Centre and Capital

After the king's armies left Bristol early in August, a degree of normality began to return, although the city was to continue paying for its disloyalty even if, as McGrath contends, most Bristolians sought only to live in peace with the new regime.[1] The Royalists were desperately short of money and munitions and were far from subtle in supplying these needs at the expense of the captured city. At one stage the ordnance office attempted, unsuccessfully, to invoke the traditional right of a victorious army to seize the city's church bells to recast into cannon.[2] However, not all Royalist demands were as picturesque, and the petty theft of the victorious soldiery was soon replaced by systematic taxation.

The seventh article of the surrender agreement negotiated by Fiennes was intended to safeguard the city's system of local government.

> That the charters and liberties of this city may be preserved; and that the ancient government thereof, and present governors and officers, may remain and continue in their former condition, according to his majesty's Charters and Pleasure.[3]

It was the king's 'pleasure' to regard Bristol as a rebel city recaptured by force of arms. Its charters were suspended and the king's servants and officers were left free to exploit the wealth and resources of the city without opposition. Although early reports that the mayor had been hanged proved unfounded,[4] a number of Bristol Councillors were placed under house arrest while the trial and execution of the Royalist conspirators was investigated.[5] There were no retaliations, either because the king recognized that there was nothing the Bristolians could have done or because the 'guilty' had the good sense to leave the city. The Councillors attempted to buy their way out of the situation in which they found themselves: on 7 July they spent £22 on a gift of wine and sugar for the injured Hopton and dispersed £151 8s 4d in 'certain monies for wounded soldiers'.[6] This was followed by similar gifts of money and luxury goods to the king and other leading Royalists, over and above the vast sums levied on the city to support the garrison and repair the defences.[7] Despite this sycophantic generosity Bristol received no preferential treatment and it was not until November 1643 that it was included in a series of proclamations of pardon covering the west of England.[8]

In February 1644 a 'Free and General Pardon' was granted to the Mayor, Burgesses and Commonalty of Bristol, which was neither free nor general as it cost the city £150 plus numerous presents to royal officials and excluded a number of individuals and crimes.[9] The pardon covered a range of offences committed between the assembly of the Long Parliament in November 1640 and the capture of the city.

> The crimes covered by the pardon include high and petty treason, rebellion, conspiracy, felony, burglary, murder, arson, premunire, riot and breach of the peace. All indictments, judgments and punishments concerning such offences are stopped, and the pardon is to be effective in all royal courts without mention of particular names or offences, and without further order to any royal officer. In addition the king restores all offenders' property forfeited to the Crown during this period.[10]

Excluded from the pardon were all those who had participated in the 'bloody and detestable murder' of Yoemans and Boucher, a number of offences relating to the king's revenue and estates and 'purloining of goods for other purposes than those of war'. The pardon closed with the offer of individual forgiveness if required in the form of 'a particular pardon in the petitioner's own name'.[11] The city regained a degree of control over its own affairs, but the real power remained in the hands of the governor and his garrison.

BRISTOL AS AN ADMINISTRATIVE CENTRE

Due to its comparatively secure and central location Bristol was ideally suited for a wide range of both military and civilian administrative activities. The city was also to serve as Hopton's headquarters during the period when he established Royal authority in the south-west,

> He was chosen (Oct. 1643) commander in chief of the west, where in half a year he got 40 garrisons well maintained, 12000 men well disciplined, £1000 a month contribution settled, above 400 old officers, soldiers and engineers out of the palatinate, the low countries and Ireland fully employed: A press to print orders, declarations, messages and other books to instruct and undeceive the people . . .[12]

Later the city was to serve as the 'capital' for the Prince of Wales and his Council when he was sent into the west to assume command early in 1645.

A Charles I half-crown (actual size) minted in Bristol in 1644. Such coins are now very rare but were produced in tens of thousands during the civil war. (By kind permission of Spink & Son Ltd)

One of the first Royalist institutions to be established in Bristol was a mint, the previous one having closed in 1549. It was established in the castle in August/September 1643 by an enterprising official named Thomas Bushell;[13] he was no stranger to such activity, having previously petitioned the king for permission to establish a mint at Aberystwyth in 1637.[14]

He had previously worked in Oxford and had brought with him to Bristol a set of dies and a skilled engraver to produce other dies specifically for use at Bristol. He was authorized to coin £100 a week using silver drawn from his own mines in Cardiganshire and others at Combe Martin; if this proved insufficient he was to purchase silver plate at 4s 4d per ounce. He was soon producing half-crowns, shillings, sixpences, groats, threepences, half-groats and pennies in silver, and after the arrival of the Prince of Wales gold unites and half-unites were also produced.[15] These coins, once the new dies were produced, were distinguished by the mint mark BR.[16] The need for money was so great that other sources of silver had to be exploited, and a forced loan of £100,000 was agreed by the Oxford Parliament in February 1644. William Wyatt, a Bristol merchant, was informed on 14 February that his contribution was to be £20 in cash or plate; in March he handed over 80 oz of plate, valued at 5s the oz, to be coined.[17] Silver was even collected in areas controlled by Parliament as the Committee for the Advance of Money discovered on the day Wyatt handed over his plate:

> Letters having been intercepted from Bristol, advising him [Lionel Plater of Greenwich and farthing token office] to bring such money and plate as he has to Bristol. It being probable he had other malignants' estates in custody, order that he be brought in custody tomorrow.[18]

The mint ceased production shortly before the arrival of the New Model Army but in May 1652 Bristol was mentioned as one of the former Royalist mints where after the surrender 'the irons were carelessly neglected and came into the hands of knaves'. These enterprising individuals were now producing coins using 'only the clipping of English silver and pewter dishes'.[19]

The 'press' being used by Hopton was also in Bristol. It moved from Shrewsbury during the autumn of 1643 and was in operation by November supplied with paper from Exeter.[20] The press, a portable one, was run by Christopher Baker, Printer to

Charles I, and was one of the first to be operated in the city. In addition to administrative paperwork for the military and civil authorities Baker found time to produce runs of a dozen different books and pamphlets in the city.[21] An example of the type of book produced in the city was *Mercurius Hibernicus*, which sought to explain and justify the Royalist truce with the Confederate Irish on the grounds that the king lacked the resources to suppress the rebels and hoped to stop the fighting in order to save lives.[22] Thomas, in his biography of John Berkenhead, suggests it is possible that a Bristol edition of *Mercurius Aulicus*, the most successful of the Royalist newssheets, might also have been produced.[23] Baker was evacuated from the city with his equipment ahead of the advancing parliamentary forces in 1645 and it was to be fifty years before another printing press was established in Bristol.[24]

Taxation was a major function of the Royalist administration in Bristol. The collection of customs dues in the port continued as previously and was

Mercurius Hibernicus:
O R,
A Difcourfe of the late Infurrection in IRELAND, diſplaying,

1. *The true caufes of it (till now not fo fully diſ-covered.)*

2. *The courfe that was taken to fuppreſſe it.*

3. *The reafons that drew on a Ceſſation of Arms, and other compliances fince.*

AS ALSO
Touching thofe Auxiliaries which are tranſ-ported thence to ferve in the prefent WARRE.

—————————*Patremque*
Mercurium *blandæ quis negat eſſe* Lyræ.

Printed at *Briſtoll,* 1·6·4·4·

Mercurius Hibernicus. *This propaganda work seeking to explain the king's policy in Ireland during the civil war era was one of the first books to be published in Bristol. (Reproduced by kind permission of Bristol Central Library)*

estimated, rather optimistically, in 1644 as being worth £200 a week.[25] Control of this revenue was to spark a dispute between Sir Edward Hyde, the Chancellor of the Exchequer, and Lord Ashburnham, the Paymaster to the King's Forces. The latter, always desperate for cash, seized the receipts of the Bristol customs, provoking an angry response from Hyde, the proper recipient. The king settled the matter in favour of the Chancellor.[26] He ordered Rupert and Hopton to tax the city to cover the costs of the garrison, defences and arms production locally.[27] To balance this the city was given trading privileges by the Royalists, partly to create a rival to parliamentary-controlled London but also to increase revenue.[28] In July 1644 a warrant was sent to the Mayor of Bristol instructing him to introduce excise payments on various commodities. At first the revenue from this tax was earmarked for local defence but soon it was being used to pay for general arms production, and by 1645 it was devoted entirely to payment for arms imports.[29]

To ensure the speedy and effective collection of contributions a warrant was issued to Edmund Turner, a cavalry officer, authorizing him to act as treasurer to the garrisons in the Bristol region.[30] Local officials were instructed to obey his orders and bring in contributions 'under such pain and penalties as shall be inflicted upon them by a council of war'. If there were any difficulties with collection the treasurer could call for assistance:

> We do also require and command all our officers and soldiers within or belonging to our said garrisons, from time to time to give their best assistance in sending forth such parties of horse or foot as you think fit and necessary for the due levying and collecting of the contributions aforesaid.[31]

Turner was responsible for collecting and accounting for weekly contributions of £850 from Somerset, £500 from Wiltshire, £300 from Gloucestershire and £150 from the City of Bristol.[32] To assist him there were two deputies, two clerks, eight collectors and three storekeepers; the cost of this organization was £24 12s 4d a week plus 'allowance for books, bag, paper, ink, pens and all such other necessities as our said service shall require'.[33]

There were a number of other military and civil service bodies in Bristol at this time. Pennington, for example, would certainly have enjoyed an establishment of assistants, clerks and storemen such as Turner's to administer the naval forces in the city. However, the most important organization was probably the ordnance office under the able and energetic direction of Richard Marsh. Responsible for the manufacture or purchase of munitions, their storage and distribution,[34] this organization grew into a highly efficient bureaucracy controlling arms production and distribution throughout the region. It became sufficiently independent to allow Marsh to challenge the authority of Hawley in his own garrison.[35] The ordnance office was not the only organization purchasing and distributing arms in Bristol, as smaller arsenals and stores were operated by various bodies at different times. The Council maintained its own magazine for the city troops at the Guildhall[36] and there may have been a separate store for arms imported in the queen's name, although Marsh appears to have accounted for these.[37] A magazine was certainly established to supply the army of the Prince of Wales in March 1645.[38]

Another administrative function of great value to the various field armies in the region was that of the base hospital. The city had provided this facility to Waller's army during the early stages of the campaign in the west, and Fiennes complained of 'hundreds of his maimed soldiers that have been cast upon my care and charge'.[39] After the siege the city housed large numbers of wounded Royalist troops and these were soon joined by increasing numbers of sick. Early in September Nicholas Luke, a parliamentary spy, reported that 'above 400 sick, lame and maymed men sent from the leaguer [Gloucester] to Bristol by Water'.[40] In February 1645 it was noted that two surgeons were paid 70s by the City Council for caring for 'many maimed soldiers'.[41] In May Secretary Culpepper wrote that large numbers of 'sick and hurt' men from the siege of Taunton had been sent to Bridgwater, Barnstaple and Dunster and that 120 of the guards had been sent to Bristol.[42] After the city was recaptured by the New Model Army it continued to function as a military hospital, and a letter to the Speaker gives an interesting description of how such hospitals were organized and staffed:

> We appointed an hospital, and placed therein so many as the house could contain, with nurses and chirurgiens fitting for them, and as our number increased we added house-room and attendants to them: which though a house of great receipt yet not sufficient to hold all our foot soldiers, we caused the horse to be quartered in the country which hath byn one addition to their burden, though not in giving free quarter – which we have paid in money for the most part – yet in disquiet of their houses, destruction of their bedding, linen and consumption of their firing which hath byn the more enforced. The generality of their wounds being fractures of bones and dismemberings by plug-shot from the enemy, expressing height of malice, rather than martial prowess.[43]

ARMS IMPORTS AND MANUFACTURES

The main sources of arms imports, both for king and Parliament, were Holland, the Spanish Netherlands, France and Denmark. The scale of these imports was vast, as a letter from the Hague to Secretary Nicholas, dated 22 November 1642, shows:

> We have sent over ten thousand foot arms, two thousand horse arms, twenty pieces of cannon, we bring over wagons and all accommodation to march as soon as we arrive, . . from Denmark there are likewise sent arms for ten thousand foot and two thousand five hundred horse and a train of artillery, and everything proportionable to the very drums and halberds. Two good men of war come their convoy.[44]

William Sands, the Royalist agent based in Dunkirk, claimed that by 1645 he had shipped almost 40,000 arms to ports in northern and south-west England.[45] However, not all these weapons reached the king's ordnance stores:

> Her Majesty [the Queen] had, from her first going into Holland dextrously endeavoured to advance the king's interest, and sent great quantities of arms and ammunition to Newcastle (though by the vigilance of the Parliament agents in those parts, and the power of their ships, too much of it was intercepted).[46]

One captured vessel making for Newcastle with a cargo from Denmark was found to contain 500 barrels of gunpowder and 4,500 sets of infantry weapons.[47]

At first sight Bristol would not appear to have been a particularly attractive port for blockade-runners trying to bring in cargoes of arms. The journey was longer than to Scarborough or Weymouth and both the Severn Estuary and River Avon were difficult to navigate. Despite this Bristol was considered by many to be a more secure destination and was to play a vital role in Royalist arms importation.[48] On 25 August 1643 Lord Percy, the Royalist General of the Ordnance, had instructed a supplier, Daniel van Hecke, to deliver his cargo, brought into Bristol on the 15th, to Richard Marsh.[49] Hecke, captain of the aptly named Dunkirk frigate *Lady of Assistance*, brought the first arms shipment into Bristol for which he was paid £1000.[50] The Royalist newssheets hailed the arrival as a triumph, and reported that the cargo included 6,000 muskets, 2,000–3,000 hand grenades and 'many thousands' of carbines, pistols and other arms.[51] Some of the cargo appears to have been of rather dubious quality and Marsh reported that many of the back- and breast-plates and all the swords would require repair before they could be issued. However, considerable quantities of arms and ammunition were issued to the navy and to the garrison at Bristol, and Marsh was further able to supply the king's field army with 600–700 sets of armour and 200 pairs of pistols.[52] In October John Scott reported to Samuel Luke that together with 800 barrels of gunpowder 'a great many arms' had arrived in Bristol from France; this may refer to the *Lady of Assistance*, but it seems strange that there was no mention of so large a quantity of powder in Royalist sources.[53] It could perhaps refer to another early arrival, a shipload of ammunition sent from Leghorn by the king's agent Robert Saintwell and Mr Wright, although equally it could have been a delivery from France or the Low Countries.[54] Another vessel definitely arrived in Bristol in November 1643, and Marsh reported that the cargo contained 140 barrels of powder, 2,500 bandoliers and 400 pairs of pistols.[55]

In addition to those shipments that landed directly in Bristol, the city also acted as an assembly and distribution centre for cargoes delivered to other ports in the south-west.[56] In January 1644 Hawley sent carts and troops from Bristol to collect gunpowder that had been landed in Weymouth from France, for use in his garrison.[57] This sparked a row with Marsh who claimed he controlled the ammunition. Marsh was already seeking to coordinate arms imports throughout the south-west, calling for reports from other ports and planning a tour of inspection.[58] Marsh was finally granted a warrant giving him the powers he wanted, but Hawley refused to hand over the gunpowder from Weymouth; finally, after Marsh threatened to refuse to issue arms to the Bristol garrison, the disputed powder was divided equally between the stores and the garrison.[59] By the closing stages of the war large quantities of arms and ammunition were being sent to Bristol from ports further to the west. Early in May 1645 Lord Jermym wrote to Lord Digby to say that a large consignment of arms was being despatched to England in a frigate commanded by Capt Haesdonck, and a substantial quantity of gunpowder shipped to Dartmouth. On the 15th the Governor of Pendennis Castle reported the safe arrival of the cargo and requested instructions as to its disposal. On the 22nd, Culpepper wrote to Digby from Bath, 'I have been careful in speeding away ammunition to Bristol,' and giving details of the deliveries.[60]

> The landing of 200 barrels of gunpowder with the promise of 800 more to come is excellent news, for before the arrival of this earnest we were almost in despair. Neither will you find 6,000 muskets, 2,000 case of pistols, 24,000lbs of match and 50,000lbs of brimstone, which I understand to be in Haesdonck's frigate to be ill news.[61]

Bristol supplied arms and ammunition to Royalist troops operating over a wide area. Shortly after the capture of the city a parliamentary agent reported that four demi-culverins had been supplied to Berkeley Castle and three other guns to Worcester.[62] The king's forces had been at least partially re-equipped from the stocks of arms and ammunition taken at Bristol before they moved against Gloucester, and the forces there were also supplied from Bristol.[63] In June 1644 the Committee of Both Kingdoms was informed that Rupert's army, then operating in Lancashire and Cheshire, had been supplied with ammunition from Bristol.[64] Large quantities of arms and ammunition were also supplied to Oxford, as were other military stores manufactured in Bristol.[65] Even the resources of some of the smaller magazines in Bristol were considerable: that under the control of the Prince of Wales still contained 2,000 pikes and 'many muskets' after the Prince's Guards had been equipped and large quantities of arms had been issued to Prince Rupert's forces.[66]

In terms of arms manufacture Bristol's contribution to the Royalist war effort was of the greatest importance. The city had a considerable capacity to produce weapons and ammunition with at least six gunsmiths active in 1642.[67] In August 1643, when the city was still in chaos after its capture, Hopton reported that Bristol could supply 200 desperately needed muskets a week.[68] By the following January Marsh had organized the production of not only 200 muskets and bandoliers each week but also 6–8 barrels of gunpowder; in April Rupert suggested that the production of arms and powder should be concentrated in Bristol rather than in Oxford.[69] By May 1645 Marsh was able to report that the city was capable of manufacturing arms to equip 20,000 men a year (15,000 muskets and 5,000 pikes).[70] In addition to arms and ammunition a range of military stores including drums, bullets, and wagons were produced in Bristol for the king's forces.[71]

The major problem Marsh faced was the shortage of hard cash to pay the producers. Roy points out that two weeks' output of muskets and bandoliers would have cost £310, a barrel of powder 50–60s and a ton of musket shot £16.[72] These costs were supposed to be met from taxes raised within the city, but there

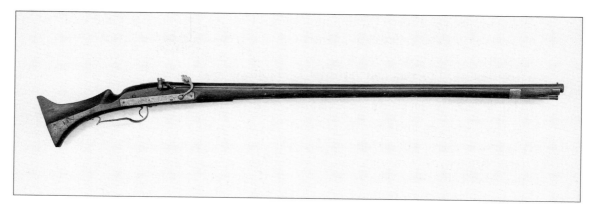

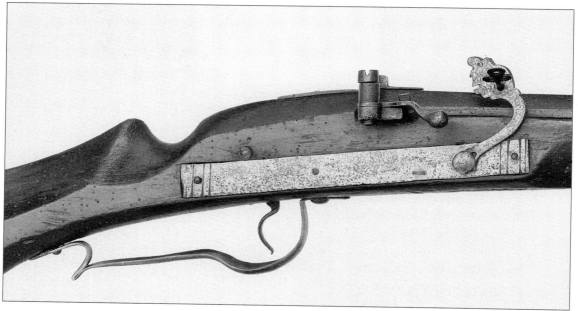

Matchlock musket. Most infantrymen in the civil war were armed with these simple but robust weapons and the vast majority of the 200-plus muskets that Bristol's gunsmiths produced each week would have been of this type. These guns had a four-foot barrel and weighed ten pounds. (Reproduced by kind permission of the Board of Trustees of the Royal Armouries. Accession No. XII. 1638)

were always competing claims for any money raised. In the establishment issued in November 1644, a sum of £350 a week was set aside for 'making of arms and ammunition', but Marsh remained desperately short of cash:

By the new establishment made for the settlement of the manufactures and garrisons of Bristol, Bath &c which began from the 1st November to this present, being 29 weeks, there was payable £10,150, and since I have received from Mr Turner the Treasurer but £2,490, being under £90 a week. The amount expected from the customs here and the contribution coming in from Somersetshire are so small that unless some present course be taken for a constant weekly payment out of the excise of Bristol or other ways, the artificers cannot continue at the work, their arrears now owing being above £1,200.[73]

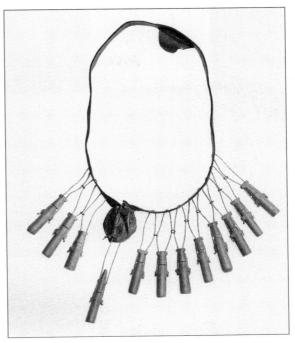

A musketeer's bandolier. This was basically a leather shoulder belt fitted with wooden containers, each of which contained a charge of gunpowder for a musket. It has been suggested that such belts were already obsolescent by the time of the civil war and were being replaced by paper cartridges. However, paper was a scarce resource and the bandolier had the great advantage of being reusable almost indefinitely. (Reproduced by kind permission of the Board of Trustees of the Royal Armouries. Accession No. XIII. 93)

There is perhaps a temptation to accept Marsh's report at face value and dismiss arms production in Bristol during the civil war as one of history's 'might have beens'. However, the sum received from the treasurer was sufficient to purchase over 3,200 muskets and, as Marsh points out, a large amount of work was undertaken on credit, the outstanding debt representing over 1,500 musketeers. William Barber, the Bristol powder-maker, petitioned for an office in the Bristol customs house after the Restoration, on the grounds that he had supplied £2,500 worth of powder without payment during the war, which represents over 500 barrels.[74] Armaments workers were excused service in the trained bands or auxiliaries and were safe from forced enlistment in the royal army – as long as they continued to produce weapons and remained on good terms with Marsh and his officers. The output of weapons from Bristol did not reach the levels Marsh hoped for, but they were still considerable and certainly of great value to the Royalist forces.

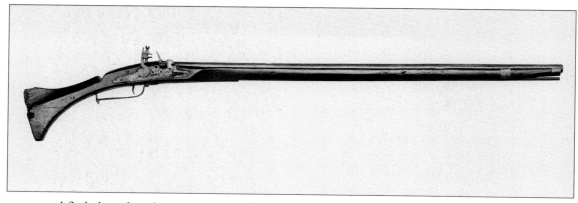

A firelock musket. A proportion of the firearms manufactured in Bristol were probably fitted with the more advanced flintlock known as a firelock. Mainly issued to dragoons or troops guarding baggage or artillery trains, such weapons were more effective than the normal matchlock. However, as they were more complex and expensive to manufacture these weapons would have been uncommon among ordinary infantry units. (Reproduced by kind permission of the Board of Trustees of the Royal Armouries. Accession No. XII. 5143)

AN ALTERNATIVE CAPITAL

On 11 March 1645 Charles Prince of Wales, then fifteen years old, arrived in Bristol to assume command of the south-western area in his father's name. His official task was to coordinate the war effort in the region, and to assist him he had a council of experienced soldiers and administrators.[75] Clarendon, a member of the Prince's council, suggests that there were other reasons for sending the heir to the throne out of the Oxford region in early 1645:

> He was now to act a part by himself, as the affairs should require, or rather he was to sit still without acting any thing; the end being, as was said before, only that the King and Prince might not be exposed at the same time to the same danger; without any purpose that he should raise any more strength, than was necessary to the security of his own person; or that indeed he should move further westward than that city.[76]

This seems to be rather an exaggeration, as the Council members sent with the prince were certainly not supernumerary courtiers assigned to baby-sitting duties. The Council included the Duke of Richmond, a close relative of the king, who had undertaken various diplomatic missions in the past and was an uncompromising supporter of the Royalist cause;[77] the Earl of Southampton, originally thought likely to support Parliament, and something of a defeatist, but 'a great man in all

When Charles Prince of Wales was sent to the south-west in 1645 as the king's general, he established his headquarters at Bristol until he was forced to abandon the city owing to an outbreak of plague. This picture shows Charles as king a few years later when he led a Royalist/Scots army which threatened Bristol prior to its defeat at Worcester. (Reproduced by kind permission of Bristol Central Library)

Edward Hyde, later Lord Clarendon, was a member of the King's Council who was later sent to Bristol to advise the Prince of Wales. His account of the war, although strongly Royalist in sympathy, contains a wealth of first-class information. (Reproduced by kind permission of Bristol Central Library)

respects and brought much reputation to the king's cause';[78] and Lord Capel, 'a man in whom the malice of his enemies could discover few faults, and whom his friends could not wish better accomplished', and later to be beheaded for his opposition to Cromwell.[79] The Chancellor of the Exchequer, Lord Culpepper, was also appointed to the young prince's Council and appears to have taken an active interest, along with Clarendon, in organizing arms supplies and sorting out problems created by competing military commanders.[80] As his chief military advisor the king chose Hopton, a man whose reputation and influence in the region were second to none,[81] despite the fact that he held the critical office of General of the Ordnance.

The origins of this plan can be found in a proposal of early 1644 that an Association should be formed by the counties of Somerset, Dorset, Cornwall and Devon.[82] The counties were to raise an army of 30,000 men, one-third of whom were to be formed into a field army under the command of Prince Maurice.[83] The king was required to supply 1,000 barrels of powder and 10,000 firearms for which the counties would pay. The cost of these arms and the wages of the army would be raised by contributions, fines and forfeitures without affecting payments to Hopton's forces or the Bristol garrison.[84] Finally it was suggested that if Wiltshire and Bristol wished to join the new Association 'they shall be received with all cheerfulness'.[85] The whole plan was clearly ludicrous: the king lacked the resources requested and conditions in the south-west meant it was highly unlikely that such an army could have been raised or supported. Hopton had already organized the defences in the region, the creation of a second army could only weaken his forces and confuse the command structure; perhaps the proposal was published simply for propaganda reasons. However, the news of the impending arrival of the Prince of Wales encouraged the original movers of the plan to try again:

> Upon the first fame of the Prince's being to visit the west and keep his court there, some gentlemen, of the best quality in the west, came to Oxford as entrusted by the rest to acquaint his majesty 'That they had now formed the design, that they formally presented to him, much better than it was; and that the four Western counties, Dorset, Somerset, Devon and Cornwall, had resolved to enter into an Association'. . . . They desired the King 'That the Prince might be made General of this Association; in order to which, they would provide for his support according to his dignity; and in the first place, take care for the raising of a good Guard of Horse and Foot, for the security of his person'.[86]

Although the king recognized that the plans were impractical, 'he was sure it could do no harm' and he did not want to offend or discourage his supporters in the south-west. The difference between what was promised and what was achieved must have been a sobering lesson for the prince and his councillors when they arrived in Bristol.

> The Prince being attended at Bristol by the Commissioners of Somerset, found no one thing provided, or one promise complied with, which had been made by them at Oxford: Of his Guards of Horse and Foot, which they assured him, for the proportion of that county, should be ready against his coming, not one man or horse provided: Of the hundred pound a week, to be allowed by them towards his Highness's support, not one penny ready, nor like to be. So that he was forced to borrow from the Lord Hopton's own private store, to buy bread.[87]

The city of Bristol welcomed their new royal resident with a gift of Canary and Gascon wines, which cost them £35 12s.[88] Prior to this the Council, at the request of Lord Hopton, had prepared accommodation for the prince and his followers, housing them in the 'Great House' at St Augustines and the Bishop's Palace. The Council guaranteed to repay five Councillors who agreed to lend beds and bedding if their property was not returned.[89] The city also purchased a dinner service for the prince's use, in pewter rather than silver, at a cost of £19. After his arrival it was decided to present the prince with £500; this was to be raised by collecting '3s and upwards' from every household. However, the state of the city's economy by this stage was such that only £430 could be collected, the remainder coming from Council funds.[91] To make matters worse, just after the prince arrived a plot to deliver the city to William Waller was discovered; unlike their Royalist predecessors the main plotters escaped to join the parliamentary forces.[92]

More worrying for the young general than his personal discomfort was the military situation he faced, particularly the divisions that existed among his father's supporters. The serious dispute between Goring and Hopton was undermining the efficiency of the royal forces in the region,[93] and even within the garrison of Bristol 'quarrels and animosities ran so high in the army as nearly to destroy all order and discipline'.[94] The main problem was too many independent or overlapping commissions held by individuals who refused to place the king's service above their own pride. The worst offender was Goring, who was strongly disliked by Clarendon, who he said would:

Drunken, unstable and an inveterate schemer, Goring was nevertheless capable of displaying considerable ability as a military commander. He did much to undermine efforts to reorganize the Royalist forces in the south-west and his defeat at Langport ended any hope of concentrating enough troops to successfully oppose the New Model Army. He retreated into Devon where he did little to oppose the Parliamentarians and ignored a royal summons to Oxford. With his health ruined by drinking and old wounds, he left for the continent and died in poverty in Madrid in 1657. (Reproduced by kind permission of Bristol Central Library)

Without hesitation, have broken any trust, or done any act of treachery to have satisfied an ordinary passion, or appetite; and in truth wanted nothing but industry (for he had wit, and courage, and understanding, and ambition uncontrolled by fear of God or man) to have been as eminent, and successful in the highest attempt of wickedness, as any man in the age he lived in, or before.[95]

In contrast his equally partisan view of Hopton suggests a serious personality clash between these men, even if they had not been competing for control of the western armies.

The Lord Hopton was a man superior to any temptation, and abhorred enough the license, and the levities, with which he saw too many corrupted. He had a good understanding, a clear courage, an industry not to be tired, and a generosity that was not to be exhausted; a virtue that none of the rest had: but in debates concerning the war, was longer in resolving, and more apt to change his mind after he had resolved, than is agreeable to the office of a commander in chief; which rendered him rather fit for the second, than the supreme command in an army.[96]

Hopton may have been the more attractive individual, but Goring was a brilliant commander (when sober), although he had alienated many local Royalists, and had to be brought under control if any order was to be imposed on the king's affairs in the west.

As Hopton clearly could not negotiate with Goring, Capel and Culpepper were sent to Wells to discuss with Goring plans for a concerted operation to reduce the parliamentary garrison at Taunton.[97] On 11 April the prince ordered Goring to send his infantry and guns to Taunton and dispatch his ill-disciplined cavalry units into Dorset or Wiltshire to harass parliamentary sympathizers rather than Royalist ones, though Goring was allowed to choose which body he accompanied. Goring complained bitterly that his army was being broken up and in a fit of temper declined to accompany either body but announced his intention to go to Bath for the sake of his health. After 'some days frolicking' he returned to Bristol and made his peace with the prince's Council.[98] Having apparently solved the most pressing problem the prince travelled to Bridgwater to meet with the Commissioners of the Western Association in an attempt to 'kick start' the promised army:[99]

all particulars were agreed upon: the several days for the rendezvous of the new levies, and the officers to whom the men were to be delivered named; and the warrants issued accordingly: all things required for the speedy reduction of Taunton ordered, and directed; so that, towards the taking of that place, and the raising of an army speedily, all things stood so fair, that more could not be wished.[100]

It seemed as if the prince and his Council were bringing order to the chaos of the king's affairs in the west, but when he returned to Bristol the prince found that Goring had gone to Oxford where he obtained from the king a letter naming him commander of the west and ordering Hopton to return to the main army.[101] The prince's Council immediately sent a messenger to the king with their version of events, but the careful work of the previous weeks was destroyed in renewed in-fighting as Goring 'expressed all possible contempt' for the members of the prince's Council. However, before this could be resolved the Prince of Wales was forced to move his headquarters, which damaged still further the fragile structures he and his councillors had created. 'He had nearly established unanimity when he was obliged to quit the city and retire to Barnstaple in Devon on account of the plague having broken out in it.'[102]

After less than three months in the 'western capital' the Prince of Wales left Bristol to avoid a serious outbreak of plague, his personal safety being considered as of greater importance than any advantage his presence and authority might bring at Bristol. Could Charles, based at Bristol, have established effective control of the king's forces in the west and organized effective resistance to the New Model Army? He was the only person in the region with sufficient authority to control Goring but as that individual was prepared to ignore orders from the king himself on occasion, even that might not have been enough.

Bristol was not simply a garrison town. It provided a wide range of administrative and military functions, many of which were critical to the Royalist war effort in the west and further afield. The tendency to look at the city simply in terms of soldiers and battles during the civil war somewhat overlooks this aspect, but to the king's cause the various support functions provided by the city were perhaps even more important.

CHAPTER 9

The Campaign of 1645

Parliament, recognizing the importance of the south-west, tried valiantly to regain control of the region. Just after the capture of the city, when it was already too late to alter the wording, an ordinance was published 'for the speedy raising and levying of money' assessing Bristol at £55 15s a week; a new committee under the direction of Fiennes was to supervise collection.[1] The author of *Mercurius Aulicus* commented that 'if the worthy members would come to these places [Oxford and other royalist towns were also included] their money lies ready for them'.[2] In July 1644 Parliament named a new local committee for the western counties, which was given the authority to raise men and money to form a regional army in August.[3] The desire to recover the west, combined with rivalries between Essex and Waller, resulted in the Lord-General leading his army into Cornwall to face catastrophic defeat at Lostwithiel.[4] Preachers sought to explain the defeat:

> O let us be humbled for our covenant breaches past and if we would not have God go on to break and blast our armies, let us not only renew our covenants (which is part of the work of this day) but let us be mindful of and faithful to our covenants; or never look to have God more with our armies.[5]

In October 1644 the city of Bristol was once again included in a parliamentary ordinance 'for relief of the army in Ireland',[6] and the following year the Western Association was reanimated under the command of Massey who was subsequently ordered to obey Fairfax.[7]

By this time the military situation was swinging in favour of Parliament. The king had lost control of the north and was facing increasing pressure from a Scots army moving south.[8] Parliament's armies had been reorganized into the New Model Army with an establishment of 22,000 men; the core of the army were veterans from the commands of Essex, Waller and Manchester, they were organized in twelve regiments of infantry, eleven of cavalry and one of dragoons.[9] Only 7,600 infantry remained from the old armies and numbers had to be made up by impressment although recruits raised by this method often deserted as soon as they reached the army. Fairfax's infantry were at least 4,000 men under establishment when the army took the field in May.[10] The cavalry, in contrast, was

*Appointed to command the New Model Army, Thomas Fairfax had previously served
in the north of England. During the Bristol campaign he made great efforts to improve
relations between Parliament and their army. After the execution of the king, Fairfax
retreated into private life in Yorkshire although like many other moderate
Parliamentarians he later became involved in plots to restore the monarchy.
(With grateful thanks to Alan Turton)*

largely composed of experienced officers and men under the direct command of Oliver Cromwell.

As the Prince of Wales marched out of Bristol towards Barnstaple the Oxford Army under Rupert captured the town of Leicester and the king announced his decision to abandon the march north and return to Oxford.[11] After two weeks' marching through the midlands the king's forces and the New Model Army clashed at the village of Naseby in Northamptonshire.[12] The battle was a disaster for the Royalist cause, the Oxford Army being effectively destroyed as a fighting force. Some 600 soldiers were killed, and 5,000 irreplaceable veteran infantry were captured, including 500 officers.[13] No fewer than 112 colours were captured, in addition to 8,000 arms and a dozen brass cannon.[14]

Fairfax now hoped to consolidate his success by ensuring that the king did not raise a new army. The south-west was the only area where the Royalists could assemble sufficient troops quickly enough to salvage their cause. Fairfax, although aware of the divisions among the western Royalists, knew that the military resources of the region represented a huge threat.

> The king's field forces for the securing of these western counties and garrisons, even from Oxford to the Mount in Cornwall, under the command of the Lord Goring, the Lord Hopton, Sir Richard Grenville and Major General Sir John Digby, brother to Lord Digby, may modestly be computed to be, in all, fourteen thousand foot and horse, besides their several garrisons secured with horse and foot.[15]

Fairfax knew that if these troops were to be united under a single commander he would face a Royalist army as strong as or stronger than that which took the field at Naseby. He had to reach the south-west before the Royalists could reorganize their forces. After recapturing Leicester on 18 June Fairfax marched his army south through Wiltshire and into Somerset.

The king and his advisors also realized that the resources of the south-west would be critical in the rebuilding of their armies. Rupert was despatched to the Prince of Wales to discuss the situation, and coordinate raising a new field army with Goring.[16] It was suggested that the cavalry that had escaped Naseby should be shipped across the Severn from South Wales to reinforce the troops already in the south-west, but such movements were complicated by parliamentary naval patrols. On 1 April the Committee of the Navy had ordered a squadron of six ships or pinnaces supported by six shallops to be prepared 'for the blocking up of Bristol'.[17] A week later it was reported that three armed colliers, the frigate *Spy* and four shallops would be dispatched to Bristol and other vessels would join them, although subsequently two shallops were diverted to other duties.[18] By July the Severn was patrolled by ships attached to Admiral Moulton's fleet, based at Milford Haven, and a number of Royalist transports were captured. The greatest success was the discovery and capture of a squadron of a dozen vessels being assembled at Steep Holm to bring reinforcements from Wales, shortly after the fall of Bridgwater.[19] When Fairfax arrived at Bristol, Moulton joined the squadron blockading the city, comprising *Lion* (40 guns), *Mayflower* (28), *Anne and Joyce* (22), *Nicholas* (12), *Defiance* and *Spy* (6), in addition to shallops capable of carrying 300 men apiece.[20] Sea communications were finally cut on 28 August when, after six days' resistance, the army captured the fort at Portishead, allowing the parliamentary ships to occupy the Kingsroode and the mouth of the river.[21]

Prior to this Rupert had arrived at Bristol to organize artillery for the new field army. He found the situation at this vital base far from encouraging:

> The auxiliary and trained bands, by interruption of trade and commerce, by the pestilence still raging there, by their poverty and pressures laid upon them, were reduced to 800; and the mariners for want of employment, betook themselves to other ports or to the enemy.[22]

Soon after Rupert's arrival news of the defeat of Goring's army reached Bristol, ending any hopes of raising a new army, and making the defence of Bristol Rupert's primary objective. He issued orders that all families were to stockpile six months' food in preparation for a siege; however, when officers inspected civilian homes it was discovered that 60 per cent of the 2,500 families remaining in Bristol had failed to provision themselves through 'indiligence or want'. He immediately ordered 2,000 bushels of grain from Wales and ordered the garrison to drive in cattle from the surrounding areas. Rupert complained he also faced a shortage of powder, although there were 130 barrels of powder available, and serious shortages of match and bullet, which the prince tried to overcome by restarting local production.[23] He began clearing hedges and buildings around the defences to deprive the attackers of cover, but Fairfax's advance was so rapid that this vital work could not be completed.

Fairfax forcemarched his army from the midlands to the south-west to raise the siege of Taunton and thereby frustrated Royalist plans to form a new army:

> Our poor foote (being impatient of the relief of their friends at Taunton) marched sixty-two miles in five days, and offered at Dorchester, after twelve miles' march that day, to march all that night to relieve Taunton.[24]

The critical battle was fought at Langport on 10 July 1645. The Royalists held a strong defensive position behind a river, protected by hedges, and Goring planned to hold this position long enough for his guns and transport to reach the safety of Bridgwater. This fitted in with Fairfax's strategy of forcing Goring to fight before the Royalists could concentrate their forces. The battle was marked by savage close-quarter fighting among the hedges and bitterly contested cavalry combats, before finally swinging in favour of the Parliamentarians.[25] Goring's army lost 300 killed and 2,000 captured. Combined with a vast number of deserters, this defeat meant that his army effectively ceased to exist as a fighting force. The significance of this defeat was immense: the parliamentary forces had frustrated the Royalists' attempt to assemble a new army strong enough to counter the New Model Army.

> First Sir observe, that had we not forgotten our weariness and all other difficulties, and hastened the work, the enemy had been reinforced with 5000 Welsh foot, 1500 of which was come over the Severn, who it is possible be our prisoners or worse.
>
> Secondly, Granville had undoubtedly brought down near as many out of Cornwall, all which we must have buckled with jointly.
>
> Thirdly, that having scattered this army, there is not an army of his majesty's in being, but such as may be with an ordinary, active power, scattered and brought to nothing.
>
> Fourthly, that if the clubmen join with us now, after this admirable success, they may be suddenly at quiet and see good days, and the west is ours.[26]

The first reports listed dozens of officers captured during the battle, in addition to 1,200 common soldiers, 500 of whom promptly changed sides. Goring retreated being harassed by clubmen 'more terrible to him than our own army' while other Royalist leaders fled to France or Wales.[27] Col. Lilburn was sent to report to Parliament and to request regular pay, recruits and supplies of shoes and stockings for the troops. The colonel asked Parliament to show its active support for the army to encourage the troops in the field.[28] Goring's army was completely shattered,

> To the account which was given of the fight and rout on the tenth, all I can add is, that Goring passed through Bridgwater on Friday morning towards Barnstaple without ordnance, with three carriages, about 3000 horse most of them unserviceable, 400 foot whereof 300 never came in the fight, 8 remaining colours, in the most perplexed condition in regard to the discontent of his shattered forces and the carriage of the country, who made so bold to bring up his rear for him, which made him put 500 of his best horse there to secure his march.[29]

After relieving Taunton Fairfax moved his forces against Bridgwater, where the well-fortified garrison controlled Royalist lines of communication between Bristol and the south-western counties. The garrison under Wyndham conducted a spirited defence, leaving much of the town a burnt-out ruin, but which did not end, as one recent account claimed, with 'most of the defenders dead'.[30]

After the general had taken this side of the town, we summoned the town, they altogether refused and fired that part of the town we had taken. The General summoned it again, and told them they should march away or else if they would yield on some further condition; they denied, said they would stand it out to the last man: the general perceived their fury, sent to them that he would give leave for all of the women and children to come out of the town: the governor returned thanks, sent his wife and many ladies out; then our men shot wild-fire into the town and fired it; whereupon, the governor sent out to the general to parley: our general refused, only he would be merciful and spare their lives; whereupon they yielded themselves prisoners.[31]

Sprigg says that only thirty men were killed during the siege[32] but the list of prisoners and material captured at Bridgwater shows the significance of the garrison:

Colonel Wyndham (Governor)
Sir Hugh Wyndham (his son)
Sir John Digby
Sir Francis Courtney
Tom Eliot (Quartermaster)
6 colonels
14 lieutenant colonels
100 other officers
2,000 common soldiers
36 pieces of ordnance
5,000 arms
800 horses
600 oxen
10 loads of ammunition
40 tons of match
All Goring's carriages and baggage
4 months' provisions

The loss of Bridgwater removed any hopes that Bristol might be reinforced from Devon or Cornwall, while parliamentary naval patrols made it increasingly difficult to bring troops from Wales. Fairfax had not only prevented the Royalists from concentrating their forces and destroyed Goring's army, he had also driven a wedge between the king's forces in the south-west and those around Bristol and Oxford. At the end of July an army chaplain was sent to Parliament to report the success of their forces:

A motive to enjoy favour for this army, will be the unparalleled presence of God with it, viz. In six weeks; two battles fought, six garrisons taken in, Leicester, Ilchester, Lamport, Burrow, Hauclot [Highworth] Bridgwater and Taunton relieved: We hope it shall not be our misery, that whilst bad men are bad unto us, good men shall be bad unto us also.[34]

There was considerable ill-feeling and distrust between the army and their political masters which Fairfax was careful to try to reduce by regular reports delivered by officers or chaplains. The army feared that Parliament would not supply the money and manpower needed to defeat the king.

The beast by nature and divine institution, after labour was to have rest and recruits, and shall not we? If now they come [reinforcements] we may fall upon Exeter and Bristol, and probably carry both. There is a terror upon the enemy.[35]

Mindful of Essex's experience the previous year, Fairfax decided to capture Bristol before moving further west. Bath was occupied without a shot being fired on 30 July,[36] and a garrison of two infantry and two cavalry regiments established there; Fairfax wrote to his father that he hoped they 'will straighten Bristol very much'.[37] Two days later one of Fairfax's chaplains wrote that he hoped the new garrison 'might be a check to Bristol' and block up Rupert.[38] Fairfax then began clearing any garrisons to the south of the city that he thought might interfere in coming operations.[39] Later, in August, Fairfax sent Hugh Peters to London to explain his strategy to Parliament:

There were many inducements (after they had taken Sherburn and Rumney) thither to go, rather than to the west: As the entreaty of the people of Somerset, which was very strong; the horrid cruelties of Prince Rupert, who began to burn all the country behind the army; the increasing of his forces, whereby he might with the help of the malignant incensed clubmen of Dorset, fall upon the rear of the army: Besides he might have spoiled most of our summer's work in those parts; and the army feared to fall into some other former errors, by only passing through the country to leave in worse case than they found them. But by taking Bristol (if God would give that blessing) the country would be cleared of them even to Exeter.

Moreover, Rupert was far more considerable than Goring and of more repute; and in the west they were very slow in their rising, though all means were used; their own differences many, and if our army had followed Goring, had he gone into Cornwall, where the whole country had been helpful to him, which they denied otherwise.

To this may be added that Bristol could not be assaulted in a better time, they wanting all things for food.[40]

The Royalists were trying to assemble an army in the Bristol area to challenge Fairfax's forces:

> Prince Rupert sent for all those foot which were levied towards a new army, and part of those that belonged to General Gerrard, to supply the garrison of Bristol: so that his majesty seemed now to have nothing in his choice, but to transport himself over the Severn into Bristol, and hence to have repaired his army in the west; which would have been much better done before, yet had been well done then; and the king resolved to do so; and that the horse under Gerrard and Langdale should find a transport over the Severn (which might have been done) and then find the way to him wherever he should be.[41]

The king was persuaded not to move to Bristol by followers who disliked Rupert and did not wish to see the king move into a region under his control.[42] Parliament were unaware of this, and on 29 August Massey and Fairfax were warned that the king was moving towards Bristol and planned to join forces with Lord Goring.[43] On the same day the Committee of Both Kingdoms passed on reports that 4,000 Royalist horse and dragoons had been observed in the Aylesbury area, marching towards Bristol via Oxford; they were to join with Goring who, it was reported, now had 10,000 horse and foot.[44] In reality, after Langport and the fall of Bridgwater there was little chance of the Royalists being able to carry out a concentration of forces to counter Fairfax and his army.

The first units of the New Model Army arrived at Bristol on 21 August and after making a careful reconnaissance they fell back to Keynsham while Fairfax established his headquarters at Hanham.[45] Cromwell reported to the House of Commons that the first units to close in on the city were Colonel Weldon's 'Taunton' brigade who 'marched to Pile Hill on the south side of the city, being within musket shot thereof, where in a few days they made good quarter, overlooking the city'.[46] Rupert began to burn outlying villages, but following the destruction of Clifton and Bedminster his parties were driven back by Parliamentarian cavalry. To protect the villages to the north of the city Commissary General Ireton was sent with five regiments of horse, one of dragoons and a detachment of 500 infantry.[47] Fairfax, still on the southern side of the Avon, was attacked by Royalist cavalry on 22 August;[48] in this action Richard Crane, the commander of Rupert's Lifeguard, was either killed or seriously wounded.[49]

Over the next two days more troops arrived from Somerset, crossing the river at Keynsham, and were deployed on the eastern side of the city. An infantry brigade under Colonel Montage was deployed between the Rivers Frome and Avon where he established his troops in positions within musket shot of the defences. To his right another infantry brigade under Rainsborough was positioned on Durdan Down with his flanks secured by the horse and dragoons under Ireton.[50] On

During the second siege, Ireton commanded a detached cavalry force which protected the villages to the north of the city and prevented a break-out by the Royalist cavalry. An opponent of radicals such as Rainsborough, he was one of those who signed the king's death warrant. He married Cromwell's daughter and served as second-in-command in Ireland. After Cromwell's recall to England he assumed command but died of fever after the capture of Limerick in November 1651. (With grateful thanks to Alan Turton)

23 August Fairfax established a new headquarters at Stoke House in Stapleton nearer to these concentrations.[51] Cromwell was to admit that these deployments resulted in the besieging infantry being thinly spread and 'our horse were forced to be upon exceeding great duty to stand by the foot'.[52] On the same day as Fairfax moved to Stapleton, the troops to the south 'began some breastworks and battery upon the hill without Temple Gate with a traverse across the way to hinder our soldiers'.[53]

The parliamentary forces tried to make contact with their 'fifth column' within the city. A letter was intercepted, signed and sealed by Fairfax and Cromwell, which offered generous terms if the city was surrendered. It suggested that if the trained bands and auxiliaries were able to seize the city for Parliament the New Model Army would not enter without their invitation. However, generosity was backed with threats:

An engineer. The construction of fortifications and siege works, and the direction of attacks upon defended cities, required the services of highly skilled experts. A military engineer in this period was a highly valued individual capable of surveying ground, designing defences and supervising their construction. This individual wears a civilian coat and breeches, and has functional shoes and stockings. Although he carries a sword he does not wear armour or buff-coat. He has surveying equipment and drawing tools and is clearly not equipped for combat. (With grateful thanks to Alan Turton)

> That they fall to some speedy resolution, and attempt for the purpose aforesaid, because else we shall fall to some attempt by our own forces and (if thereby through God's blessing it be taken) we shall hardly be able to withhold the soldiers from doing violence and damage to the city which we earnestly desire and study to prevent.[54]

After this letter, instructions to the City Council to deliver the city were also intercepted and Rupert ordered 'several suspected or active persons to be restrained which prevented this design'.

Seeing his opponents thinly spread, Rupert launched a series of probing attacks or sallies against them. On the day Fairfax moved to Stoke House a party of Royalist horse attacked the pickets in Rainsborough's sector but accomplished little before they withdrew.[55] The next day a stronger force attacked from Prior's Hill and

Troops under Col. Rainsborough's command captured the fort at Prior's Hill during the second siege. His account of this action is one of the most detailed of contemporary descriptions. After the war he was active in radical politics and became a leading member of the Leveller movement. He was killed by a Royalist raiding party in an inn at Doncaster while directing the siege of Pontefract Castle. (Reproduced by kind permission of Bristol Central Library)

surprised dragoons on picket duty; however, the arrival of cavalry and infantry reinforcements quickly drove the attackers back to the line with losses.[56] It was not until the 26th that another sally was attempted. This time, having found Rainsborough's position too strong, the Royalists turned their attention to Wheldon on the Somerset side. The attack was launched at four in the morning and caught the besiegers by surprise, according to Sprigg 'through the negligence of the officer that then had the command there'. Ten Parliamentarians were captured and a similar number killed. By way of compensation during a minor skirmish that afternoon the Parliamentarian horse captured the mortally wounded Bernard Aspley, a senior Royalist officer in the Bristol garrison.[57] On the 27th the Royalists sallied around Lawfords Gate but the Parliamentarians had advanced knowledge of the attack and it was quickly repulsed; a similar and equally unsuccessful attempt was made the next day.[58] The last and by far the most determined attack against the besieging forces was launched by 1,000 cavalry and 600 infantry from the Royal Fort on 1 September. Mist and rain concealed their movements, giving the Royalists the advantage of surprise but once again the picket line was quickly reinforced and the Royalists, under Rupert's personal command, were pushed back. In the skirmish a parliamentary captain was killed and Colonel Okey of the Dragoons was captured.[59]

What had these attacks achieved? Rupert claimed they 'succeeded according to design' and Royalist newssheets presented them as triumphs:

Sunday afternoon, Aug. 24. His Highness Prince Rupert sallied forth with 300 horse and 500 foot, killed 37, in an instant, and disordered the rebels whole body, Capt. Richardson commanded the forlorn hope. Tuesday morning early (Aug. 26.) His Highness sallied forth at Ratcliffe Gate with 120 horse and 300 foot, fell on the rebels guard at Bedminster, killed six score, cut off their whole guard, pursued them quite through the streets, and brought off seven score arms; Colonel Slingsby commanded the foot, Thursday noon (the rebels being at dinner) His Highness sallied forth near Lawfords Gate with 500 foot and 50 horse, slew eight score rebels, cut off the whole guard, brought off all provisions, clothes and arms; Colonel John Russell commanded here. (The Pamphlets at this sally grant 18 files cut off.) Saturday last His Highness early sallied at Watergate Fort with 400 horse and 120 foot, fell on the body of Rebels quarters, slew their foot, killed three officers (a major and two captains) brought in Colonel Okeley himself and most of his regiment. The Post (at this sally) confesses but 60 prisoners, Colonel Cary commanded the horse.[60]

In contrast Cromwell dismissed Rupert's attacks as trivial, saying that the New Model Army lost only thirty men during them all.[61] Markham suggests that while there were only limited losses to both sides these attacks 'kept the besiegers constantly on their guard' and thus wore down the attacking forces.[62] It seems likely that Rupert's main objectives were to disrupt the Parliamentarian army's preparations for an assault and to gather information on the strength and efficiency of the forces surrounding Bristol. From Rupert's point of view the information gained was far from encouraging. Even when his troops had the advantage of surprise their attacks were quickly contained and in every case they were forced to retreat. By 2 September Rupert knew he was facing a strong, well-organized army whose leaders were unlikely to panic or make foolish errors in combat.

Any hope that these attacks might disrupt the preparations of the besiegers was also to prove unfounded. By the end of August the Committee of Both Kingdoms had issued orders that recruits should be impressed to bring Fairfax's army up to strength and by 8 September these levies were assembling at Reading and the army was instructed to sent officers to collect them.[63] Four days earlier a body of 2,000 local volunteers arrived to join the besieging army and on the 5th another twelve companies of such reinforcements came into the camp.[64] These local partisans appear not to have been fully trusted by the army commanders although they were posted to the front line in support of Rainsborough's Brigade.

It was not a little grieving [for] the enemy within to see the forwardness of the country to come to our assistance; for which reason (and to lay an effectual caution against their revolt) it was held fit to make use of those forces from the country, rather than for any considerable service [that] could be expected of them.[65]

These volunteers were probably not particularly effective as fighting troops but as Latimer suggests they provided an invaluable labour force for the besieging forces.[66] By 3 September a parliamentary correspondent reported to London that preparations were progressing well.

Great store of ladders are brought into the leaguer unto Sir Thomas Fairfax's quarters by the country, and the first and second of September instant at night every soldier on the guards was commanded to take a faggot, many cannon baskets are made.[67]

On 9 September Sir Henry Vane wrote to his father, then serving as one of the parliamentary commissioners to the Scots at Berwick:

The state of our forces before Bristol is indifferent well, considering the time of year and the wet and cold nights they meet with. They have not as yet any infection amongst them that they know of. They resolved to storm the town the latter end of last week, since which we have not heard from them. In case they did not succeed they intend to block it up and take the field against Goring.[68]

At what point did Fairfax decide to carry the city by assault rather than siege? The decision appears to have been taken on 2 September at a council of war attended by the general officers of the army, regimental commanders and senior naval officers.[69] At first it seems there were serious divisions within the council as to tactics:

We had a council of war concerning the storming of the town, about eight days before we took it; and in that there appeared great unwillingness to the work, through the unseasonableness of the weather, and other great difficulties. Some inducement to bring us thither, was the report of the good affection of the townsmen to us, but that did not answer expectation. Upon a second consideration, it was overruled for a storm, which no sooner concluded, but difficulties were removed, and all things seemed to favour the design: and indeed there hath been seldom the like cheerfulness in officers and soldiers to any work like this, after it was resolved on.[70]

The question of the tactics to be adopted was referred to a sub-committee who were instructed to present a plan the following morning for consideration by the full council.[71]

Having demonstrated that they could contain Rupert's garrison, why did Fairfax and his fellow officers choose to risk the heavy losses of an assault rather than pursuing the slower but less costly method of investment? In part the reasons were those given by Cromwell: the army was not suffering from sickness but for how long would that continue during a cold wet autumn? Also, the longer the New Model Army remained tied down in front of Bristol the greater was the possibility that the Royalists could assemble a relief force.[72] However, there were also political reasons. Westminster wanted a speedy end to the war rather than have their main army bogged down in a prolonged siege while the Royalists remained active in other areas. Firth suggests that Fairfax and his officers simply preferred assault tactics to a gradual approach.[73]

The report of the planning committee was presented the next day. An attack against the strengthened northern defences was deemed too costly and therefore the assault would be launched from the south and east. Weldon's brigade, supported by three regiments of cavalry,[74] was to attack the southern walls. Montague, supported by two regiments of horse, was to attack around Lawfords Gate and the line between the Rivers Frome and Avon.[75] North of the Frome as far as Prior's Hill Fort, Rainsborough's troops, also supported by two regiments of horse, were ordered 'to storm the fort itself as the main business'.[76] Rainsborough was to detach a regiment of foot and one of horse to skirmish with the Royalists around the Royal Fort to prevent them reinforcing the line elsewhere, and another 200 men were to reinforce an attack by sailors from the fleet against the Water Fort. A brigade of horse and dragoons was stationed on Durdham Down to prevent the Royalists breaking out of the city and escaping northwards, and two of these regiments of horse and the

Officers of both sides wore very much what they wished, although there is some indication that scarlet coats and breeches were popular with both Royalists and Parliamentarians. This particular New Model Army officer's suit is heavily decorated with silver or gold lace and is worn beneath a sleeveless buff-coat and a large silk sash which is held at the shoulder by a bunch of black ribbons. Black ribbons also decorate his fashionable 'sugar loaf' hat. He wears an iron gorget around his throat as a sign of his officer status. On his hands he wears fringed and laced gauntlets and on his feet square-toed bucket-topped boots lined with laced boot-hose. The walking cane he carries is not just highly fashionable but can also be used to reprimand disobedient soldiers. (With grateful thanks to Alan Turton)

dragoons were to attack the line around Brandon Hill to prevent troops being moved to other sectors of the line.[77] Having agreed this plan, the army began collecting ladders and other materials, moving them into the forward areas.[78]

Having agreed with his officers to assault the city, Fairfax wrote to Rupert on 4 September, demanding the surrender of the city.

> Sir: for the service of the Parliament, I have brought their army before the city of Bristol, and do summon you in their names to render it, with all the forts belonging to the same, into my hands, for their use.
>
> Having used plain language, as the business requires, I wish it may be effectual unto you as it is satisfactory to myself, that I do a little expostulate with you about the surrender of the same, which I confess is a way not common, and which I should not have used, but in respect to such a person and to such a place. I take into consideration your royal birth and relation to the crown of England, your honour, courage, the virtues of your person and the strength of that place which you may think yourself bound and able to maintain.[79]

Fairfax went on to explain that Parliament's dispute was not with the king but with his 'evil councillors' and encouraged the prince to deliver the city to avoid bloodshed and needless destruction. Such a surrender would result in the 'restoring of you to the endeared affection of the Parliament and people of England, the truest friends your family hath in this world'. According to tradition, when Rupert received this letter he was supposed to have said 'God damn me! it's a summons' and to have immediately called for a cup of sack.[80] However, when he replied the next day Rupert did not reject the demand out of hand:

> Sir, I received yours by your trumpeter. I desire to know whether you will give me leave to send a messenger to the king, to know his pleasure in it.
>   Your Servant
>   Rupert[81]

This reply was clearly considered by a Council of War, as it was the next day before Fairfax replied, rejecting consultation of the king on the grounds of delay and demanding a definite answer to his summons.[82] Rupert assembled his own Council of War to discuss what should be their next course of action and it was agreed that proposals should be sent to Fairfax to enable negotiations to be extended:

> We might strengthen our works within, hear from the king, and had he [Fairfax] assented to our demands we should have required a confirmation of them by the Parliament, which protraction of time would have been to our advantage.[83]

The Royalist terms were delivered to Fairfax on 7 September, with a rather less than honest answer:

Sir, whereas I received your letter for the delivery of the city, forts and castle of Bristol; and being willing to join with you for the sparing of blood, and preserving his majesty's subjects, I have, upon these grounds, and none other, sent you the following propositions.[84]

Rupert sent draft articles. The main points of disagreement were contained in articles 10, 11 and part of 13.

10. That the lines, forts, castle and other fortifications about or in the city of Bristol, be forthwith slighted, and the city stated in the same condition it was before the beginning of this unnatural war: and that hereafter the Parliament during this war place no garrison in it.

11. That no churches be defaced: that the several members of the foundation of the cathedral shall quietly enjoy their houses and revenues belonging to their places, and that the ministers of this city may likewise enjoy their benefices without trouble.

13. . . . that no mulct or fine be imposed upon any person mentioned in this article [mayor, sheriffs, aldermen and citizens] upon any pretence whatsoever, or questioned for any act or thing done or committed before the day of our marching forth.[85]

Fairfax replied that 'some things were doubtfully expressed; other things inconsistent with the duty I owe to them I serve'.[86] As Rainsborough reported to Parliament after the siege 'the essential articles are: exception from sequestration; cathedral men to continue; against which there is an ordinance; the works to be demolished and no garrison hereafter; which may be inconvenient'.[87] Fairfax was careful not to reject the proposals and suggested that commissioners be appointed by both sides to discuss terms for surrender. Rupert, desperately playing for time, requested that any points of disagreement should be put in writing, which was done, but Rupert still refused to name commissioners. Finally, on 9 September, after sending a final message demanding the immediate acceptance of the terms offered, Fairfax issued orders for an assault to be made the next day.[88] Throughout this exchange the New Model Army had continued to mass troops: had Fairfax been as cynical as Rupert? Certainly the Parliamentarians were fully aware of Rupert's strategy:

There can be but two things, in my opinion, induces the Prince to offer conditions; either he is not able to defend the place, and in fear of Sir Lewis

Dives conditions, if he is driven for refuge into the Royal Fort; or else, he doth do it to gain time, till his counter-scarfes and inner lines be finished, which he is very active in making day and night; or that he expects aid from the king or Goring, neither of which are moving this way, as our intelligence is.[89]

However, both sides could later claim they had tried to avoid bloodshed and accuse the other of negotiating in bad faith.

On the night of 9/10 September preparations were made for an assault. Around midnight Fairfax moved from his headquarters to the forward area to supervise the final arrangements.[90] Just before the infantry moved into their assault positions they were paid the 6s bonus promised for service at Bridgwater,[91] although raising this much cash had taxed the inventiveness of the parliamentary commissioners:

> Certificate by Col Herbert and Harcourt Leighton, Commissioners of Parliament for the Army, that the day before Bristol was taken, they were ordered by Lord General Fairfax, to issue out the money which they and Colonel Pinder had received for goods sold in Bridgwater after it was stormed, amounting to £681 13s (besides plate worth £1,200 sent to the treasurers) to pay the officers of the foot regiments the 6s gratuity formally promised the foot soldiers by the General. They had to borrow £1,300 on account from the Treasury (Mr Grosvenor then being deputy to Captain Blackwell, and Mr Bilton delivering it to them) which not sufficing they were obliged to add £100 from the money received to buy horses for the army, all which moneys were paid by them at Stapleton, near Bristol, on the 9th of September 1645.[92]

From this it appears that the infantry regiments of the New Model Army at Bristol contained just under 7,000 common soldiers, plus perhaps 800–900 officers – not many more than Rupert had deployed during the first siege. The tactics employed required the careful assembly and organization of hundreds of men in darkness in those final hours before the assault:

> Ordered to storm in three places, viz. Two hundred men in the middle, two hundred on each side, as forlorn hopes, to begin the storm; twenty ladders to each place, two men to carry each ladder, and have 5s apiece; two sergeants, that attended the service of the ladders, to have 20s a man; each musketeer that followed the ladder to carry a faggot, a sergeant to command them, and to have the same reward; twelve files of men with firepikes and pikes to follow the ladders to each place where the storm was to be; those to be commanded by a Captain and a Lieutenant; the Lieutenant to go before with five files, the Captain to second him with the other seven files; the two hundred men that were appointed to second the storm to furnish each party of them twenty

pioneers, who were to march in their rear; the two hundred men, each to be commanded by a field officer, and the pioneers by a sergeant; (those pioneers were to throw down the line and make way for the horse) the party that was to make good the line, to possess the guns and turn them; a gentleman of the ordnance, gunners and matrosses, to enter with the parties; the drawbridge to be let down; two regiments and a half to storm after the foot, if way be made.[93]

At two in the morning a huge bonfire was lit at Fairfax's command post on Ashley Hill and the nearby battery fired four heavy guns at Prior's Hill Fort as the signal for the assault to begin. Rainsborough describes the troops as 'shouting with joy' and said that in the early stages of the assault 'the service was very hot'; Sprigg noted that the assault was 'terrible to the beholders'.[94] One veteran of the attack recalled the Royalists had been warned by a deserter that an attack was imminent: 'the enemy stood ready cocked, and the gunners by their guns.'[95] In his own account of the assault Rupert mentions that he had 'received intelligent a little before it' and thus 'all were in readiness to receive them'.[96]

In the south the carefully organized assault columns found the ditch and walls as much an obstacle as the Cornish had two years before: the ladders were too short to reach the top of the walls.[97] Despite the courage and determination of the troops they only, as one contemporary put it, 'alarmed the enemy'.[98] The attackers finally fell back, having accomplished nothing but the loss of a hundred men and several officers killed or wounded.[99]

Although frequently presented as two brigade-sized attacks, the assaults on the eastern defences were carried out by pairs of infantry regiments who quickly breached the defences at a number of points, disorganizing the defenders and preventing effective reinforcement. They probably adopted tactics similar to those used by the units to the south, with each regiment forming an assault column. Montague's and Pickering's attacked the defended position around Lawfords Gate:

a great double work well filled with men and cannon, presently entered, and with great resolution beat the enemy from their works, and possessed their cannon: their expedition was such, that they forced the enemy from their advantages without any considerable loss to themselves, they laid down bridges for the horse to enter.[100]

Sprigg said that the troops at Lawfords Gate 'recovered twenty-six guns and took many prisoners in the works' and that they opened the way for their supporting cavalry.[101] Rainsborough commented that they 'took 16 pieces in the several works and half moons they gained by storming'.[102] Supported by infantry who had breached the line to the north of them and by cavalry of Fairfax's regiment under Major Desborough, the attackers pushed the surviving defenders back into the city and secured access to

During excavations on the site of the medieval defences at Tower Harratz on the southern wall it was discovered that the old defensive tower had been demolished and replaced by a structure identified as a seventeenth-century artillery redoubt. There is also evidence that this position was extended, perhaps during the Royalist occupation. During the first siege it was noted that 'at Tower Harris over the Bridge' the Parliamentarians mounted a saker and two minions. These guns, and those in a similar position in the second siege, would have been able to sweep the ditch and base of the wall. (Copyright Bristol Museum and Art Gallery)

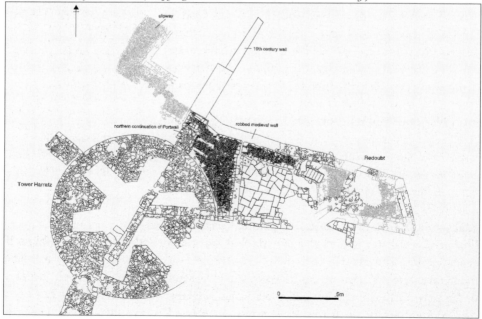

one of the gates into the city 'against Castle Street'.[103] Rupert admitted that 'many officers and men were taken or killed' at Lawfords Gate but suggested that this was because the enemy entered the line 'where the townsmen and new Welsh were',[104] while Bernard de Gomme argued that the defences in this sector were not as formidable as parliamentary accounts suggest.[105]

The infantry regiments of Hardress Waller and Thomas Fairfax attacked further up the line towards the River Frome, at a point where de Gomme says the line was weak and 'decayed' and the ditch only 5 feet wide and deep.[106] They appear to have been able to breach the line quickly and move into the rear of the defenders of Lawfords Gate, preventing them escaping or Rupert reinforcing them. The regiments of Skippon and Birch attacked the line just north of the River Frome and 'entered with good resolution, where their post was possessing the enemy's guns, and turning them'.[107] John Birch left a vivid description of the assault at this point. The Royalists were ready for them and the flash of artillery fire lit up the attackers:

> which continued for about a quarter of an hour, the otherwise being as dark as ever I saw; yet God so blessed you that you entered in that very place; and about 90 were killed or taken that kept that place: but not without some hazard; whole volleys discharging, when you had but the breadth of the trench of, and many case shot. But God was with you then, and enabled you, when you were in, to keep it.[108]

Once the line was taken the pioneers quickly created a passage for the supporting cavalry under Maj. Bethel, who led the first successful cavalry breakthrough of the assault. This was fortunate as soon afterwards they were attacked by 500 Royalist cavalry 'appointed to scour the line'.[109] A cavalry mêlée resulted in which it was noted Bethel 'did behave himself very gallantly, and was shot in the thigh, had one or two shot more, and had his horse shot under him'.[110] He was reinforced by the regiments of Whaley and Rich and part of Grave's. In the face of such numbers, and realizing that their infantry had been driven from the line, the Royalists retreated to the Royal Fort and Coulston's Fort.[111]

This New Model Army infantryman wears the issue coat and breeches trimmed in his regimental colour, and low-heeled shoes. For the assault he has been issued with grenades instead of his normal pike or musket and carries a length of slowmatch to ignite the fuses. The use of grenades and other 'fireworks' was a notable feature of both sieges. (With grateful thanks to Alan Turton)

In the north operations were mainly intended to tie down the defenders and prevent Rupert moving men to other areas. The planned attack on the Water Fort by sailors from the fleet, who had been waiting in boats at Vincent's Rock since the 5th, was frustrated by adverse tidal conditions, and they landed to join Rainsborough's attack.[112] Half of Pride's Regiment was detached with orders to skirmish with the garrison of the Royal Fort; it was, however, noted that 'afterwards they took a little fort of Welshmen'.[113] The dragoons were also deployed to skirmish with the Royalist defenders of Brandon Hill, while on Durdham Down a brigade of horse under Ireton was kept in reserve in case Rupert tried to escape from the city with his cavalry.

However, the most bitter fighting of the night occurred around Prior's Hill Fort which was attacked by the regiments of Rainsborough and Hammond supported by those men of Pride's regiment not employed at the Royal Fort.[114] The fort was the key to the whole defensive line:

> obtaining this strong fort, without which all the rest of the line to Frome river would have done us little good; and indeed, neither horse or foot would have stood in all that way, in any manner of security, had not the fort been taken.[115]

Hammond's Regiment attacked the line below the fort to cut the garrison's line of retreat and allowed cavalry to enter, preventing reinforcements reaching the fort from the city.[116] This was probably the attack which Rupert erroneously describes as carrying Stokes Croft Gate where the Mayor of Bristol was killed leading the city troops.[117] Rainsborough's Regiment attacked the fort itself[118] and their colonel was full of praise for his men 'which piece of service was as bravely performed, as ever a thing was done by man'. Sprigg describes the attackers 'plying them hard with musket shot in at the portholes'.[119] After hand-to-hand fighting, ladders were brought forward but once again they were not long enough as the fort was 'exceeding high, a ladder of thirty rounds scarce reaching the top thereof', and even Cromwell admitted that the attackers began to lose hope of taking the fort.[120] However, men of Hammond's Regiment attacked the weaker inner face of the fort and were able to gain access by climbing through firing ports.[121]

The mood of the Parliamentarian infantry was ugly. They had fought the defenders for over two hours with the Royalists 'playing fiercely with great and small shot upon our men'.[122] They began to slaughter the defenders, a fact which Parliamentarian accounts made no effort to deny.[123]

> In the end we forced the enemy within to run below into the inner rooms of the work, hoping to receive quarter; but our soldiers were so little prepared for to show mercy, by the opposition that they met withal in the storm, and the refusal of quarter when it was offered, that they put to the sword the commander (one Major Price, a Welshman), and almost all the officers, soldiers

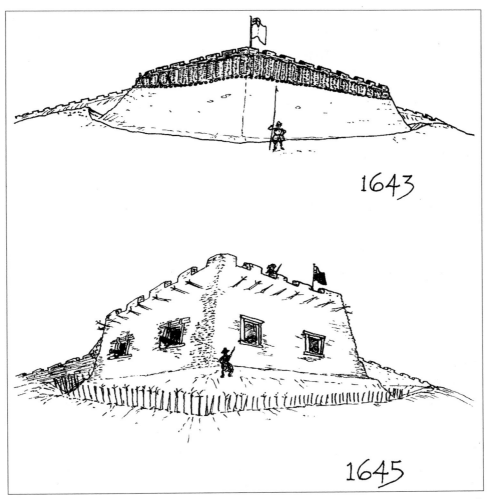

Artist's impression of Prior's Hill Fort during the first and second sieges of Bristol. The extent of rebuilding and strengthening of these northern forts is clearly shown. (With grateful thanks to Alan Turton)

and others in the fort, except a very few, which at the great entreaty of some of our officers, had their lives spared.[124]

Maj. William Price of Pilleth, Radnorshire, was known to local Parliamentarians as 'the Prince of Radnorshire', and the fort's garrison was probably recruited from this area.[125] It is also possible that Rainsborough's men were taking revenge for losses at the siege of Sherborne where a number of officers were killed by Royalist snipers equipped with birding pieces.[126] As dawn broke the last Royalist resistance was crushed and the fort was firmly in parliamentary hands. It was critical that the fort was captured before dawn, as in daylight the defenders could have been supported by artillery in the castle and the forts along the high ground. The potential effect of this was seen shortly after the fort's capture when Fairfax and Cromwell were standing on the parapet of the fort, discussing the next stage of the attack: a cannon shot from the castle landed between them, showering them with dirt but leaving them unharmed.[127] Rupert now faced a difficult decision:

> then the day breaking we found them in full possession of the line and fort which caused our horse and foot to retire to the Great Fort, who were presently ordered into the city to make that good, leaving other works insufficiently manned, Coulston's Work, Brandon Hill, and the new redoubt without the line, finding ourselves in this condition and considering the engagement of those within the city and castle and that Lord Hawley, Sir Matthew Appleyard, Col Slingsby and their men were in danger of being cut off, the enemy between us and them, his highness moved the officers to entertain a treaty this time, before they were lost.[128]

While Rupert and his officers discussed the possibility of surrender, the victorious troops were engaged in trying to extinguish a number of fires in the city; theses may have been deliberately started or simply a consequence of the fighting. This proved extremely difficult and Cromwell reported that the fires 'begat a great trouble to the General and all of us fearing to see a great city burnt to ashes before our faces'.[129] As the fire-fighting continued, a messenger arrived from Rupert at about 9.00 a.m. asking that surrender negotiations should begin at once. Fairfax agreed on condition that the Royalists quenched the fires within the city.[130]

The commissioners nominated by Fairfax were Colonels Montague, Rainsborough, and Pickering. They met Rupert's representatives Mynne, Tillyer and Vavasour but the negotiations were not easy. At one point the Royalists refused to agree that all firearms should be surrendered. The matter was referred to the full Council of War of the garrison who sent instructions that 'it is our general opinion that if better conditions could not be granted, we assent to the leaving of the firearms of the private soldiers'.[131] At another stage Rupert threatened to break off the negotiations owing to 'some insolencies of the soldiers' unless he obtained satisfaction from Fairfax.[132] However, the result was inevitable and the conditions finally agreed upon were reasonably generous: the bulk of the garrison was to be disarmed but the troops were granted the courtesies and honours of war and allowed to march away to Oxford.[133]

On 11 September Prince Rupert and his forces evacuated the city of Bristol. The occasion was recorded by a Parliamentarian correspondent:

> Yesterday, according to the articles, Prince Rupert marched out in this manner, having drawn all his foot into the Royal Fort and the Castle, his horse, standing

in the green under the fort, within the line, those wagons appointed for him being laden with his baggage, in all not above eight.

He drew out part of his horse and foot before his wagons and part following, himself next with his lifeguard of firelocks came forth, all in red coats before him and his lifeguard of horse following, accompanied by some lords, viz Cromwell, Grandison etc. Colonel Hammond's regiment of foot standing at the port to receive the keys of the fort and marched in, Lieut-General Cromwell, Col Montague, Col Rainsborough and some other officers waited at the port of the fort for his coming out, and waited upon him to the general, who stood with the convoy of horse without the line, and accompanied him over Durdum Down, being almost two miles: The Prince was clad in scarlet, very richly laid with silver lace, mounted upon a very gallant black Barbury horse; the General and the Prince rid together, the General giving the Prince the right hand all the way; the number of the Princes foot was about 2000, the horse with the designated number of 250 and the lifeguard altogether, made 400: I think there might be noblemen and gentlemen to the number of at least three hundred more.[134]

Rupert marched out to disgrace and criticism from the uncle in whose cause he had fought so loyally; relations rapidly deteriorated to the point where the prince and his supporters chose to leave for the continent.[135] In the ranks of the New Model Army and at Westminster the capture of Bristol served to antagonize relations between Presbyterians and Independents. Cromwell's report of the capture of the city was published by order of the Commons but comments seen as critical of the Presbyterian faction in Parliament were carefully censored.[136] However, in October 1645 a pamphlet appeared, without a printer's name, which made public the lieutenant-general's views:

Presbyterians, Independents, all had here the same spirit of faith and prayer, the same presence and

A Declaration of Prince Rupert. *Just as Fiennes had tried to explain his actions at Bristol, so too did Rupert. He was no more successful and after being disgraced and criticized by the king he left for the continent with a party of supporters. (Reproduced by kind permission of Bristol Central Library)*

answer, they agree here, know no names of difference; pity it is, should it be otherwise anywhere: all that believe, have the real unity which is most glorious, because inward and spiritual in the body and to the head.[137]

The following April the army chaplain Hugh Peters preached a sermon to both Houses of Parliament, the Aldermen of London and the Assembly of Divines; this was not only pro-Independent in tone but used Bristol on a number of occasions to demonstrate the 'special providences' that had attended their cause.[138] The Independents successfully argued that Fiennes should be fully pardoned for surrendering the city on the grounds that:

All the enemy's actions and councils have turned to our advantage, and we have been gainers by our losses generally: As in the loss of Bristol, we found the way to take it by the loss, at first view we saw it was not tenable with so little force, which easily acquits that wise and valiant gentleman that surrendered it.[139]

CHAPTER 10

For Parliament Again

As Rupert and his troops evacuated the city the New Model Army reoccupied it in the name of Parliament. Plague was raging and Sprigg left the following description of conditions in the city:

> more like a prison than a city, and the people more like prisoners than citizens; being brought so low with taxations, so poor in habit, and so dejected in countenance; the streets so noisome, and the houses so nasty as that they were unfit to receive friends or freemen till they were cleansed.[1]

The Parliamentarians had previously experienced no serious outbreaks of sickness in their ranks but this was unlikely to continue if they remained in or near the city.[2] Fairfax dispatched Rainsborough to capture Berkeley Castle, which fell on 25 September, effectively clearing Gloucestershire of Royalists. A week later Fairfax marched to Bath and 'rested there some four or five days for the better recovery of his health (as was need), having been much wearied out, and spent with that great business of Bristol'.[3] Cromwell, with a strong detachment, was sent to reduce Royalist garrisons in Wiltshire and Hampshire, capturing Devizes on 23 September and Basing House a month after Bristol fell.[4] Fairfax himself moved west, liberating Somerset, pushing into Devonshire by mid-October, capturing Tiverton Castle on the 19th and raising the siege of Plymouth in early January.[5]

Four days after Rupert left, the City Council met to elect new officials. Asked for advice, Fairfax suggested that the ancient custom in such matters should be observed. The council demonstrated its independence, or stupidity, by electing Francis Creswick, a well-known Royalist, as mayor. To balance this two Parliamentarians, Richard Vickris and Luke Hodges, both expelled in 1643, were reinstated by the Council.[6] On 2 October the council decided to give a £5,000 gratuity to the soldiers of the New Model Army; this sum was to be raised by confiscating the goods of all 'foreigners' in the city at the surrender, supplemented by a rate on the citizens. Bristol was once again trying to buy its way out of trouble. Two days later the 'gift' was increased to £6,000 to try to pacify the soldiers. On 8 October two parliamentary Commissioners wrote to Westminster warning that there were problems:

In Bristol, where the plague was increasing, the inability of the writers to relieve the sick and wounded begot daily mutinies and desertions, and but for the gratuity raised for the troops ruin would have fallen on the city from the soldiers' appetites. It had been hoped that funds would be obtained from the wealth of the enemy; but the city was found to be a den of thieves, the goods of escaped Royalists being claimed under pretended transfers or for pretended debts. The citizens, moreover, refused to buy such prize goods as had been found.[7]

By 12 November only £1,500 had been raised, and the military authorities demanded the city rate books so that troops could gather the money. The Council promised that the money would soon be available, but it was not until February that the total amount was paid, much of it in the form of silver plate rather than coin.[8]

Sycophantic generosity was no more effective in winning over Parliament than it had been previously with the king. The pro-Royalist sympathies of many members of the Bristol Corporation were well known and a purge was ordered by an Ordinance of 28 October. This removed from office the newly elected mayor, five other Alderman and seven common Councillors.[9] The vacancies were to be filled with 'well-affected' persons and those imprisoned or sequestered for opposition to Parliament were to be disqualified. Another Ordinance dated 1 November ordered the restoration to the Council of Richard Aldworth, Luke Hodges and Richard Vickris (the later two had been reinstated in September) who had been 'removed without lawful cause'.[10] Just as the Councillors learned that the new regime had neither forgiven their enemies nor forgotten their names, so former Royalists found themselves facing heavy fines. In October 1645 Thomas Miller 'of the Customs, Bristol' compounded on the Bristol articles, claiming that he had held the post for eleven years and had a wife and several small children to support but had never been in arms against Parliament; it was agreed that he should not be fined.[11] Thomas Brown of Boston in Lincolnshire was less fortunate:

> 1 November 1645. Begs remission of his offence, or admission to an easy composition. In June 1643, was sent for by his uncle at Bristol for preferment in marriage, the city being then under the Parliament's command; but before his arrival, it surrendered to the King. Was stayed by Prince Rupert, and compelled to take up arms for the king. When Parliament retook Bristol, came to London, submitted to the Speaker, and paid £20. on the propositions.
> 23 December. Fined £260
> 9 March 1646. Fine accepted by the House, abating £60, the former setting of £260. being an error in the report.[12]

Bristol Royalists were called before a tribunal who investigated the value of the estates of 'delinquents' and fixed the fines to be paid in lieu of sequestration.[13]

Thomas Colston admitted in April 1646 that he had commanded the city's trained bands, but claimed he had since 'been conformable to the orders of Parliament'; his case was referred to a sub-committee and it appears he was not fined.[14] William Bevan, who had been active in both the Royalist plot and the first siege, claimed that he had 'laid down his arms' ten months before Fairfax arrived and had paid the various fines and contributions imposed upon him; the Committee for Compounding considered this sufficient and no order was made against him.[15] However, three other expelled councillors who compounded on the same day were heavily fined.[16] In July 1649 another group of former councillors tried, to claim exemption under the articles of surrender at Bristol; although this was rejected there is no evidence that any of this group was fined.[17]

A number of Royalists living in Bristol petitioned the Committee in the following years although most of them were relatively minor individuals.[18] A pamphlet listing those who had compounded for their estates named only seven Bristolians, including just three of the expelled councillors, as having been fined by 1655.[19] Why were so few of the king's supporters punished by the victorious Parliamentarians? A letter from John Ash and Edmund Prideaux in November 1647 suggests that prosecutions were not being pressed:

> When we were with you in Michaelmas 1646, you informed us that there were several gentlemen in Bristol liable to sequestration, but that you thought it better there should only be an engagement taken from them to prosecute their composition, and sequestration forborne. We assented, but most of them do not compound, and yet are free from sequestration; whereby we and you are in danger of censure, as the Committee at Goldsmith's Hall is resolved to take some course therein. We desire you to bring them to speedy composition or sequester them, that we and you may not incur trouble for neglect of duty.[20]

Were Bristolians trying to protect their fellow citizens? Certainly the Committee for Compounding thought so. They wrote to the Mayor and Aldermen of Bristol in February 1652.

> We hear from the county committee that you wish none but yourselves to manage things of this kind. We know not how far any not yet detected are concerned therein, but we believe there is a desire rather to conceal than punish offenders. We confirm the power of our commissioners, and have ordered them to proceed vigorously, and you are to suffer them to act in your precincts, and to give them all assistance. We shall take a strict account of your carriage herein.[21]

The number of Royalists who escaped fines seems to suggest that the authorities in Bristol were at least turning a blind eye if not actively protecting their fellow citizens.

Commander of the infantry in the Earl of Essex's army and later in the New Model Army, Phillip Skippon did not take part in the second siege of Bristol as he was recovering from serious wounds received at Naseby. He was appointed governor of the city by Parliament. (Reproduced by kind permission of Bristol Central Library)

Although initally a regiment of foot was left to garrison the Royal Fort[22] no regular units of Fairfax's army were to be permanently stationed in the city. The garrison was formed from 1,500 foot and two troops of horse recruited locally for that purpose.[23] As early as 15 September exiled Bristolians in London were suggesting that Philip Skippon, the commander of the New Model Army's infantry, should be appointed Governor of Bristol.[24] An Ordinance of Parliament dated 3 December 1645 named Skippon as governor and placed heavy levies on Bristol and the surrounding area to cover the costs of a new garrison.[25] Another ordinance of the same date allowed £5,000 towards the raising of forces in the city; this appears to refer to the infantry regiment of Samuel Kem.[26] By August 1646, when the king was finally in the hands of Parliament, it was considered safe to reduce the Bristol garrison to 800 infantry and a single troop of horse.[27] In November the 'city regiment' was reduced to five companies.[28]

In January 1647 the king, who had surrendered to the Scots in the hopes of being able to drive a wedge between the allies, had been handed over to his Parliament and in March Harlech Castle, the last Royalist garrison outside Ireland, surrendered. Peace had returned. In Bristol the garrisons of the castle and great fort were reduced to just 250 men, the city itself was disgarrisoned and the ring of defensive works and the other forts 'slighted' to render them indefensible.[29] The previous November 1,000 infantry under the command of Colonels Needham and Grey were shipped from Bristol to Dublin to reinforce the army fighting the Royalists and their Irish allies.[30] Bristol had always been an important port in the Irish trade and had often seen such movements of men to and from Ireland. Both sides tried to ship men and material through the city. In

December 1648 Captain Plunkett, who had 'revolted and joined with the Irish rebels', tried to ship two small cannon from London to Ireland via Bristol, although this particular consignment was discovered by a Customs officer.[31] A letter to Capt. Bishop of the Bristol garrison from the Council of State in April 1649 shows how some of the king's supporters reached Ireland:

> Cornet Pinke and other suspicious persons are lately come to Bristol, to be transported into Ireland, and have contracted with the master of a ship bound for New England, to be landed in Munster, for which they are to pay £10 a man. Their ordinary discourse is nothing but bitter invectives against Parliament, and the manner of their living so extremely riotous that there is just ground of suspicion that they go thither to join a disaffected party, but fly from hence to avoid inquiry about a robbery lately committed in London, in which a great sum of money and many precious goods were taken from Mons. Le Mot. We therefore desire you to apprehend Pinke and his assistants, seize his and their horses and arms, and search them and all trunks, boxes &c belonging to them, for money, rings, jewels, letters and papers and secure them and their persons until further orders. You are also to examine the master of the ship in which they are going, and if he refuses to give any account concerning them, to stay his ship until he does so. As they intend going away next week you must use expedition.[32]

However, before Parliament could concentrate on the campaign in Ireland there was renewed fighting in England and Wales. The Second Civil War broke out in March 1648, when Col. Poyer, a parliamentary officer, declared for the king and secured the town of Pembroke.[33] Bristol was clearly endangered by this sudden revival of Royalist activity, and in May parliamentary warships were ordered to take into custody a large sum of money then in Bristol ready to be transported to Ireland.[34] The Committee of Both Houses ordered reinforcements and supplies of ammunition for Bristol, as well as £500 to be spent on repairing and provisioning the great fort and castle.[35] However, the threat from Wales evaporated in July when Poyer, lacking cavalry and threatened by approaching parliamentary forces, surrendered in the hope of obtaining mercy. He was taken to London, tried and shot.[36]

The Scots army that had invaded England in support of the Stewarts was defeated at Preston, and the Royalist revolt at Colchester was crushed by the end of August. Under the control of the Independent faction began to consolidate its position. In December the Presbyterian faction was purged from Parliament on the grounds that they were now in alliance with the king. Charles was brought to trial in January 1649 by a specially formed 'High Court of Justice'. He was found guilty of High Treason and sentenced to death; he was executed on 30 January. In March 1649 Cromwell was appointed Lord-Lieutenant of Ireland and commander-in-chief of the army there: the last centre of Royalist resistance was

1653.
OLIVER CROMWELL
LORD PROTECTOR
of England Scotland
and Ireland

*Oliver Cromwell was second-in-command to Fairfax at the siege of Bristol.
He was to pass through the city on his way to assume command of the army in
Ireland and as Lord Protector removed the garrison of the city and ordered
the demolition of the defences. He is shown here as Lord Protector in 1653.
(With grateful thanks to Alan Turton)*

to be reduced. On 27 June the Council of State wrote to James Powell, their agent in Bristol:

There are many forces now ready for transport to Ireland, and the exigency of affairs there requires their presence. To expedite them you are to stay all ships in the ports of Bristol, Minehead, Barnstable and Appledore, fit for transportation of horse and foot for Dublin, agree with them either by the month or freight, and order them to Milford Haven, where the horse and men are to be shipped.[37]

A week later the Council sent Powell details of the ships required to carry Cromwell's army to Ireland:

The ships shall enter into pay when they have fallen down to Kingsroad, and are there ready to sail to Milford Haven. Much more shipping than that in your paper will be needed, and some of less burthen; as of 30, 40 or 50 tons; therefore the names of such vessels had better be returned. Take care that water casks be provided at the State's charge, and such quantity put on board every ship fit to carry horses – of which number there will be more than you seem to intimate – as shall contain water enough for 10 days at least. For the proportion of horse they can carry, pails are also to be provided, to water the horses aboard, and rings to tie them to the ship's side, and slings to ship them with.[38]

Bristol became one of the main bases supporting the army in Ireland. On 14 July Cromwell himself arrived in Bristol to take ship for Ireland, and the City Council, always seeking to impress the powerful, entertained their visitor and presented him with a butt of sack.[39] On 31 July Col. Hagget was ordered to assume the government of the city and raise a second garrison company under his own command, with £500 being allocated to repair the defences. In the event of 'imminent danger' Hagget was authorized to raise a regiment in the city among those of 'approved fidelity', but this was only to be paid when upon actual service.[40] Over the coming months shipments of foodstuffs and clothing were made to Dublin or Munster,[41] and in March 1650 Powell was ordered to assist Col. Ryves in raising and transporting six companies of infantry to Ireland, but the letter warned that the profiteering would no longer be tolerated:

The council notices that the rates paid by you last winter for transportation of foot and horse to Munster are excessively dear, considering what is paid from Chester to Dublin, which is about the same distance Bristol is from Youghall, the State paying but 2s 6d for every footman and 10s for every horseman from Chester; let them speedily understand the lowest rates for transportation of each foot and horse soldier to Munster, advising with the governor and mayor of

Bristol, and such others as you think fit; and upon return of the rates, you shall receive orders to press any vessel for service that refuses to go upon these terms.[42]

During 1650 the defences of the city were repaired at a cost of £1,000 which, it was noted, was to be repaid from the sale of Royalist estates, and the quantity of gunpowder held in the city increased from forty to sixty barrels.[43] In March 1651 orders were issued for 1,352 soldiers to be drawn from garrisons in England and Wales to bring units in Ireland up to strength; 462 of these were ordered to be shipped from Bristol, along with the 80 men of Capt. Purye's company of the Bristol garrison.[44] In May Powell was ordered to make arrangements to ship 4,000 impressed recruits from Bristol to Munster.[45] However, by now the war in Ireland was approaching its final stages, and the focus of attention was to shift back to England as a new menace emerged.

In August 1651 Charles II invaded England with a Scots army. Marching down the west coast he occupied Worcester and appeared to be considering an advance towards Bristol. Early in the crisis 100 men were drawn out of the Bristol garrison to form part of a field regiment but the men quickly returned.[46] Local militia units were mobilized to defend the city, known Royalists were arrested and it was ordered that all ships in Bristol be sent down to the Kingsroode to prevent their capture if the city fell to the Scots.[47] Later in the month Lt-Col. Clark was instructed to move the ten companies under his command from Exeter to Bristol although Clark himself was subsequently sent to Plymouth to replace Blake, who had been ordered to sea with the fleet.[48] At the end of the month the Council of State wrote to the authorities in Bristol:

We hear, both by your letters and those of others, of the readiness in you, the people and the forces of your city, to be active in this exigency for preservation of your city against the enemy. Considering the importance of the place, we had given orders for such forces as could to march towards you, and your appearance in great readiness to defend yourselves no doubt discouraged the enemy to press any further that way to attempt you.[49]

A few days after this letter was written Cromwell destroyed the Royalist threat, shattering the Scottish army at Worcester and pursuing the remnants through Yorkshire.

The only Scots to reach Bristol were prisoners of war. This was nothing new: after Preston, Bristol merchants had requested permission to 'transport 500 of the prisoners to the plantations'; this was granted.[50] After Worcester, most of the prisoners were concentrated in Bristol and orders to this effect were sent to the parliamentary Governors of Liverpool, Chester, Shrewsbury, Stafford and Worcester:

That you may have no further trouble with prisoners in your custody, we have thought fit that they should be sent to Bristol, in order to their disposal abroad.

Send all in your power under the quality of captains, lieutenants and cornets, to Shrewsbury, or the most fit place on the Severn, where they are to be put in vessels to be carried down to Bristol.[51]

At Bristol Col. Scrope was ordered to make arrangements to accommodate the prisoners until they were transported. He was instructed to allow 2½d each for food, which Scrope was assured 'we will see is repaid'.[52] A letter in December shows there were delays in shipping the prisoners:

The mayor and aldermen report an infectious disease among the Scottish prisoners. Aldworth must remove them to places where there will be least danger of infection, and you must pay 4d a day each for their subsistence to privates, and 5s a week to officers. These prisoners were to have been carried to plantations, but were left behind; inquire what merchants have left them, that some course may be taken.[53]

Despite these difficulties the merchants of Bristol, discovering how profitable prisoners of war could be as a cargo, went on to ship substantial numbers of Irish to the plantations in the West Indies after July 1652.[54]

After the Third Civil War the government felt secure enough to begin reducing the army and disbanding garrisons throughout England. As early as 21 February 1650 the Council of State had considered 'the state of the fortifications at Bristol, and particularly whether the castle and fort are necessary for the safe-keeping of the city'.[55] These discussions had been interrupted by the outbreak of the Third Civil War but on 3 January 1653 the Council of State asked the Irish and Scottish Committee to consider 'the order of Parliament concerning the disgarrisoning of Bristol Castle and Fort and other places, and report'.[56] However, Cromwell wrote to Col. Scrope, the Governor of Bristol, telling him to disregard instructions to disband the troops in the castle and fort and to await further orders.[57] On 15 March an order was issued by the Ordnance Committee to Anthony Robbins to visit a number of garrisons, including Bristol, to collect all artillery and ammunition for transfer to the Tower of London.[58] On 6 April the Irish and Scottish Committee ordered that the gunpowder then in the castle and fort at Bristol was to be shipped to Ireland when the garrison were removed from the city. Nine days later the committee was instructed by the Council of State to confer with the Lord–General and the Mayor of Bristol about dismantling the castle.[59] By July payments were being made to Commissary Thomas Fowler for bringing guns and arms from Bristol, although Robbins, the official sent to organize the collection, complained bitterly that he had not been paid for his work.[60]

On 27 December 1654 Col. Scrope was ordered by Cromwell to withdraw most of his men from the castle into the Royal Fort and on the following day a warrant was issued to the Corporation 'to dismantle and demolish the castle within the city of Bristol'.[61] The city authorities formed a committee to oversee the demolition. Work continued until the end of the following year, reducing the walls and keep to ground level and laying out new streets on the site.[62] While work on the castle continued, an order was issued in July 1655 by the Council of State that 'all provisions of war in Bristol to be removed to Chepstow Castle, and the Royal Fort demolished'.[63] By June 1656 a Royalist agent reported that there were only sixty soldiers at Bristol, despite the fact that the city was the magazine for the local militia, and a considerable number of prisoners were held there.[64]

These unsettled years were to see new ideas in politics and religion emerging as forms of government were discussed and rejected following the execution of the king. There had been radical religious groups in Bristol even before the war and these had grown in numbers and influence. By 1646 Thomas Edwards noted that 'emissaries of the sectaries' were active in Bristol and Wales.[65] After the war the question of religious belief became entwined in the political life of the period, as Kem warned his regiment during a sermon he preached as a farewell to his troops:

> It is a sad time, but this is more sad omen of worser times, even the rabble of opinions in this city of Bristol; of which many say, that as the sword hath slain many, so hath error many more in a few months time.[66]

Kem was probably referring to supporters of the various religious groups who increasingly opposed the Presbyterian faction in their attempts to negotiate with the king and obtain a long-term settlement. A petition to the Council of the Army demonstrates that some Bristolians held strong views on this subject:

> We were filled with sorrow, when we saw the abominable apostasy and degenerate actings of the majority of the House of Commons, who after we had bought their security with our most precious blood and treasure, should by their treating with the king, so cruelly sell us into the blood and revenge of him and his desperate confederates, so contrary to their first principles and declarations, and to justice and equity, esteeming the effusion of the most excellent English blood, to be but just homage to his lusts and tyranny, and all their unhappiness to be an equitable tribute to his will and pleasure.[67]

Later, in common with other former Royalist areas, the Levellers began to win support in Bristol for their radical programme of religious and land reform.[68] Quakers also became a conspicuous and troublesome group in Bristol during the 1650s with the mixture of religious zeal and apocalyptical sense of God's imminent return to judge man.[69] They were to be joined by even more extreme individuals such as the Bristol grocer who embraced the beliefs of the Ranters and declared that 'the Bible was the plague of England'.[70]

A political and religious radical and an early Quaker, James Naylor was seen as subversive and dangerous by the authorities. Following an incident in Bristol in 1656 he was subjected to savage punishment for blasphemy in London and Bristol. (Left) a small contemporary print showing Naylor branded with the letter B for Blasphemer; (right) a much better, and far more lifelike, picture of Naylor (sadly the original does not copy well). (Reproduced by kind permission of Bristol Central Library)

Perhaps the most extreme manifestation of both religious belief and intolerance in Bristol in these years concerns the behaviour of James Naylor, a northerner and former soldier, who progressed through the west country proclaiming that Christ was in him. His followers accepted this as a literal truth and began to treat Naylor, who was clearly mentally unstable, as the son of God. This behaviour horrified conventional Christians of all shades of opinion, but his entry into Bristol on 24 October 1656 was simply too much to ignore:

On departing from Bedminster for Bristol on the 24th, a procession was formed on that part of the road reserved for carts, where, says an observant spectator, the mud reached to the knees of the impassioned pedestrians; and Naylor, on horseback, was escorted by his friends into the city amidst singing and screams of rejoicing. Soon after he had reached the White Lion Inn, in Broad Street, the scandalised magistrates gave orders for the arrest of all the strangers, and on the following day they were examined at the Tolzey, where Naylor repeatedly proclaimed his Messianic character, whilst one of his female adorers positively asserted that two days after her death he had restored her to life.[71]

Having no idea what to do with this troublesome and unwelcome guest the Bristol magistrates sent details to London, and received orders to send him to Parliament. MPs spent six weeks denouncing the hapless Naylor and worked themselves into a hysterical frenzy, many of them demanding the sentence of death for his blasphemies. Cromwell tried to moderate the situation and Naylor's life was spared but the punishment he suffered was horrendous:

> it was resolved that the hapless manic should be exposed for two hours in the pillory at Westminster, and for the same time in London, after being whipped from one city to the other (310 lashes were inflicted during this); that he should have his tongue bored through with a red hot iron, and his forehead branded with the letter B; that he then be sent to Bristol, where he was to ride through the streets on a bare-backed horse and be publicly whipped, and that he should then be carried to London and kept in solitary confinement, debarred the use of pen and paper, and compelled to earn his food by hard labour, until Parliament thought fit to release him.[72]

The crowds in both London and Bristol displayed respect and solidarity with the victim of this sadistic punishment, who by all accounts underwent the ordeal with great courage and fortitude. However, he never recovered from the horrific injuries he suffered and died three years later aged 43.[73]

It would be wrong to present this period as one of continual crisis. The city was slowly returning to normal, and as early as October 1646 the Council organized poor relief and paid off the arrears of salary owed to officials; soon after, they arranged the revival of the mayor's fishing trip, a perambulation of the boundaries and a duck hunt.[74] Latimer's account of these years contains increasing references to the Council's concern with repairing war damage, collecting rents and sorting out old debts rather than matters of national politics.[75] Trade revived, although Irish and Royalist privateers remained a menace. In at least one case the Bristol merchantman *Recovery* returned to port having captured the *Royal James* frigate which had attacked her.[76] By February 1654 the city's manufacturers appear to have recovered from the war, and parliamentary agents in Bristol were reporting that shipbuilding and gunpowder production were going well.[77]

By the mid-1650s wine was being imported in smaller quantities than in pre-war years but the Merchant Venturers wharfage books show a wide range of commodities being imported from French, Spanish and Dutch ports. Following Cromwell's suppression of Ireland, trade was begining to revive with Irish ports in commodities such as tallow, barrel staves, preserved meat, fish and skins.[78] As the cattle trade with Ireland was severely disrupted by the prolonged conflict the number of ships trading there declined in these years, a reduction made permanent by legislation against the live cattle imports in the 1660s. There was considerable growth in the trans–Atlantic trade: in 1636/7 America and the West Indies were the destination of 4.1 per cent of ships leaving Bristol and in 1637/8 they were the points of origin of just 2.5 per cent of those discharging cargo.[79] By the late 1650s shipping to these regions accounted for one–seventh (14.2 per cent) of the total shipping and this increased rapidly as the century progressed until by the 1680s it represented between a third (33 per cent) and a quarter (25 per cent).[80] The decline in wine imports was more than matched by an increase in sugar and tobacco which enjoyed high prices on the European market.[81]

The Royalists continued to form conspiracies, many of which were infiltrated by Cromwell's intelligence organization under Thurloe. In March 1658 the English ambassador in Paris wrote to Thurloe to inform him that the Royalists were planning an attack on Plymouth which they believed would be supported by a rebellion in the Bristol and Gloucester region.[82] In September 1658 the hopes of the Royalists were raised by the news that the Lord Protector Cromwell was dead and had been succeeded by his son Richard. A sense of crisis now gripped the republicans and preparations began to resist a potential Royalist revival:

Council hearing of the designs against us of the common enemy, thinks fit, for your safety and that of the city wherein you live, to send down commissions to enlist arm, and muster 6 companies of foot from amongst the well–affected inhabitants of Bristol,

Col. John Okey commanded the dragoon regiment of the New Model Army at the second siege of Bristol, where he suffered the indignity of being captured by the defenders during a skirmish. In the closing weeks of the Protectorate Okey was made responsible for security in the Bristol region. As one of those who had signed the king's death warrant, he fled to Europe at the restoration but was arrested in Holland and returned to England with two other regicides. He was executed on 9 April 1662. (Reproduced by kind permission of Bristol Central Library)

whereof you are each to command one, and to put yourselves in an attitude of defence such as enable you to withstand any attacks.[83]

On 29 July Col. Okey was ordered to deploy his forces to protect Bristol and Gloucester, and to search the houses of known opponents of the regime for arms, as a Royalist insurrection was feared in the region.[84] On 2 August Okey received a letter from Whitehall thanking him for his fidelity and efforts in suppressing the Royalist plot in the Bristol region and instructing him to get the Bristolians to secure their city.[85] On 14 September the Council of State ordered that two infantry regiments, recently brought back from Flanders, should be broken up into companies to reinforce certain strategic garrisons, and Bristol was to receive three of these companies.[86] The value of these reinforcements may have been limited, as Secretary Nicholas wrote from Brussels to Mr Lipe:

Thanks for your long delayed letter, and your care of my troublesome business. Before the king's departure, he and your friends here were perfectly acquainted with your and Mr Clayton's great industry in the business of Bristol, and other of his Majesty's services, and I am glad that there is still so great hope of that important place. I hear that the foot companies in Bristol are part of those men that were called out of France, and not ill-affected to the interest of the King.[87]

In February 1660 General Monk staged a successful *coup d'état* and was appointed commander-in-chief by Parliament. The change in policy can be seen in a letter sent to Okey at Bristol on the day Monk assumed control:

Having received information that, contrary to the Parliament's last declaration, you have removed men out of their houses at Bristol, imprisoning some and threatening to send others to Chepstow Castle, we have thought fit to advise you of the said information, to the end that we may receive an account of the ground of your proceedings therein. We desire that nothing of that nature may be done without order of Parliament, the Lord-General, or the Council of State, unless in case of sudden insurrections, and that you have especial care that the military powers do not trench upon the civil authority, or the inhabitants of the city, in the rights and privileges which by law they ought to enjoy, so far as possibly may consist with the public peace.[88]

In April Charles issued the declaration of Breda and a month later Parliament proclaimed him King Charles II of England. On 25 May he landed in triumph at Dover after having crossed the channel aboard the warship *Naseby*, which had been quickly and diplomatically renamed *Royal Charles*. The civil war was over and England was once again ruled by a king.

CHAPTER 11
Conclusion

The events of the Restoration period lie beyond the scope of this book. By 1660 Bristol was entering a period of rapid economic growth, based on the importation of colonial products such as tobacco and sugar, soon to be supplemented by the 'triangle trade'. Understandably, Bristolians were keen to put the war behind them and concentrate on making money and enjoying themselves. For Bristol and Britain the civil wars had not been a romantic episode nor a heroic adventure, but a bitter hard-fought conflict waged at great cost in terms of damage to property and disruption of trade and manufacturing, to say nothing of the loss of life. The possession of Bristol, the second city of the kingdom, was recognized as critical by both Royalists and Parliamentarians, and no effort was spared to gain and retain control of the city. Bristolians could not ignore the war: hundreds served, or were forced to serve, in the forces of the two factions, and many lost their lives through military action or disease. Many tried to side with the winners, only to be caught on the wrong side when the city changed hands but others were deeply committed to one faction or the other.

At the outbreak of the war Bristol was wealthy and prosperous, enjoying the benefits of a long-term improvement in trade. There were, of course, problems: royal policy caused friction and damaged certain groups, although these tended to be manufacturers rather than merchants. Interestingly there was no organized resistance to the king's imposition of Ship Money during the 1630s; perhaps Bristol, being dependent upon seaborne trade, could see the advantages in having a strong navy to suppress piracy. The crisis that led to conflict in England was not internal in origin but external: war with the Scots and rebellion in Ireland shattered the fragile structure of Charles's personal rule and encouraged his enemies into open opposition.

As the split between king and Parliament escalated from a war of words to armed conflict, Bristol, in common with other areas, tried to remain neutral, avoiding offending either side but refusing to participate. This policy was not wholly passive: the city also made serious preparations to defend itself should it become necessary. In a sense, the city saw itself as being at war with both sides. However, the protective cordon of non-participation was permeable and the Council was unwilling or unable to prevent citizens going to the assistance of the Parliamentarians in Somerset. The Royalists were equally flexible when it came to neutrality, maintaining contacts with the king's faction and possibly supplying them with arms and money. As the conflict became an open military contest, attitudes began to harden and the fiction of neutrality became increasingly difficult to maintain. The city was too important to be allowed to remain isolated from events occurring elsewhere in Britain.

The period of neutrality ended when Bristol was occupied by parliamentary forces with the active assistance of their supporters within the city. Royalist resistance was badly organized and poorly supported, the leaders apparently underestimating both strength and commitment of the parliamentary faction in the city. The early stages of the parliamentary occupation were dominated by Thomas Essex – potential traitor or simply a moderate supporter of Parliament? Certainly the man who replaced him, Nathaniel Fiennes, was very much a hard-liner, almost a stereotypical 'roundhead'; was there a personality clash or was it simply a matter of personal jealousy? The military situation in the Bristol region by the early spring of 1643 meant that parliamentary leaders could not afford to give Essex the benefit of the doubt. He was removed and packed off to the Lord-General to explain his behaviour while Fiennes took control of Bristol, his first act as governor being to suppress a mutiny among Essex's infuriated troops.

The importance of the Severn region was recognized in Westminster, and Parliament's most successful field commander, Sir William Waller, was sent to organize its defence. He inflicted damaging reverses on his opponents but faced increasing pressure from Wales, Oxford and the south-west. Bristol served as the base for Waller's operations, supplying money, men, arms and ammunition to maintain and expand his army. In Bristol Fiennes made frantic efforts to construct defences and strengthen the city's garrison, despite a serious shortage of money. Waller saw Bristol as a pool of reserves for his army and frequently called for reinforcements, seriously weakening the defending force. Waller's defence of his actions, quite logically, was that a strong field army represented the best possible protection for Bristol. Unfortunately he made a serious miscalculation, stripping the garrison of men and then allowing the Royalists to destroy his field force.

One reason Fiennes needed to retain at least some troops in Bristol was the internal threat posed by the Royalist 'fifth column' within the city; not everyone had welcomed the arrival of a parliamentary garrison and some were actively plotting to expel it. The king's supporters were in contact with Oxford from an early date and plans were formulated to admit a force of Royalist troops, in the same way as Col. Essex's had been admitted into the city in December. The conspirators were a diverse group, merchants and manufacturers rubbing shoulders with seamen, labourers and carters. Potentially the most dangerous group consisted of disgruntled members of Thomas Essex's old regiment who resented the treatment of their colonel. Almost certainly the plot was infiltrated from an early stage but the parliamentary authorities allowed it to run its course to ensnare as many Royalists as possible. Either by luck or careful counter-intelligence work the plotters were surprised at their assembly points and imprisoned; further arrests followed of individuals known to be sympathetic to the plotters.

Although the conspiracy can appear almost comic the repression that followed it was brutal and heavy-handed. Fiennes used the plot as an excuse to strike at all the king's supporters in the city. Among the Parliamentarians there was near-hysteria: rumours circulated that the Oxford troops had orders to slaughter the city's inhabitants and the plotters had marked the doors of their supporters who were to be spared. To a contemporary Englishman such detail would have been reminiscent of the St Bartholomew's Day massacres in Paris when the Catholics slaughtered the Huguenots. This reinforced the view that the king's supporters were murderous papists in the mould of the brutal Spanish 'Cavalieros' who persecuted Protestants in the Low Countries. In view of this and the fact that the plotters were captured in a treacherous conspiracy rather than in a fair fight, the judgment at their trial was a foregone conclusion, as were the death sentences passed on the leaders. The threats and counter-threats that passed between the Earl of Firth and Fiennes displayed a level of bitterness and viciousness not normally associated with this 'war without an enemy'. By all accounts the leaders of the conspiracy met their deaths with commendable courage but their deaths would cost Bristol much suffering and money when the city changed hands.

The destruction of Waller's army at Roundway Down was arguably the most complete military defeat of the war; even at Naseby the Royalists were able to extract the bulk of the cavalry to fight again. But at Roundway the main Parliamentarian force in the western counties lost three-quarters of its manpower as casualties, prisoners or deserters, together with all the artillery, ammunition and stores and the bulk of its arms. The king's generals seized the opportunity and concentrated most of their field forces in the south of England in a single army under the command of Prince Rupert. Fiennes found himself in an unenviable position: most of his garrison units had been destroyed or badly shattered while serving with Waller's army, and he was frantically attempting to replace them. His position was not hopeless: the city's defences were strong, with good stocks of arms to equip the new troops, and there was no shortage of food or ammunition in the city. The newly formed units were based around officers and soldiers from Waller's army, who acted as trained cadre troops, so the situation was not as dire as it first appears.

After a brief period of skirmishing the Royalist commanders decided to capture the city by a general assault rather than a formal siege. The basis for this decision included the fact that the ground on the northern side of the city was unsuitable for entrenching, there were shortages of artillery and ammunition, and a serious outbreak of disease had weakened Rupert's army. The plan called for a carefully coordinated attack on both north and south, but this was thrown into confusion by the premature attack by Cornish troops on the southern defences. The assault was a disaster: five of the six attacking columns were quickly repulsed with heavy losses among officers and men. Even the column which succeeded in breaching the line could easily have been repulsed, but by a combination of luck and mismanagement the breach was eventually secured and troops repulsed at other points moved forward to fight their way through the suburbs. The breaching of the line did not cause the defenders' morale to collapse and the advancing Royalists found themselves increasingly bogged down in costly street battles against opponents sheltering inside houses and behind barricades. However, Fiennes appears to have panicked and ordered the precipitate evacuation of those sectors of the line still held by his men; failing to employ his considerable reserves in a counter-attack, he offered to surrender. The battle was going so badly for the king's supporters that they assumed this was a trick and the fighting continued, with the defenders enjoying some success, until a second offer of surrender was received and taken seriously. The disbelief of the attackers was matched by the fury of the defenders, many of whom were to accuse their commander of cowardice, incompetence or even treason.

After the capture of the city the Royalist troops behaved badly and both the retreating garrison and the civilian population were abused and plundered, much to Rupert's embarrassment. As a city where Royalists had only recently been publicly hanged in the main street, some rough treatment was to be expected from an army who had been living in the open and whose pay was in arrears. In fact although a great deal was made of the 'sack of Bristol', compared to the treatment of captured cities in the European wars of this period the king's men were relatively restrained. There was a serious row among the commanding generals who captured Bristol as to who should govern the king's newly regained subjects; the potential seriousness of this dispute can be judged by the king's decision to go to Bristol in person to settle the matter. Bristol's political elite tried to buy their way out of a very difficult position with generous gifts to the king and his officers; this did not have the desired effect but, rather like giving starving wolves a small piece of meat, it made them hungry for more. Bristol was to pay very heavily for its 'disloyalty' once the king regained control of the city.

Among the supporters of Parliament the news of the loss of the second city of the kingdom with its vast military resources was an unprecedented blow and for the first time moderates began to question the possibility of military victory and suggested negotiations with the king. For Fiennes the loss of Bristol was an unmitigated personal disaster: he made reports to the Lord-General and to Parliament that were not only inaccurate but deliberately misleading, in the vain hope of protecting his honour and his neck. He was quickly and publicly challenged. He and his family attempted to silence the critics but only antagonized their opponents, who included the powerful Presbyterian faction in Parliament, Waller's supporters, disgruntled Bristolians and Radicals who were outraged by Fiennes's use of family influence to protect himself. Finally it was recognized that the only way to end the controversy was to bring the matter to trial; although initially the court seemed to favour Fiennes it eventually found him guilty on a lesser charge.

Almost as soon as it was captured Bristol became a major centre for recruiting and organizing Royalist armies, centred as it was between the main recruiting areas of Wales and the south-west, while offering plentiful accommodation and strong defences. It was an ideal point for the assembly and training of new units. Bristol was to see the continuous arrival and departure of troops, and the citizens became accustomed to strange accents and, in the case of some of the Welsh and Cornish levies, strange languages. Significant field forces under the command of Hopton or Rupert were assembled in the city on a number of occasions either for independent operations or to reinforce the king's main army. In the aftermath of Naseby the king sent Rupert to the Bristol region to organize and equip a new army, the city and its resources representing the last hope of turning the tide against Fairfax's army.

Bristol was the base for a Royalist naval force, created from shipping and personnel in the city. Although never able to challenge parliamentary naval supremacy, the Bristol squadron contested control of the Severn Estuary and shipped thousands of troops from Ireland. During the war commanders such as Slingsby and Wake raided parliamentary shipping in the name of the king with flotillas of Bristol vessels. The city became the centre of a network of permanent garrisons in Gloucestershire and Somerset with a permanent establishment of troops to man them to ensure that this critical region remained firmly under control. The Royalists reconstructed the city's defences, improving them in the light of the experience gained in capturing the city. The basic line remained unchanged but the forts were rebuilt and the number of guns greatly increased. The most spectacular feature of the new defences was the Royal Fort, a huge pentagonal bastioned work which was not simply a fort to defend the city but a citadel to overawe it if required.

Bristol was not simply a gigantic barracks. It also served as the administrative centre for the south-west and organizations established within the city were crucial to the Royalist war effort. The facilities developed by the Royalists ranged from a mint producing coin to pay the army to a hospital to care for the sick and wounded. To ensure sufficient cash was raised to keep the armies and other organizations functioning, a well-developed system of local taxation was created, with a staff of officials to collect and administer it. Although the king's supporters are sometimes stereotyped as be-feathered, carefree young men, the clerks and officials in the stores and counting houses operated with an efficiency that kept the king's armies in the field for almost five years. The city served as Hopton's headquarters for much of 1643/4 and not surprisingly when the Prince of Wales was appointed to command the western counties he established his residence and council at Bristol, giving the city, briefly, the status of an alternative Royalist capital.

Bristol was also the centre of a complex regional organization controlled by the Ordnance Office, the body responsible for supplying the king's forces with arms and ammunition. Bristol became a major *entrepot* for arms shipped from the continent and a major assembly/distribution centre for munitions landed at other ports in the south-west. These imports were crucial to keeping the king's armies in the field and were further supplemented by local production in the Bristol area; while not reaching the level some optimists had hoped for, this did much to reduce the shortage of firearms among the king's infantry. The arsenals established in Bristol not only supplied recruits and field forces assembling in the city with arms and ammunition but also sent regular supplies to Oxford and even further afield. In terms of the Royalist war effort as a whole Bristol was far more than simply a garrison town.

The turning point of the war, as hindsight now makes clear, was the destruction of the king's main field army at the battle of Naseby. However, the king did not recognize this and ordered the creation of a new army by merging various forces in the western counties, dispatching Rupert to create this Royalist 'New Model Army'. Fairfax realized the importance of the western region and marched immediately from the midlands to frustrate Royalist plans. Fairfax fought Goring's army at Langport, destroying it as a fighting force and ending plans to use this body as the core of the new army. Bristol could no longer serve as the assembly point and magazine of a new army but was to act as a fortress to tie down Fairfax's army while the king assembled an army from his scattered troops in the west and around Oxford. Fairfax, mindful of the experience of the Earl of Essex the previous year, decided to capture the city before proceeding to liberate the west; he had no wish to find a new army assembled and armed at Bristol operating in his rear while he faced the still formidable remnants of the king's forces in the field.

Fairfax prepared carefully to attack Bristol. Outlying garrisons were captured to remove any threat to lines of supply and communication, while all available units were brought to the Bristol region. After his forces were assembled he opened negotiations, which were conducted in bad faith by both sides. Rupert simply tried to gain time while Fairfax continued to prepare for an assault despite discussing surrender terms. The garrison was stronger than during the first siege with the defences improved during the Royalist occupation, and Fairfax's army was only slightly stronger than that which Rupert had commanded in 1643 but was far better equipped, particularly in terms of artillery. Although the Parliamentarians should have learned from Rupert's mistakes in 1643, this did not happen in all cases; a brigade was thrown against the southern defences, as the Cornish had been, with the same disastrous results. However, the New Model Army did not attempt to attack the heavily defended northern ridge, but instead turned their attention to the eastern fortifications which were successfully carried in a night assault. At daybreak Rupert still held the castle and Royal Fort and although he had lost far more men than Fiennes had done, he was still in a position to continue the defence. However, he recognized that Fairfax would simply attack each of the northern forts in turn, and when their supporting guns were silenced he would carry the central city by general assault. The king had ordered him to hold to the last but Rupert, realizing that further resistance could only delay rather than prevent the loss of the city, surrendered to save his troops. As a consequence of this logical assessment of the situation Rupert faced the fury of the king and was disgraced, regardless of his previous service.

Bristol remained a parliamentary garrison for the rest of the war. After the surrender of the last of the king's forces the number of troops slowly reduced as peace returned. Although Bristol was not to face a full-scale assault again, the peace of these years was disturbed by military operations near enough to pose a threat. During the Second Civil War the revolt of the parliamentary garrison of Pembroke was seen as a threat to Bristol, at least for a short period of time. The city became an important base for the army under Cromwell and his successors in Ireland; the garrison was increased and defences were repaired, doubtless owing to fears of Royalist attempts to disrupt the flow of supplies and reinforcements. The Scottish invasion of the Third Civil War looked at one stage as if it might reach Bristol and there were frantic efforts to prepare the city for defence, but in the end the invaders were shattered at Worcester and the only Scots to reach Bristol were prisoners being shipped to the West Indies by enterprising Bristol merchants. The city remained a centre of Royalist intrigue and many plots were aimed at gaining possession or assumed support from the Bristolians; although none of these came to fruition it is notable that in the final chaotic months of the Protectorate regular troops were again stationed in the city.

It would be wrong to present the years after the civil war as one prolonged crisis: peace and normality returned and Bristolians began rebuilding their city and their fortunes. Few Bristol Royalists were punished for their actions, a fact noted by the new regime; in general the elite seemed to try to protect each other from the effects of ill-advised political actions. Trade revived and if the profitable importation of Irish cattle was disrupted this was compensated for by increased imports of sugar and tobacco from North America and the West Indies. The city's defences were eventually demolished, including the castle, which was turned over to the city; the Council cleared the site and laid out new streets which survived until the air raids of the Second World War. The good citizens may have been influenced or irritated by the new and often extreme views in politics and religion that emerged in the aftermath of the war, but in general life settled down quickly.

The civil war was not a happy time for Bristolians. It has been suggested that in a large part this was due to their own behaviour and their sycophantic desire to remain on good terms with the winning side. In fairness the city changed political allegiance on three occasions in four years: from neutral to Parliament, from Parliament to Royalist, and from Royalist to Parliament, and trying to make peace with the dominant group can be regarded as a survival strategy. Control of Bristol and its resources was of great importance in this war, and the significance of its capture to the Royalists cannot be exaggerated. The king might have been able to continue the war if Rupert had been repulsed in July 1643 but it would not have been easy, and he might well have had to retreat to the northern counties. Likewise Fairfax's refusal to leave the city in Royalist hands shows that its value was fully understood by the king's opponents. If the king were to assemble and equip a new army, possession of the city was vital. Wars are messy and traumatic events in human affairs and the conflict between Charles I and his Parliament was no exception. The experience of Bristol in these years was certainly not romantic: both sides ruthlessly exploited the city's financial, military and industrial resources in an effort to gain victory. Whatever else Bristol had, it had its fill of 'interesting times' during these years.

Notes

1 Introduction

1. Sellers & Yeatman, *1066 and All That*, pp. 71–2.
2. Ollard, *War without an Enemy*.
3. Hibbert, *Cavaliers and Roundheads*, p. 116.
4. Porter, *Destruction in the English Civil Wars*, p. 14.
5. Ibid.
6. Ibid; Stoyle 'Whole streets converted to ashes' in Richardson, *The English Civil War: local aspects*, pp. 129–44.
7. Clarendon, *History of the Great Rebellion*, book VII, pp. 297–8.
8. McGrath, 'Bristol and the Civil War', in Richardson, *English Civil War*, p. 121.
9. Fiennes, *Relation*; Fiennes, *Letter to my Lord General*.
10. Walker, *An Answer to Nathaniel Fiennes Relation*; Prynne & Walker, *Trial of Nathaniel Fiennes*.
11. de Gomme, 'Siege and Capture of Bristol'.
12. Seyer, *Memoirs*, p. 403.
13. Ibid, pp. 407–14.
14. Robinson, *Sieges of Bristol*.
15. Gardiner, *History*, vol. 1, pp. 179–80.
16. Latimer, *Annals*, pp. 177–81.
17. Wedgwood, *The King's War*, pp. 117–220.
18. Rodgers, *Battles and Generals*, pp. 90–4; Young & Holmes, *Military History*, pp. 138–41.
19. Robinson, *A Shocking History*, pp. 44–5; Roy, *Ordinance Papers*, p. 483.
20. McGrath, 'Bristol in the Civil War', p. 104.
21. Robinson, *Sieges of Bristol*, p. 49.
22. McGrath, *Bristol in the Civil War*, p. 52.
23. *Mercurius Belgicus*, 11 September 1645.
24. Clarendon, *Great Rebellion*, book IX, p. 691.
25. Prynne & Walker, *Trial of Nathaniel Fiennes*, pp. 50–1.
26. Turner, E., 'Remarks', p. 129.
27. Luke, *Journal*, p. 15.
28. Ibid, p. 218.
29. McGrath, *Bristol and the Civil War*, pp. 2–7.
30. Underwood, *Revel, Riot and Rebellion*, p. 164.
31. McGrath, 'Bristol and the Civil War', pp. 120–1.

2 Peace, Neutrality and War

1. Bettey, *Bristol Observed*, p. 46.
2. Vanes, *Overseas Trade*, p. 170.
3. McGrath, *Merchants and Merchandise*, p. 280.
4. Vanes, *Overseas Trade*, p. 170; McGrath, *Merchants and Merchandise*, p. 280.
5. Farr, *Shipbuilding*, p. viii.
6. Mayoral Audit Books.
7. Maps of Bristol, Bristol Central Library.
8. McGrath, *Merchants and Merchandise*, p. ix ff.
9. Sacks, 'Corporate Town', pp. 88–96.
10. Ibid.
11. Roy, *Royalist Ordinance*, pp. 9–10.
12. *SPD*, 1637–8, p. 96.
13. *SPD*, 1631–3, p. 195.

14. *SPD*, 1633–4, p. 244.

15. Ibid, pp. 277, 493.

16. Ibid, p. 559.

17. *SPD*, 1634–5, pp. 502, 507.

18. *SPD*, 1637–8, p. 5.

19. Ibid, p. 32.

20. Ibid, p. 150.

21. *SPD*, 1638–9, p. 134.

22. *SPD*, 1625–49, pp. 595–6.

23. *SPD*, 1639, pp. 83–4.

24. Latimer, *Annals*, p. 121.

25. *SPD*, 1635, p. 35.

26. Ibid, p. 99.

27. Latimer, *Annals*, pp. 121–2.

28. Ibid, pp. 122–3.

29. Ibid, pp. 118–19.

30. Ibid.

31. Latimer, *Annals*, p. 132; *SPD*, 1634–5, p. 581.

32. Latimer *Annals*, pp. 132–3; *SPD*, 1635–6, pp. 297, 408.

33. Latimer, *Annals*, p. 133; *SPD*, 1639–40, pp. 406, 531.

34. *SPD*, 1638–9, pp. 513–14.

35. *SPD*, 1637–8, p. 284.

36. *SPD*, 1640, pp. 487, 544.

37. *Exceeding True News* (London, 7 Sept. 1642).

38. Latimer, *Annals*, p. 156.

39. Anon, *More Good News*, pp. 5–6.

40. Latimer, *Annals*, p. 156.

41. Aldworth, R., *A Letter sent to the Right Worshipful William Lenthall*, pp. 6–8.

42. Wedgwood, *The King's Peace*, pp. 292–6.

43. Latimer, *Annals*, pp. 152, 147.

44. Ibid, p. 155.

45. Mayoral Audit Books.

46. Latimer, *Annals*, p. 158.

47. Firth & Rait, *Acts and Ordinances*, 5 March 1642/3.

48. Parliament, *A Declaration of the Lords and Commons* (London, 10 August 1642).

49. Clarendon, *Great Rebellion*, book III, p. 188.

50. Ibid, book VI, p. 3.

51. Peachy & Turton, *Old Robin's Foote*, p. 4.

52. Davies, G., 'The Parliamentary Army', p. 54.

53. Anon, *Copy of the Commission*, p. 4.

54. Hutton, *Royalist War Effort*, p. 52.

55. Latimer, *Annals*, p. 157.

56. Clarendon, *Great Rebellion*, book VI, p. 3.

57. Horner, *Hertford his Letter*, p. 1.

58. Proud, *True and Sad Relation*, pp. 2–3.

59. Ash, *A Perfect Relation*, p. 5.

60. Anon, *A Relation of all Passages and Proceedings*, p. 3.

61. Clarendon, *Great Rebellion*, book VI, p. 6; Hopton, *Bellum Civile*, p. 9.

62. Ball, *Declaration*, p. 1.

63. Anon, *A True and Joyful Relation*, pp. 4–5.

64. *Exceeding True News* (London, 7 Sept. 1642), p. 2.

65. Latimer, *Annals*, p. 158.

66. McGrath, *Bristol and the Civil War*, pp. 11–12.

67. Ibid, pp. 5–6.

68. Russell, *Causes of the English Civil War*, pp. 21–2, 226.

69. Latimer, *Annals*, p. 152.

70. Anon, *The Somerset petition with an answer*, p. 3.

71. Anon, *A collection of sundry petitions*, p. A2.

72. Latimer, *Annals*, p. 166.

73. Anon, *The humble petition of the city of Bristol*.

74. Ibid, p. 4.

75. Anon, *An abstract of some letters*.

76. Latimer, *Annals*, p. 163.

77. Sanderson, *Complete History*, p. 581.

78. Ball, *Declaration*, p. 1.

79. Latimer, *Annals*, p. 160.

80. Ibid, pp. 162–4.

81. Ball, *Declaration*, pp. 1–2.

3. *Parliamentarian Bristol*

1. Latimer, *Annals*, p. 163.

2. Ball, *Declaration*, p. 2.

3. Peachy & Turton, *Old Robin's Foote*, p. 6.
4. Ball, *Declaration*, p. 2; Anon, *Letter from Exeter*, p. 7.
5. McGrath, *Merchants and Merchandise*, pp. xxvii–xxviii.
6. Ball, *Declaration*, p. 2; Anon, *Letter from Exeter*, p. 7.
7. Ball, *Declaration*, p. 3.
8. Sanderson, *Complete History*, p. 581.
9. Ball, *Declaration*, p. 9.
10. Ibid.
11. Anon, *Letter from Exeter*, p. 7.
12. Sanderson, *Complete History*, p. 581; Ball, *Declaration*, p. 4; Anon, *Letter from Exeter*, p. 7.
13. Anon, *Letter from Exeter*, p. 7.
14. Ibid, pp. 7–8.
15. Peachy & Turton, *Old Robin's Foote*, p. 6.
16. Langrish, *Full Declaration*, p. 17.
17. *Mercurius Aulicus*, 10 February 1643.
18. Luke, *Journal*, p. 8.
19. Langrish, *Full Declaration*, pp. 13–15.
20. Ibid, p. 20.
21. *Mercurius Aulicus*, 22 February 1643.
22. Langrish, *Full Declaration*, p. 3.
23. Ibid, p. 11.
24. Anon, *The Earl of Essex his letter*, p. 6.
25. Clarendon, *Great Rebellion*, book V, p. 507.
26. Parliament, *A Declaration* (London, 26 January 1642/3).
27. Clarendon, *Great Rebellion*, book III, p. 186.
28. Langrish, *Full Declaration*, p. 3.
29. Walker, *Check to Brittanicus*, p. 5; Walker & Prynne, *Articles of impeachment and accusation*, article 1; Prynne & Walker, *Trial of Nathaniel Fiennes*, pp. 14, 18–19, 28–36.
30. Langrish, *Full Declaration*, p. 5; Luke, *Journal*, p. 22.
31. Langrish, *Full Declaration*, p. 5.
32. Firth & Rait, *Acts and Ordinances*, 11 February 1642/3.
33. Wedgwood, *The King's War*, pp. 170–1, 181–2.
34. Ibid, p. 201.
35. Clarendon, *Great Rebellion*, book VII, pp. 278–86.
36. Fiennes, *Letter to my Lord General*, pp. 5–6.
37. Fiennes, *Relation*, p. 5.
38. Prynne & Walker, *Trial of Nathaniel Fiennes*, p. 78.
39. Needham, *Check to the Checker*, p. 2.
40. Prynne & Walker, *Trial Catalogue: Deposition of Lt Col Paleologos and Lt Col Andrews*, p. 9.
41. Aldworth, *A letter sent to the right worshipful, William Lenthall*, p. 4.
42. Latimer, *Annals*, p. 158.
43. Ibid, p. 161.
44. Luke, *Journal*, p. 16.
45. Anon, *A Brief Relation*, pp. 2, 4.
46. Seyer, *Memoirs*, p. 306.
47. Russell, J., *Civil War Defences*, pp. 28–9.
48. Roy, *Ordinance Papers*, p. 262.
49. Russell, J., *Civil War Defences*, p. 30.
50. Fiennes, *Relation*, p. 28.
51. de Gomme, 'Siege', p. 25; Prynne & Walker, *Trial Catalogue: Testimony of Major Edward Wood*, p. 11.
52. Roy, *Ordinance Papers*, p. 262.
53. Fiennes, *Relation*, pp. 4–5; Aldworth, *A letter to Mr Speaker*, p. 4.
54. Seyer, *Memoirs*, pp. 302–3; Latimer, *Annals*, pp. 176–7.
55. de Gomme, 'Siege', pp. 184–5; Roy, *Ordinance Papers*, pp. 261–3.
56. de Gomme, 'Siege', p. 184.
57. Latimer, *Annals*, pp. 162, 177.
58. de Gomme, 'Siege', p. 184; Roy, *Ordinance Papers*, p. 262.
59. Seyer, *Memoirs*, p. 302.
60. de Gomme, 'Siege', p. 184; Roy, *Ordinance Papers*, p. 262.
61. Fiennes, *Relation*, p. 4.
62. de Gomme, 'Siege', p. 184.
63. Fiennes, *Relation*, p. 25.
64. Fiennes, *Letter to the Lord General*, p. 5.
65. *Mayoral Audit Books*, 17 December 1642.

66. Ibid, 24 December 1642, 30 December 1642. 16 January 1643, 19 January 1643, 2 February 1643, 20 February 1643.

67. Ibid, 2 March 1643, 4 March 1643, 7 March 1643, 13 March 1643.

68. Ibid, 1640 to 1649.

George Knight	£3,676	7s	11d
John Taylor	£2,595	14s	½d
John Lock	£5,697	5s	10d
Richard Aldworth	£16,380	3s	11d
Humphry Hook	£5,193	7s	9½d
Alexander James	£4,350	12s	½d
John Gunning	£2,510	0s	0d
Richard Vickris	£2,599	18s	7d
Gabril Sharman	£3,510	7s	9d
William Cann	£2,726	9s	½d

69. Firth, *Acts and Ordinances*, 14 February 1643.

70. Ibid, 27 March 1643, 7 May 1643.

71. Nott, *Deposition Books*, p. 13.

72. Fiennes, *Relation*, p. 23.

73. Peachy & Turton, *Fall of the West*, p. 602.

74. Langrish, *Full Declaration*, p. 1.

75. Luke, *Journal*, p. 15.
Col Essex 600 officers and men
    Troop of Col Essex (not named)
Col Popham's the like number
    Troop of Col Cole
Col Hungerford 500 (newly joined the garrison)
    'A third troop likewise'

76. Langrish, *Full Declaration*, p. 3.

77. Fiennes, *Extraordinary delivery*, p. 2.

78. Fiennes, *Relation*, pp. 14, 22.

79. Ibid, pp. 4–5; Peachy & Turton, *Fall of the West*, pp. 606–10.

80. Clarendon, *Great Rebellion*, book VII, p. 279.

81. Ibid.

82. Young & Holmes, *English Civil War*, pp. 134–8.

83. Walker, *An Answer*, pp. 3–4; Fiennes, *Reply to a Pamphlet*, pp. 6–7.

84. Fiennes, *Relation*, p. 6.

85. Fiennes, *Reply to a Pamphlet*, p. 7.

86. Prynne & Walker, *Trial Catalogue*: Testimony of Maj. Allen, pp. 13–14.

87. Peachy, S., *Storming of Bristol*, pp. 11–26; According to this reconstruction the garrison had the following units:

Col John Fiennes Foote	300–400 men
Nathaniel Fiennes Foote	500 men
City Volunteer units	1000–1200 men
Remnants of Waller's Foot*	400 men
Garrison of Malmesbury	200 men
5–6 troops of Horse and 2–3 companies of Dragoons	300 men

(* Popham's, Hungerford's, Essex's, Cook's, Carey's and other units.)

88. Prynne & Walker, *Trial Catalogue*: Deposition of Henry Hazzard, p. 21.

89. de Gomme, 'Siege', p. 185; Roy, *Ordinance Papers*, pp. 261–3.

90. Sprigg, *Anglia Rediviva*

Bridgwater 44 guns	Bristol 151 guns
Dartmouth 106 guns	Dennis Fort 22 guns
Exeter 75 guns	Barnstaple 35 guns
Oxford 36 guns	Worcester 25 guns
Pendennis 95 guns	Raglan 23 guns

91. McGrath, *Merchants and Merchandise*, pp. 212–14.

92. Nott, *Deposition Books*, pp. 11–12.

93. Luke, *Journal*, p. 60.

94. *SPD*, 10 July 1646, p. 453; de Gomme, 'Siege', p. 193.

95. Peachy & Turton, *Fall of the West*, pp. 602–5.

96. Mayoral Audit Books.

97. Peachy & Turton, *Fall of the West*, pp. 602–5.

98. Fiennes, *Relation*, p. 6.

99. McGrath, *Merchants and Merchandise*, p. 90.

100. Ibid, pp. 82–3.

101. Luke, *Journal*, p. 16.

102. Fiennes, *Relation*, p. 6.

103. Roy, *Ordinance Papers*, p. 22.

104. Mayoral Audit Books.

105. Ibid.

106. Walker, *An Answer*, p. 11; Fiennes, *Reply to a Pamphlet*, p. 14.

107. Walker, *An Answer*, p. 11.

108. Fiennes, *Relation*, p. 10; Walker, *An Answer*, p. 11.

109. Prynne & Walker, *Trial of Nathaniel Fiennes*, p. 78.

110. Clarendon, *Great Rebellion*, book VII, pp. 231–2.

111. *SPD*, 14 July 1643.

4. The Royalist Plot

1. Seyer, *Memoirs*, p. 341.

2. Anon, *Several Examinations*, Examination of John Preston, pp. 11–12.

3. Ibid, Robert Yoemans' Confession, p. 2.

4. Ibid, Examination of George Teage, p. 5; Examination of John Boucher, p. 8.

5. Anon, *Two State Martyrs*, pp. 7–8.

6. Ibid, pp. 9–10; Luke, *Journal*, p. 16.

7. Anon, *Two State Martyrs*, p. 11.

8. *Mercurius Aulicus*, 10 February 1643.

9. Anon, *The humble petition of the city of Bristol*.

10. Fiennes, *Extraordinary delivery*, p. 5.

11. Anon, *Several Examinations*, Robert Yoemans' Confession, pp. 2–3.

12. Ibid, Examination of Master Robert Yoemans, p. 10.

13. Seyer, *Memoirs*, pp. 359–62.

14. Anon, *Letter sent from Bristol*, pp. 7–8.

15. Fiennes, *Extraordinary delivery*, 'Letter from a most Reverend Minister', p. 13.

16. Ibid, 'From the fort at Brandon Hill', p. 8.

17. Tombs, J., *Jehovah Jireh*, p. 4.

18. Ball, *Declaration*, p. 3.

19. Luke, *Journal*, p. 16.

20. Fiennes, *Extraordinary delivery*, 'Letter from R.A.', p. 5.

21. Ibid, 'Letter from the fort at Brandon Hill, p. 8.

22. Tombs, *Jehovah Jireh*, p. 5; Seyer, *Memoirs*, p. 360.

23. *Mercurius Aulicus*, 14 March 1643.

24. Anon, *Two State Martyrs*, p. 14.

25. Anon, *Several Examinations*, Robert Yoemans' Confession, p. 2.

26. McGrath, *Bristol in the Civil War*, p. 23.

27. Fiennes, *Extraordinary delivery*, 'Fiennes letter to Lord Saye', p. 3.

28. Peachy & Turton, *Fall of the West*, pp. 649–51.

29. Ibid, pp. 628, 634, 649–50.
Lieutenant Colonel Andrews – present at siege of Bristol;
Major Paleologus – serving in Francis Thompson's regiment by 28/5/43, present at siege of Bristol;
Captain Devereux – serving in Fores' dragoon regiment by April 1643, commanding own regiment by December

30. Tombs, *Jehovah Jireh*, p. 4; Fiennes, *Extraordinary delivery*, 'Letter from R.A.' p. 5; 'Letter from E.H.', p. 7; Langrish, *Full Declaration*, p. 7.

31. Seyer, *Memoirs*, pp. 342–4.

32. Tombs, *Jehovah Jireh*, p. 5.

33. Langrish, *Full Declaration*, p. 8.

34. Seyer, *Memoirs*, p. 343.

35. Langrish, *Full Declaration*, p. 7.

36. Ibid, p. 5; Anon, *Several Examinations*, Evidence of Capt. Jeremy Buck, p. 6.

37. Anon, *Several Examinations*, Evidence of Capt. Jeremy Buck, pp. 6–7.

38. Langrish, *Full Declaration*, p. 5.

39. Fiennes, *Extraordinary delivery*, 'Letter from a Reverend Minister', pp. 12–14.

40. Langrish, *Full Declaration*, p. 5; Fiennes, *Extraordinary delivery*, p. 12.

41. Ibid, 'Letter from a most Reverend Minister', pp. 12–13.

42. Ibid, 'From the fort at Brandon Hill', p. 4.

43. Seyer, *Memoirs*, p. 348.

44. Ibid, p. 349.

45. Roe, *Military Memoir*, p. 2.
46. Anon, *Several Examinations*, pp. 2–3.
47. Tombs, *Jehovah Jireh*, p. 3.
48. Ibid, p. 6.
49. T.P., *Eban Ezar*.
50. *Mercurius Aulicus*, 17 March 1643.
51. Ibid, 19 March 1643.
52. Ibid, 31 March 1643.
53. Anon, *Several Examinations*, March–May 1643.
54. Clarendon, *Great Rebellion*, book VII, p. 247; Seyer, *Memoirs*, p. 349.
55. Officers forming the Court Martial at Bristol:
    Col Nathaniel Fiennes
        (Governor of Bristol)
    Col Richard Cole
        (Deputy-Lieutenant of Somerset)
    Lt-Col Walter White
        (N. Fiennes Foot Regiment)
    Lt-Col James Ford
        (Pophams Foot Regiment)
    Lt-Col John Clifton
    Maj John Chamneys
        (Pophams Foot Regiment)
    Capt Thomas Hippesley
        (Pophams Foot Regiment)
    Capt Martin Husbands
    Capt Thomas Rawlins
        (N. Fiennes Horse Regiment)
    Lt/Capt? Richard Hippesley
        (Pophams Foot Regiment)
    Capt Thomas Eyre
        (N. Fiennes Foot Regiment)
    Capt? Thomas Goodere
        (Independent Volunteer Company?)
    Capt? James Hean
    Capt? Thomas Wallis
    Capt William Bowel
        (Pophams Foot Regiment)
    Capt? Robert Baugh
        (Bristol Volunteers?)
56. Seyer, *Memoirs*, p. 350.
57. Anon, *Brief Relation*, pp. 1–2.
58. *Mercurius Aulicus*, 22 May 1643.
59. Seyer, *Memoirs*, p. 378.
60. Ibid, p. 379.
61. Ibid, p. 380.
62. Ibid, pp. 350–1.
63. Anon, *Two State Martyrs*.
64. Ibid, pp. 26–7.
65. Ibid, p. 29.
66. Ibid, pp. 31–2.
67. *Mercurius Aulicus*, 4 June 1643.
68. Luke, *Journals*, p. 89.
69. Latham, *Bristol Charters*, 24 February 1643/4.
70. *Mercurius Aulicus*, 4 August 1643.
71. Anon, *Two State Martyrs*, p. 27.
72. Ibid, p. 32.
73. *Mercurius Aulicus*, 15 June 1643.
74. Seyer, *Memoirs*, pp. 359–62.
75. *Copy of a Letter sent from Bristol*, pp. 6–7.
76. Seyer, *Memoirs*, p. 352; Fiennes, *Relation*, p. 25.
77. Fiennes, *Relation*, p. 25.
78. Seyer, *Memoirs*, pp. 359–62; de Gomme, 'Siege', p. 198; *SPD*, Committee for Compounding, p. 1555.
79. McGrath, *Bristol in the Civil War*, p. 23.
80. T.P., *Eban Ezar*.
81. Nicholl, C., *The Reckoning: the murder of Christopher Marlowe* (London, 1992).
82. Anon, *Two State Martyrs*, p. 32.

5. *The First Siege of Bristol*

1. Roy, *Ordinance Papers*, pp. 226–8.
2. Ibid, pp. 198–9, 472.
3. Ibid, p. 240.
4. Anon, *Two Letters*, p. 5; Roy, *Ordinance Papers*, p. 39.
5. Peachy, *Storming of Bristol*, p. 27; Roy, *Ordinance Papers*, p. 22.
6. Clarendon, *Great Rebellion*, book VI, p. 143.
7. Roy, *Ordinance Papers*, pp. 40–1.

8. Ibid, pp. 99–100.

9. Ibid, pp. 107–8.

10. Ibid, pp. 19, 28–32, 123, 124, 126, 130, 132–3, 140.

11. Ibid, p. 26.

12. Ibid, pp. 8–9, 35–6.

13. Ibid, p. 28.

14. Davies, 'The Parliamentary Army', pp. 38–40; Peachy & Turton, *Old Robin's Foote*, pp. 8–10.

15. Fairfax, *Memoirs*, pp. 9–62.

16. Powell, *The Navy*, pp. 203–4.

17. Clarendon, *Great Rebellion*, book VII, p. 228.

18. Ibid, pp. 227–8.

19. Atkyns, R., in *Military Memoirs*, pp. 10–11.

20. Clarendon, *Great Rebellion*, book VII, p. 227.

21. Eddershaw, *Civil War in Oxfordshire*, pp. 101–3.

22. Clarendon, *Great Rebellion*, book VII, p. 243.

23. Prynne & Walker, *Trial of Nathaniel Fiennes*, p. 48.

24. Cantile, *History of the Army Medical Department*, p. 26.

25. Clarendon, *Great Rebellion*, book VII, pp. 260–1.

26. Clarendon, *Great Rebellion*, book VII, p. 264; Eddershaw, *Civil War in Oxfordshire*, pp. 104–5.

27. Essex, *Letter to Master Speaker*, pp. 2–3.

28. Young & Holmes, *The English Civil War*, pp. 96–7; Wedgwood, *The King's War*, p. 201; Clarendon, *Great Rebellion*, book VII, pp. 260–3.

29. Ibid, pp. 267, 268–9.

30. Ibid, pp. 274–5.

31. Clarendon, *Great Rebellion*, book VII, pp. 175–6; Wedgwood, *The King's War*, p. 211.

32. Anon, *Great and Glorious Victory*, pp. 1–4; Atkyns, in *Military Memoirs*, pp. 12–28.

33. Aldworth, J., *Copy of a Letter*, pp. 2–4.

34. Clarendon, *Great Rebellion*, book VII, pp. 278–9.

35. Anon, *Great and Glorious Victory*, pp. 2–4.

36. Ibid.

37. Clarendon, *Great Rebellion*, book VIII, p. 282.

38. Anon, *Great and Glorious Victory*, p. 5.

39. Clarendon, *Great Rebellion*, book VII, p. 284.

40. Ibid.

41. Anon, *True Relation of the Late Fight*, pp. 2–5.

42. Clarendon, *Great Rebellion*, book VII, pp. 286–8; Hopton, *Bellum Civile*, pp. 292–3.

43. Young & Holmes, *Civil War*, p. 116; Wedgwood, *The King's War*, p. 171.

44. Young & Holmes, *Civil War*, pp. 133–7; Wedgwood, *The King's War*, pp. 215–16.

45. Clarendon, *Great Rebellion*, book VII, pp. 290–1.

46. Davies, 'Parliamentary Army', pp. 40–1; Clarendon, *Great Rebellion*, book VII, pp. 292–3.

47. Roy, *Ordinance Papers*, pp. 255–7.

48. de Gomme, 'Siege', p. 183.

49. Clarendon, *Great Rebellion*, book VII, p. 293.

50. Seyer, *Memoirs*, p. 403.

51. Young, *Edgehill*, p. 89.

52. Hutton, *Royalist War Effort*, pp. 35–6.

53. de Gomme, 'Siege', pp. 182–3.

54. Ede-Barrett, S., *Storm of Bristol*, pp. 1–3; Peachy, S., *Storming of Bristol*, pp. 6–7.

Regiment (Original area of recruitment)

Lord General's (Lincolnshire)

John Savage (Earl Rivers) (Cheshire)

Richard Molineux (Lancashire)

Gilbert Gerrard (Lancashire)

Ralph Dutton (Gloucestershire)

John Owen (North Wales)

John Bellasie (Yorkshire & Nottingham)

Edward Stradling (South Wales)

Henry Lunsford (Somerset & South Wales)

Charles Lloyd (Denbighshire & Flint)

Edward Fitton (Cheshire)

Jacob Aspley (Herefordshire)

Richard Bowle (Staffordshire)

Richard Herbert (Montgomeryshire/ Shropshire)

55. Clarendon, *Great Rebellion*, book VII, pp. 28–31.

56. Young, *Edgehill*, pp. 89–90.

57. Roy, *Ordinance Papers*, pp. 422, 477.

58. Ibid, p. 442; Eddershaw, *Civil War in Oxfordshire*, p. 103.

59. Stewart, 'Military Surgeons', pp. 153–4.

60. Roy, *Ordinance Papers*, pp. 103–4.

61. Ibid.

62. Fiennes, *Relation*, p. 6.

63. Clarendon, *Great Rebellion*, book VII, p. 311.

64. Roy, *Ordinance Papers*, pp. 226–8, 241–2, 255–9.

65. Interview with my father William Lynch, on the subject of horses, 4 March 1989.

66. de Gomme, 'Siege', p. 183.

67. Roy, *Ordinance Papers*, pp. 255–7.

68. Ibid, p. 490.

69. de Gomme, 'Siege', pp. 184–5.

70. Roy, *Ordinance Papers*, pp. 32–3, 258.

71. de Gomme, 'Siege', pp. 189–90.

72. Roy, *Ordinance Papers*, pp. 261–3.

73. Clarendon, *Great Rebellion*, book VII, p. 275.

74. Atkyns, in *Military Memoirs*, p. 12.

75. Lloyd, *Memoirs*, p. 658.

76. Clarendon, *Great Rebellion*, book VII, p. 275; Atkyns, in *Military Memoirs*, p. 12.

77. Newman, *Royalist Officers*, note 67.

78. Clarendon, *Great Rebellion*, book VII, p. 275; Atkyns, in *Military Memoirs*, App. II.

79. Clarendon, *Great Rebellion*, book VII, p. 226.

80. Clarendon, *Great Rebellion*, book VII, p. 274.

81. Bamfield, *Apology*, p. 6.

82. Anon, *Great and Glorious Victory*, pp. 2–4.

83. Ibid, p. 3.

84. Atkyns, in *Military Memoirs*, p. 17.

85. Anon, *Great and Glorious Victory*, pp. 6–8.

86. Anon, *True Relation of the Late Fight*, pp. 2–5.

87. Aldworth, *Copy of a Letter*, pp. 3–4.

88. Anon, *True Relation of the Late Fight*, pp. 1–2.

89. Clarendon, *Great Rebellion*, book VII, p. 290.

90. Ibid, p. 293.

91. de Gomme, 'Siege', pp. 183–4.

92. Clarendon, *Great Rebellion*, book VII, p. 293.

93. de Gomme, 'Siege', p. 186.

94. Walker, *An Answer*, p. 7.

95. de Gomme, 'Siege', p. 186.

96. Prynne & Walker, *Trial Catalogue*: Testimony of William Stroode, pp. 7–8.

97. de Gomme, 'Siege', p. 158.

98. Clarendon, *Great Rebellion*, book VII, p. 294.

99. Fiennes, *Relation*, pp. 27–8.

100. This was a common problem in this period when uniforms varied in accordance with the taste of the commanding officer or the availability of clothing or cloth. Although by mid-1643 the 'Oxford' troops were receiving 'suits' of clothes supplied by Thomas Bushel in red, blue or white the situation remained chaotic. Not only were red and blue common Parliamentarian colours, but Peachy & Turton's conclusion about the Earl of Essex's army can equally be applied to the king's. 'During almost the whole of the war it was probably common for regiments to have a variety of different coloured coats in the ranks. One colour might predominate, but difference in lining colours and even coat colours from mixed issues, draughts from other regiments or recruits were likely.' Peachy & Turton, *Old Robin's Foote*, p. 43.

101. Fiennes, *Relation*, pp. 27–8.

102. de Gomme, 'Siege', pp. 188–9.

103. Bamfield, *Apology*, pp. 6–7.

104. de Gomme, 'Siege', p. 180.

105. Ibid, p. 181.

106. Ibid, p. 190.

107. Ibid, p. 191.

108. Clarendon, *Great Rebellion*, book VII, p. 265.

109. de Gomme, 'Siege', pp. 105–6.
    The Left Column:
    Basset's Regiment
    Grenville Regiment
    Godolphin's Regiment
    The Main Column:
    Slanning's Regiment
    Trevelian's Regiment
    Mohun's Regiment
    The Right Column:
    Buck's Regiment
    Hertford's Regiment
    Maurice's Regiment

110. Clarendon, *Great Rebellion*, book VII, p. 295.

111. de Gomme, 'Siege', p. 196.

112. Clarendon, *Great Rebellion*, book VII, p. 295.

113. de Gomme, 'Siege', pp. 182–3.
    Lord Grandison's Brigade:
    Lord General's Regiment
    Earl River's Regiment
    Molyneux's Regiment
    Gerard's Regiment
    Dutton's Regiment
    Owen's Regiment

114. Ibid, pp. 182–3.
    Colonel Bellasie's Brigade:
    Bellasie's Regiment
    Stradling's Regiment
    Lunsford's Regiment
    Lloyd's Regiment

115. Ibid, pp. 182–3.
    Lord Wentworth's Brigade:

Fitton's Regiment
Astley's Regiment
Bowle's Regiment
Herbert's Regiment

116. de Gomme, 'Siege', p. 183.

117. Prynne & Walker, *Trial Catalogue:*
    Deposition of Sarg-Maj Wood, pp. 9–10;
    Testimony of Capt. Henry Lloyd, p. 20.

118. Ibid, deposition of Thomas Stephens, p. 6;
    Notes on evidence of Lieut-Col Clifton,
    p. 19; Deposition of Anthony Gale,
    pp. 23–4; Confessions of defendant's
    witnesses, p. 36; Testimony of Anthony
    Nicolls, p. 37.

119. de Gomme, 'Siege', p. 192.

120. Prynne & Walker, *Trial Catalogue:*
    Deposition of Robert Bagnall, p. 15;
    Deposition of Sarg-Maj Hill, pp. 22–3;
    Testimony of Richard Winston, pp. 29–30;
    Testimony of James Coles, p. 30;
    Deposition of Michael Spark, p. 35;
    Confessions of defendant's witnesses,
    p. 36; Testimony of Capt. Councell, p. 37.

121. de Gomme, 'Siege', p. 192.

122. Prynne & Walker, *Trial Catalogue:*
    Deposition of Col Thomas Stephens, p. 7;
    Deposition of Sarg-Maj Wood, p. 10;
    Deposition of Capt. Robert Bagnall, p. 15;
    Deposition of Sergeant William Hill, p. 23;
    Deposition of Stephen Radford, p. 24;
    Testimony of William Deane, p. 26;
    Deposition of William Whitborne, p. 34;
    Testimony of Capt. Councell, p. 37;
    Deposition of Jeremy Holloway, p. 39.

123. de Gomme, 'Siege', p. 193.

124. Prynne & Walker, *Trial Catalogue:*
    Deposition of Sarg-Maj Wood, p. 10;
    Deposition of Henry Hazzard, pp. 21–2;
    Deposition of Anthony Gale, p. 24;
    Deposition of Thomas Mundy, p. 27.

125. de Gomme, 'Siege', p. 185.

126. The attempt to provide such weapons in
    contemporary armies can be illustrated by

developments such as Swedish 'leather guns', Dutch 'drakes' and Scottish 'frames'.

127. de Gomme, 'Siege', p. 193.

128. Clarendon, *Great Rebellion*, book VII, p. 295.

129. Prynne & Walker, *Trial Catalogue*: Deposition of Dorothy Hazzard, p. 33.

130. Ibid, Deposition of Joan Batten, pp. 31–2.

131. Kitson, *Prince Rupert*, pp. 136–7.

132. Prynne & Walker, *Trial of Nathaniel Fiennes*, pp. 81, 86; *Trial Catalogue*: Deposition of Arthur Williams, p. 29; Confessions of defendant's witnesses, p. 36.

133. de Gomme, 'Siege', p. 196; Hopton, *Bellum Civile*, Slingsby's Relation, pp. 92–4.

134. de Gomme, 'Siege', p. 184.

135. Ibid, pp. 194–5.

136. Prynne & Walker, *Trial Catalogue*: The sum of Col Alexander Popham, p. 4; Depositions of Paleologus and Andrews, p. 9.

137. Ibid, Testimony of Nicholas Cowling, p. 20; Deposition of Henry Hazzard, p. 21.

138. Ibid, Deposition of Arthur Williams, p. 29; Confessions of defendant's witnesses, p. 36.

139. Ibid, Deposition of Joan Batten, p. 31.

140. Ibid, Deposition of Sarg-Maj Wood, p. 10; Deposition of Capt. Bagnall, p. 17.

141. Fiennes, *Relation*, p. 8.

142. Prynne & Walker, *Trial Catalogue*: Testimony of Colonel Stroode, p. 9.

143. Ibid, Deposition of Anthony Gale, p. 24.

144. Ibid, Deposition of Sarg-Maj Wood, p. 10; Deposition of Capt. Bagnall, pp. 17–18; Deposition of Sarg Gale, p. 24; Testimony of William Deane, pp. 26–7; Deposition of William Whitborne, p. 34.

145. Clarendon, *Great Rebellion*, book VII, pp. 295–6.

146. Prynne & Walker, *Trial Catalogue*:

Deposition of Thomas Mundy, p. 27; Testimony of Samuel Wood, p. 40.

147. Ibid, Deposition of Sarg-Maj Wood, p. 13; Deposition of Sarg-Maj Allen, p. 14; Testimony of Capt. Lloyd, p. 20; Testimony of Edward Baynton p. 3; Testimony of Thomas Thomas, p. 35.

148. Ibid, Testimony of James Cole, pp. 30–1; Testimony of Joseph Proud, p. 31; Deposition of Joan Batten, p. 32; Deposition of Ethelred Huddy, p. 32; Deposition of Mary Smith, p. 33.

149. Clarendon, *Great Rebellion*, book VII, p. 296; Fiennes, *Relation*, pp. 10–11.

150. Prynne & Walker, *Trial Catalogue*: Deposition of Thomas Stephens, p. 7; Deposition of William Stroode, p. 8; Deposition of Sarg-Maj Wood, p. 11; Deposition of Sarg-Maj Allen, p. 14; Deposition of Capt. Bagnall, p. 15.

151. de Gomme, 'Siege', p. 201.

6. *Repercussions*

1. Clarendon, *Great Rebellion*, book VII, p. 317.

2. Ibid, pp. 317, 330.

3. Ibid, p. 335.

4. Ibid, p. 334.

5. Charles I, *His majesties declaration to all his loving subjects.*

6. Lloyd, *Memoirs*, p. 243.

7. Clarendon, *Great Rebellion*, book VII, pp. 335–6.

8. Kitson, *Prince Rupert*, pp. 141–3.

9. *SPD*, 1641–3, p. 473.

10. Clarendon, *Great Rebellion*, book VII, p. 297.

11. Ibid, p. 296.

12. Prynne & Walker, *Trial Catalogue*: Deposition of William Stroode, pp. 8–9; Deposition of Sarg-Maj Wood, p. 11; Testimony of Sarg-Maj Allen, p. 14;

Deposition of James Powell, p. 25;
Deposition of Thomas Mundy, p. 27;
Testimony of Dorothy Hazzard, p. 33;
Deposition of Thomas Taylor, pp. 38–9.

13. Clarendon, *Great Rebellion*, book VII,
    p. 297.
14. Anon, *The Tragedy of the King's Army's
    Fidelity* (London, 1643), pp. 3–9.
15. Roe, *Military Memoir*, p. 46; Ede-Barrett,
    Storm of Bristol, p. 25.
16. de Gomme, 'Siege', p. 198.
17. Prynne & Walker, *Trial Catalogue*:
    Testimony of William Stroode, pp. 8–9;
    Deposition of Capt. Robert Bagnall, p. 6;
    Deposition of Thomas Mundy, pp. 27–8;
    Deposition of Able Kelly, p. 29; Deposition
    of Richard Winston, p. 30; Testimony of
    Dorothy Hazzard, p. 33; Confessions of
    defendant's witnesses, pp. 36–7;
    Deposition of Thomas Taylor, pp. 38–9.
18. Ibid, Deposition of Sarg-Maj Wood, p. 11.
19. de Gomme, 'Storm', p. 198.
20. Anon, *Tragedy*, p. 2.
21. Clarendon, *Great Rebellion*, book VII,
    p. 297.
22. Anon, *Tragedy*, p. 4.
23. Copy of a letter from Prince Rupert to
    Thomas Lloyd, Bristol Central Library
    (B28526).
24. Stewell, *Answer to the purchasers*, pp. 9–26.
25. Davy, *Letter sent*, p. 4.
26. Ashley-Cooper, *A copy of the king's message*,
    pp. 5–6.
27. Anon, *Tragedy*, p. 6.
28. Ibid.
29. Ibid.
30. Ibid.
31. Luke, *Journal*, p. 152.
32. *Certain Informations*, 11–18 September
    1643, p. 271.
33. Nott, *Deposition Books*, pp. 14–15.
34. Ibid, p. 15.
35. Clarendon, *Great Rebellion*, book VII, p. 305.

36. Ibid, p. 306.
37. Clarendon, *Great Rebellion*, book VII,
    pp. 307–8; Hopton, *Bellum Civile*,
    pp. 58–9.
38. Ibid.
39. Clarendon, *Great Rebellion*, book VII,
    p. 308.
40. Ibid, pp. 308–9.
41. Hopton, *Bellum Civile*, p. 59.
42. Dunne, 'Manuscript History'.
43. *Mercurius Aulicus*, 4 August 1643.
44. Mayoral Audit Books.
45. Latimer, *Annals*, pp. 181–2; Nott,
    Deposition Books, vol. 1, p. 14.
46. *SPD*, 29 May 1643.
47. Luke, *Journal*, pp. 130–1.
48. Ibid.
49. Fiennes, *Relation*; Fiennes, *Letter to my
    Lord General*.
50. Fiennes, *Relation*, pp. 3–4.
51. Ibid, pp. 13–27.
52. Prynne & Walker, *Trial Catalogue*:
    Testimony of Edward Baynton, pp. 2–3;
    Testimony of Alexander Popham, p. 4;
    Testimony of Thomas Stephens, p. 7;
    Testimony of William Stroode, pp. 7–8;
    Testimony of Nicholas Cowling, pp. 20–1;
    Deposition of Henry Hazzard, p. 21;
    Testimony of William Deane, p. 27;
    Testimony of Richard Lindon and
    Edmond Wathin, p. 30.
53. Fiennes, *Relation*, pp. 3, 5–6, 12–13.
54. Prynne & Walker, *Trial Catalogue*:
    Testimony of Edward Cook, pp. 6–7.
55. Fiennes, *Relation*, p. 5.
56. Prynne & Walker, *Trial Catalogue*:
    Deposition of Thomas Stephens, p. 7;
    Deposition of Edward Wood, p. 10;
    Deposition of Arthur William, p. 29.
57. Fiennes, *Relation*, pp. 6–7.
58. Prynne & Walker, *Trial Catalogue*:
    Testimony of Joseph Proud, p. 31;
    Deposition of Joan Batten, p. 32;

Deposition of Ethelred Huddy, p. 32;
Deposition of Michael Sparks, p. 35.

59. de Gomme, 'Siege', p. 198.

60. Ibid, pp. 186–9, 195; Prynne & Walker,
     Trial Catalogue: Testimony of William
     Stroode, pp. 7–8.

61. Fiennes, *Relation*, p. 8.

62. Prynne & Walker, *Trial Catalogue*:
     Deposition of Sarg-Maj Wood, p. 10;
     Deposition of Capt. Bagnall, p. 17.

63. Ibid, Testimony of William Stroode, p. 9.

64. Fiennes, *Relation*, p. 8.

65. de Gomme, 'Siege', pp. 191–3.

66. Fiennes, *Relation*, p. 9.

67. Prynne & Walker, *Trial Catalogue*:
     Testimony of Edward Stephens, p. 3;
     Testimony of William Stroode, p. 8;
     Deposition of Thomas Stephens, p. 7;
     Deposition of Sarg-Maj Wood, pp. 10–11;
     Testimony of Sarg-Maj Allen, p. 14;
     Deposition of Capt. Bagnall, p. 15.

68. Fiennes, *Relation*, p. 11.

69. de Gomme, 'Siege', pp. 194–5.

70. Fiennes, *Relation*, p. 8.

71. Ibid, p. 9.

72. Prynne & Walker, *Trial Catalogue*:
     Deposition of Henry Hazzard, p. 21.

73. Ibid, Testimony of Thomas Piry, p. 4.

74. Roy, *Ordinance Papers*, pp. 255–6.

75. Fiennes, *Relation*, p. 10.

76. de Gomme, 'Siege', pp. 187–9.

77. Prynne & Walker, *Trial Catalogue*:
     Deposition of Sarg-Maj Wood, pp. 11–12.

78. Fiennes, *Relation*, p. 10.

79. Roy, *Ordinance Papers*, pp. 255–7.

80. Fiennes, *Relation*, pp. 3, 5–6, 12–13.

81. Walker, *An Answer*.

82. *Dictionary of National Biography*: Clement
     Walker.

83. Prynne & Walker, *Trial Catalogue*:
     Testimony of Thomas Piry, pp. 5–6;
     Testimony of John Stephens, p. 6.

84. Ibid, Testimony of Samuel Brown, p. 5.

85. Clarendon, *Great Rebellion*, book VII,
     p. 409.

86. Manuscript letter, Bristol Record Office.

87. Clarendon, *Great Rebellion*, book VII,
     p. 409.

88. *SPD*, 26 October 1643.

89. Walker & Prynne, *Articles of impeachment
     and accusation*, p. 10.

90. Ibid, p. 3.

91. Prynne & Walker, *Trial of Nathaniel
     Fiennes*, p. 6.

92. Ibid.

93. Ibid, p. 67.

94. Ibid, p. 68.

95. Ibid, p. 54.

96. Ibid, p. 54.

97. Prynne & Walker, *Trial Catalogue*:
     introduction, p. 1.

98. Ibid, Evidence of Capt. Bagnall, p. 20.

99. Ibid, Deposition of Sarg-Maj Wood, p. 12.

100. Clarendon, *Great Rebellion*, book VII,
     p. 410.

101. Walker, *Check to Britannicus*, pp. 6–7.

102. Ibid; Needham, *Check to the Checker of
     Britannicus*.

103. Clarendon, *Great Rebellion*, book VII,
     p. 410.

7. Bristol and the Royalist Armies

1. Luke, *Journal*, p. 131.

2. Ibid, p. 130.

3. Seyer, *Memoirs*, p. 143.

4. Prynne & Walker, *Trial of Nathaniel
    Fiennes*, p. 77.

5. Roy, *Ordinance Papers*, p. 484.

6. Luke, *Journal*, p. 131; Newman, *Royalist
    Officers*, note 95.

7. Roy, *Ordinance Papers*, pp. 272–4;
    de Gomme, 'Siege', pp. 182–3; Hopton,
    Bellum Civile, p. 60.

8. Hopton, *Bellum Civile*, p. 60.

9. Ibid.
10. Luke, *Journal*, pp. 148, 150.
11. Hopton, *Bellum Civile*, p. 60.
12. Clarendon, *Great Rebellion*, book VII, p. 312.
13. Luke, *Journal*, p. 217.
14. *Mercurius Aulicus*, 25 May 1644.
15. *SPD*, 1641–3, p. 565.
16. Prynne, *The Popish Royal Favourite*, p. 71.
17. Davy, *Letter sent*, pp. 1–3.
18. Hopton, *Bellum Civile*, pp. 62–3.
19. Prynne, *The Popish Royal Favourite*.
20. Ibid, p. 74.
21. Latimer, *Annals*, p. 191.
22. Hopton, *Bellum Civile*, p. 63.
23. Ryder, *Army for Ireland*, pp. 29–31.
24. Luke, *Journal*, pp. 190, 197, 218.
25. Adair, *Cheriton 1644*, p. 9.
26. Clarendon, *Great Rebellion*, book VIII, pp. 467–8.
27. Adair, *Cheriton 1644*, pp. 28–9; Luke, *Journal*, p. 173.
28. Luke, *Journal*, p. 176.
29. Roy, *Ordinance Papers*, pp. 377–8.
30. Clarendon, *Great Rebellion*, book VII, pp. 308–9.
31. Roy, *Ordinance Papers*, pp. 377–8.
32. Ibid, pp. 379, 498.
33. Adair, *Cheriton 1644*, p. 28.
34. Roy, *Ordinance Papers*, pp. 378, 511.
35. Ibid.
36. Ibid.
37. Ibid, p. 377.
38. Ibid, p. 322.
39. Newman, *Royalist Officers*, nos 182, 1369, 1491.
40. Clarendon, *Great Rebellion*, book VIII, p. 486.
41. Ibid, p. 502.
42. Symonds, *Diary*, p. 53.
43. Kitson, *Prince Rupert*, pp. 211–12.
44. *SPD*, 1644, pp. 467, 469–70, 473, 474–5, 511.
45. Ibid, p. 512.
46. Ibid, vol. 1644–5, pp. 16–17.
47. Ibid, p. 29.
48. Clarendon, *Great Rebellion*, book VIII, p. 541.
49. Kitson, *Prince Rupert*, pp. 215–16.
50. *SPD*, 1644–5, pp. 79–80.
51. Ibid, p. 83.
52. Turner, 'Remarks on the military history', pp. 125–7; for Parliamentary rates of pay see Roe, *Military Memoir*, pp. 67–8.
53. *SPD*, 1631–3, p. 135.
54. *SPD*, 1637–8, p. 284.
55. Nott, *Deposition Books*, p. 11.
56. Fiennes, *Relation*, p. 6; Mayoral Audit Books: April 1642, June 1643.
57. Luke, *Journal*, p. 150.
58. Roy, *Ordinance Papers*, p. 391.
59. Mayoral Audit Books, 1 June 1644.
60. Latimer, *Annals*, p. 192.
61. Roy, *Ordinance Papers*, p. 52.
62. Mayoral Audit Books, 12 and 21 September 1644.
63. Latimer, *Annals of Bristol*, p. 193.
64. Symonds, *Marches*, p. 211.
65. *SPD*, 5 September 1644.
66. Newman, *Royalist Officers*, no. 318.
67. Ibid, no. 1405.
68. Rupert, *Declaration*, p. 6.
69. Clarendon, *Great Rebellion*, book VIII, p. 603.
70. Ibid, book IX, p. 633.
71. Ibid, pp. 639–40.
72. Ibid, p. 633.
73. Markham, *Lord Fairfax*, p. 246; Latimer, *Annals*, p. 197.
74. Kitson, *Rupert*, p. 258.
75. Rupert, *Declaration*, pp. 5–6.
76. Rupert's personal retinue probably included: Lifeguard of Horse = 150 men (nominally part of Bristol garrison); Company of Firelocks = 50–100 infantry; Regiment of Foot = 500 infantry (at Bridgwater by July 1645).

77. Kitson, *Rupert*, pp. 253–4.

78. Clarendon, *Great Rebellion*, book IX, p. 670.

79. Ibid, p. 678.

80. Powell, *The Navy*, p. 43; Seyer, *Memoirs*, p. 413; de Gomme, 'Siege', p. 198.

81. Luke, *Journal*, p. 127.

82. Thomas, *Birkenhead*, p. 109; *Mercurius Aulicus*, 4 August 1644.

83. Powell, *The Navy*, pp. 44–5; Smith, *Several Letters*, pp. 1–2.

84. Smith, *Several Letters*, p. 3.

85. Luke, *Journal*, pp. 129, 146.

86. Ibid, p. 150; *SPD*, 1660–1, p. 16.

87. *SPD*, 1641–3, p. 565; Prynne, *The Popish Royal Favourite*, p. 71.

88. Powell, *The Navy*, p. 89.

89. Ryder, *English Army for Ireland*, pp. 29–31.

90. Prynne & Walker, *Trial Catalogue*: Deposition of Mary Smith, p. 34.

91. Seyer, *Memoirs*, pp. 320–1.

92. Copy in Bristol City Library, GC10204.

93. *Mercurius Aulicus*, 13 October 1644.

94. Ibid, 27 January 1645.

95. Powell, *The Navy*, pp. 146–7.

96. Green, *Deposition Books*, vol. I, Introduction.

97. McGrath, 'The Merchant Venturers', p. 78.

98. Ibid, pp. 79–80; McGrath, *Merchants and Merchandise*, pp. 310–14.

99. Lynch, 'Bristol Shipping and Royalist', pp. 263–4.

100. Damer-Powell, *Bristol Privateers*, pp. 70–85, 86–9.

101. Ibid, pp. 73, 78, 135–6, 184–7.

102. Aldworth, *Copy of a Letter*, p. 3.

103. McGrath, *Merchants and Merchandise*, pp. 150–1.

104. Roy, *Ordinance Papers*, pp. 261–3; Green, *Deposition Books*, pp. 11–12.

105. Archibald, *Wooden Fighting Ships*, pp. 120–1.

106. Luke, *Journal*, p. 131.

107. de Gomme, 'Siege', p. 184; Rupert, *Declaration*, pp. 9–10.

108. Russell, *Civil War Defences*, pp. 13–16.

109. Rupert, *Declaration*, pp. 9–10.

110. Russell, *Civil War Defences*, p. 27.

111. Seyer, *Memoirs*, p. 302; Turner, 'Remarks', p. 126.

112. Seyer, *Memoirs*, p. 302; Turner, 'Remarks', p. 126; Parker, 'Tyndall's Park', p. 131.

113. Latimer, *Annals*, p. 162; Turner, 'Remarks', p. 126.

114. Roy, *Ordinance Papers*, pp. 261–3; Turner, 'Remarks', pp. 126–7.

115. Parker, 'Tyndall's Park', p. 131.

116. Latimer, *Annals*, p. 190.

117. *SPD*, 1644–5, 15 June 1644.

118. Turner, 'Remarks', pp. 126–7.

119. Rupert, *Declaration*, p. 9.

120. Turner 'Remarks', pp. 126–7; Sprigg, *Anglia Rediviva*, table after p. 356.

8. *Manufacturing Centre and Capital*

1. McGrath, *Bristol in the Civil War*, pp. 2–6.

2. Roy, *Ordinance Papers*, pp. 371, 508.

3. Clarendon, *Great Rebellion*, book VII, p. 296.

4. Luke, *Journal*, pp. 130–1.

5. *Mercurius Aulicus*, 4 August 1643.

6. Mayoral Audit Books.

7. Latimer, *Annals*, pp. 181–2.

8. Charles I, *Pardon to the City of Bristol* 10/11/1643

   Other Pardons in Series:
   Wiltshire 2/11/1643
   Gloucestershire 3/11/1643
   Somerset 9/11/1643
   Devonshire 9/11/1643
   Exeter 9/11/1643
   Dorsetshire 16/11/1643

9. Latimer, *Annals*, p. 184; Latham, *Bristol Charters*, pp. 166–7.

10. Ibid, p. 166.
11. Ibid, p. 167.
12. Lloyd, *Memoirs*, p. 243.
13. Grinsell, *Bristol Mint*, pp. 14, 32.
14. *SPD*, 1637, p. 301.
15. Grinsell, *The Bristol Mint: The History and Coinage*, p. 32; Grinsell, *The Bristol Mint: A Historical Outline*, pp. 17–18.
16. Latimer, *Annals*, p. 188.
17. *SPD*, 1643–4, p. 14.
18. *SPD*, Committee for Advance of Money, p. 125.
19. *SPD*, 1651–2, p. 262.
20. Thomas, *Birkenhead*, p. 51.
21. Woolrich, *Printing*, p. 2.
22. Philerenus, *Mercurius Hibernicus*.
23. Thomas, *Birkenhead*, p. 51.
24. Woolrich, *Printing*, p. 2.
25. Turner, 'Remarks', p. 127.
26. Latimer, *Annals*, pp. 185–6.
27. Roy, *Ordinance Papers*, p. 38.
28. Latimer, *Annals*, pp. 187–8.
29. Roy, *Ordinance Papers*, p. 39.
30. Turner, 'Remarks', pp. 121–4.
31. Ibid, pp. 123–4.
32. Ibid, p. 127.
33. Ibid, p. 124.
34. Roy, *Ordinance Papers*, pp. 43–7.
35. Ibid, pp. 385, 388–9, 515, 517.
36. Ibid, p. 391.
37. Ibid, pp. 50, 340, 502, 507.
38. Ibid, p. 52.
39. Fiennes, *Letter to my Lord General*, pp. 5–6.
40. Luke, *Journal*, p. 146.
41. Mayoral Audit Books.
42. *SPD*, 1644–5, p. 493.
43. Firth, *Cromwell's Army*, p. 261.
44. Sanderson, *Complete History*, pp. 595–6.
45. Roy, *Ordinance Papers*, pp. 512–13.
46. Clarendon, *Great Rebellion*, book VI, pp. 142–3.
47. Rodgers, *Battles and Generals*, p. 95.
48. Roy, *Ordinance Papers*, p. 381.
49. *SPD*, 1643, p. 479; *Mercurius Aulicus*, 15 August 1643.
50. Roy, *Ordinance Papers*, p. 507.
51. *Mercurius Aulicus*, 15 August 1643.
52. Roy, *Ordinance Papers*, pp. 365–6, 507.
53. Luke, *Journal*, p. 163.
54. *SPD*, Committee for Advance of Money, p. 374.
55. Roy, *Ordinance Papers*, p. 370.
56. Ibid, pp. 320, 340, 366, 370, 385, 387–8, 388–9, 392–3, 394–6, 405–7, 409, 426.
57. Ibid, 385, 388–9.
58. Ibid, p. 515.
59. Ibid, pp. 515–16, 517.
60. *SPD*, 1644–5, pp. 464, 494, 511.
61. Ibid, p. 511.
62. Luke, *Journal*, p. 146.
63. Ibid, pp. 133–4.
64. *SPD*, 1644, pp. 256, 258.
65. Roy, *Ordinance Papers*, pp. 130, 135, 136.
66. Ibid, pp. 39ff.
67. Mayoral Audit Books.
68. Roy, *Ordinance Papers*, p. 38.
69. Roy, *Ordinance Papers*, pp. 388, 391; Kitson, *Rupert*, p. 175.
70. *SPD*, 1644–5, p. 511.
71. Roy, *Ordinance Papers*, pp. 38, 389, 436.
72. Ibid, p. 38.
73. *SPD*, 1644–5, p. 511.
74. Latimer, *Annals*, p. 298.
75. Hutton, *Royalist War Effort*, pp. 172–3.
76. Clarendon, *Great Rebellion*, book VIII, p. 624.
77. Ibid, book VI, pp. 198–9.
78. Ibid, pp. 200–1.
79. Ibid, book XI, p. 275.
80. *SPD*, 1644–5, p. 511; Clarendon, *Great Rebellion*, book IX, p. 634.
81. Ibid, p. 560.
82. Anon, *The Association*.
83. Ibid, p. 7.
Devon was to supply 13,500 men

Cornwall to supply 4,500 men
Somerset to supply 9,000 men
Dorset to supply 3,000 men
The Field Army to Comprise:
8,000 foot
1,500 horse
500 dragoons

84. Ibid, p. 7.
85. Ibid, p. 10.
86. Clarendon, *Great Rebellion*, book VIII, p. 603.
87. Ibid, book IX, p. 633.
88. Mayoral Audit Books.
89. Latimer, *Annals*, p. 194.
90. Ibid.
91. Latimer, *Annals*, p. 194; Mayoral Audit Books.
92. Seyer, *Memoirs*, p. 428; Latimer, *Annals*, p. 195.
93. Clarendon, *Great Rebellion*, book IX, pp. 631–2.
94. Dunne, 'Manuscript History'.
95. Clarendon, *Great Rebellion*, book VIII, p. 555.
96. Ibid, p. 482.
97. Ibid, book IX, p. 634.
98. Ibid, p. 633.
99. Ibid, pp. 638–41.
100. Ibid, p. 640.
101. Ibid, pp. 659–60.
102. Dunne, 'Manuscript History'.

9. *The Campaign of 1645*

1. Firth & Rait, *Acts and Ordinances*, 3 August 1643.
2. *Mercurius Aulicus*, 12 August 1643.
3. Firth & Rait, *Acts and Ordinances*, 1 July 1644; Parliament, *Ordinance . . . for Associating Wilts, Dorset, Somerset, Devon and Cornwall*.
4. Hibbert, *Cavaliers and Roundheads*, p. 182; Wedgwood, *The King's War*, pp. 331–8;

Young & Holmes, *English Civil War*, pp. 204–12.
5. Newcombe, *A Sermon tending*, p. 41.
6. Firth & Rait, *Acts and Ordinances*, 18 October 1644.
7. Ibid, 24 May 1645, 26 August 1645.
8. Sprigg, *Anglia Rediviva*, pp. xi–xvi.
9. Firth, *Regimental History*.
10. Young & Holmes, *English Civil War*, p. 230.
11. Ashley, *Naseby*, p. 61.
12. Ibid, pp. 67–98; Hibbert, *Cavaliers and Roundheads*, pp. 206–11; Wedgwood, *The King's War*, pp. 422–8; Young & Holmes, *English Civil War*, pp. 236–50.
13. Ashley, *Naseby*, p. 90.
14. Sprigg, *Anglia Rediviva*, p. 336.
15. Ibid, pp. xii–xiii.
16. Clarendon, *Great Rebellion*, book IX, pp. 677–8.
17. *SPD*, 1645–7, p. 636.
18. Ibid, p. 637.
19. Powell, *The Navy*, p. 106.
20. Ibid, p. 107.
21. Sprigg, *Anglia Rediviva*, p. 102.
22. Rupert, *Declaration*, p. 6.
23. Ibid, p. 7.
24. Fairfax, *A Letter sent to the right honourable William Lenthall*, p. 4.
25. Hibbert, *Cavaliers and Roundheads*, pp. 220–1; Wedgwood; *The King's War*, pp. 438–9; Young & Holmes, *English Civil War*, pp. 254–7.
26. Fairfax, *A True Relation of a Victory*, pp. 3–4.
27. Fairfax, *A letter to the honourable William Lenthall*, pp. 5–6, 8.
28. Lilburn, *A more full relation*, p. 7.
29. Anon, *A continuation of the proceedings*, p. 1.
30. Kitson, *Rupert*, p. 253.
31. Bedford, *A brief relation*, pp. 3–4.
32. Sprigg, *Anglia Rediviva*, after p. 336.

33. *Mercurius Britannicus*, pp. 823–4.

34. Peters, *Report from the Army . . . 26 July*, p. 4.

35. Anon, *Great and Glorious Victory*, p. 5.

36. Newman, *Royalist Officers*, no. 182.

37. Fairfax, *Two Letters*, p. 3.

38. Bowells, *Proceedings* (no. 6), August 1.

39. Sprigg, *Anglia Rediviva*, following p. 336.

	Date Captured	Prisoners/killed	Guns	Arms	Commander
Bath	30 July	140	6	400	Thomas Bridges
Sherborne	15 August	340	19	600	Lewis Dives
Nunney	20 August	–	–	100	Apt Turberville
Portishead	28 August	–	6	140	–

40. Peters, *Report from Bristol*, pp. 1–2.

41. Clarendon, *Great Rebellion*, book IX, p. 678.

42. Ibid.

43. *SPD*, 1645–7, p. 94.

44. Ibid, pp. 96, 98.

45. Markham, *Fairfax*, p. 247.

46. Cromwell, *Letter to the House*, p. 3.

47. Ibid, p. 1; Markham, *Fairfax*, p. 247.

48. Sanderson, *Complete History*, p. 247.

49. Rupert, *Declaration*, p. 10; Newman, *Royalist Officers*, no. 386.

50. Cromwell, *Letter to the House*, pp. 1–2.

51. Markham, *Fairfax*, p. 247; Sprigg, *Anglia Rediviva*, p. 100.

52. Cromwell, *Letter to the House*, p. 4.

53. Rupert, *Declaration*, p. 10.

54. Ibid, p. 13.

55. Markham, *Fairfax*, p. 248; Sprigg, *Anglia Rediviva*, p. 100.

56. Ibid.

57. Sprigg, *Anglia Rediviva*, p. 101.

58. Ibid, p. 102; Markham, *Fairfax*, p. 248.

59. Sprigg, *Anglia Rediviva*, p. 104; Markham, *Fairfax*, pp. 248–9; Cromwell, *Letter to the House*, p. 4.

60. *Mercurius Aulicus*, Thursday 4 September.

61. Cromwell, *Letter to the House*, p. 2.

62. Markham, *Fairfax*, p. 249.

63. *SPD*, 1645–7, pp. 99, 121.

64. Sprigg, *Anglia Rediviva*, pp. 110–11.

65. Ibid, p. 110.

66. Latimer, *Annals*, p. 198.

67. Anon, *Heads of some notes*, p. 6.

68. *SPD*, 1645–7, p. 123.

69. Sprigg, *Anglia Rediviva*, p. 104; Markham, *Fairfax*, p. 249.

70. Cromwell, *Letter to the House*, p. 4.

71. Sprigg, *Anglia Rediviva*, p. 104.

72. Cromwell, *Letter to the House*, p. 3.

73. Firth, *Cromwell's Army*, p. 172.

74. *Weldon's Brigade*:

Weldon's regiment of foot

Ingoldsby's regiment of foot

Fortescue's regiment of foot

Herbert's regiment of foot

Cromwell's regiment of horse

Pye's regiment of horse

Sheffield regiment of horse

75. *Montague's Brigade*:

Montague's regiment of foot

Fairfax's regiment of foot

Pickering's regiment of foot

Waller's regiment of foot

Desborough's regiment of horse

Grave's regiment of horse

76. *Rainsborough's Brigade*:

Rainsborough's regiment of foot

Skippon's regiment of foot

Hammond's regiment of foot

Birche's regiment of foot

Pride's regiment of foot

Riche's regiment of horse

Walley's regiment of horse

77. *Ireton's Cavalry Brigade*:
    Ireton's regiment of horse
    Butler's regiment of horse
    Fleetwood's regiment of horse
    Okey's Dragoons
78. Sprigg, *Anglia Rediviva*, p. 111; Anon, *Heads of some notes*, p. 6.
79. Sprigg, *Anglia Rediviva*, p. 108; Rainsborough, *True Relation*, p. 4.
80. Robinson, *Sieges*, p. 41; Latimer, *Annals*, p. 200.
81. Sprigg, *Anglia Rediviva*, p. 110; Rainsborough, *True Relation*, pp. 6–7.
82. Ibid.
83. Rupert, *Declaration*, p. 16.
84. Sprigg, *Anglia Rediviva*, pp. 111–14; Rainsborough, *True Relation*, pp. 7–11.
85. Sprigg, *Anglia Rediviva*, pp. 111–14; Rainsborough, *True Relation*, pp. 9–10.
86. Sprigg, *Anglia Rediviva*, p. 114.
87. Rainsborough, *True Relation*, p. 13.
88. Sprigg, *Anglia Rediviva*, p. 113.
89. Rainsborough, *True Relation*, pp. 12–13.
90. Sprigg, *Anglia Rediviva*, p. 115.
91. Ibid, p. 106.
92. *SPD*, 1625–49, p. 688.
93. Sprigg, *Anglia Rediviva*, p. 105.
94. Rainsborough, *True Relation*, p. 19; Sprigg, *Anglia Rediviva*, p. 116.
95. Birch, *Memoir*, p. 22.
96. Rupert, *Declaration*, p. 28.
97. Cromwell, *Letter to the House*, p. 6; Rainsborough, *True Relation*, pp. 19–20; Sprigg, *Anglia Rediviva*, p. 119.
98. Rainsborough, *True Relation*, p. 20.
99. Cromwell, *Letter to the House*, p. 6.
100. Ibid, p. 5.
101. Sprigg, *Anglia Rediviva*, p. 116.
102. Rainsborough, *True Relation*, p. 19.
103. Cromwell, *Letter to the House*, p. 5.
104. Rupert, *Declaration*, p. 28.
105. Ibid, p. 9.
106. Ibid.
107. Cromwell, *Letter to the House*, p. 6.
108. Roe, *Memoir*, p. 22.
109. Ibid.
110. Cromwell, *Letter to the House*, p. 6.
111. Sprigg, *Anglia Rediviva*, pp. 116–17.
112. Ibid, pp. 110, 116.
113. Ibid, p. 116.
114. Cromwell, *Letter to the House*, p. 5; Rainsborough, *True Relation*, p. 19; Sprigg, *Anglia Rediviva*, pp. 116–17.
115. Cromwell, *Letter to the House*, pp. 5–6.
116. Ibid, p. 5.
117. Rupert, *Declaration*, p. 28.
118. Cromwell, *Letter to the House*, p. 5.
119. Sprigg, *Anglia Rediviva*, p. 117; Rainsborough, *True Relation*, p. 19.
120. Cromwell, *Letter to the House*, p. 5.
121. Sprigg, *Anglia Rediviva*, p. 117.
122. Ibid.
123. Cromwell, *Letter to the House*, p. 5; Rainsborough, *True Relation*, p. 19.
124. Sprigg, *Anglia Rediviva*, p. 117.
125. Newman, *Royalist Officers*, no. 1168.
126. Firth, *Regimental History*, p. 419.
127. Markham, *Fairfax*, p. 252.
128. Rupert, *Declaration*, p. 28.
129. Cromwell, *Letter to the House*, p. 6.
130. Sprigg, *Anglia Rediviva*, p. 119.
131. Rupert, *Declaration*, p. 31.
132. Ibid.
133. Rainsborough, *True Relation*, pp. 21–4; Sprigg, *Anglia Rediviva*, pp. 119–20; Rupert, *Declaration*, pp. 29–30.
134. Iremaine, *An exact relation*, p. 1.
135. Clarendon, *Great Rebellion*, book IX, pp. 690–1, 693–5; Hibbert, *Cavaliers and Roundheads*, pp. 231–2; Kitson, *Rupert*, pp. 263–6; Wedgwood, *The King's War*, pp. 460–2, 469, 471–3.
136. Cromwell, *Letter to the House*.
137. Anon, *Strong motives*, pp. 7–8.
138. Peters, *God's doings*, pp. 21, 23, 27.
139. Ibid, p. 23.

10. For Parliament Again

1. Sprigg, *Anglia Rediviva*, p. 129.
2. Iremaine, *An exact relation*, p. 3.
3. Sprigg, *Anglia Rediviva*, p. 133.
4. Hibbert, *Cavaliers and Roundheads*, pp. 229–32; Wedgwood, *The King's War*, pp. 465–7.
5. Sprigg, *Anglia Rediviva*, p. 335.
6. Latimer, *Annals*, p. 205.
7. Ibid, p. 206.
8. Ibid, pp. 205–6.
9. *SPD*, 1645–7, p. 208.
10. Ibid, 1 November 1645.
11. *SPD*, Committee for Compounding, p. 933.
12. Ibid, p. 942.
13. Latimer, *Annals*, pp. 215–16.
14. *SPD*, Committee for Compounding, p. 1191.
15. Ibid, p. 1555.
16. Ibid, pp. 12, 1556–7; Richard Gregson, Richard Long, Ezekiel Wallis.
17. Ibid, pp. 1629–30, 1972; Francis, Creswick, Alexander James, Humphrey Hooke.
18. Ibid, vols 2–4, pp. 1013, 1586, 1629–30, 1652, 1972, 1884, 2959.
19. Dring, *Catalogue*
    Arundell, Edward, merchant, £50;
    Boucher, John, merchant, £135;
    Gregson, Richard, gentleman, £105;
    Jones, Gilbert, chancellor, £43 5*s*;
    Alexander, James, merchant, £669 10*s* 11*d*;
    Long, Richard, merchant, £600;
    Wallis, Ezekiel, gentleman, £177 10*s*.
20. *SPD*, Committee for Compounding, p. 73.
21. Ibid, p. 545.
22. Iremaine, *An exact relation*, p. 3.
23. Firth, *Regimental History*, p. 431.
24. Latimer, *Annals*, p. 204.
25. Parliament, *Appointment of Sarg-Maj Skippon*.
26. Latimer, *Annals*, p. 209.
27. Ibid, p. 213; Firth, *Regimental History*, p. 431.
28. Kem, *Orders given out*, p. 2.
    Maj Kem
    Capt-Lieut Richards
    Capt Hart (Senior Capt)
    Capt Grig
    Capt Pope
    Capt Roe
29. Latimer, *Annals*, p. 217.
30. *SPD*, 1645–7, pp. 487–8.
31. *SPD*, 1655, pp. 382–3.
32. *SPD*, 1649–50, p. 75.
33. Newman, *Royalist Officers*, no. 1162.
34. *SPD*, 1648–9, pp. 54–6.
35. Ibid; Latimer, *Annals*, pp. 220–1.
36. Newman, *Royalist Officers*, no. 1162.
37. *SPD*, 1649–50, p. 210.
38. Ibid, p. 223.
39. Latimer, *Annals*, p. 226.
40. *SPD*, 1649–50, p. 256.
41. Ibid, pp. 553, 555–8.
42. *SPD*, 1650, pp. 62–3.
43. Ibid, pp. 306, 580.
44. *SPD*, 1651, p. 100.
45. Ibid, pp. 185–7.
46. *SPD*, 1651, p. 329.
47. Latimer, *Annals*, p. 233.
48. *SPD*, 1651, pp. 356–7.
49. Ibid, p. 385.
50. Latimer, *Annals*, p. 223.
51. *SPD*, 1651, pp. 443–4.
52. Ibid, p. 443.
53. *SPD*, 1651–2, p. 44.
54. Latimer, *Annals*, p. 223.
55. *SPD*, 1650, p. 8.
56. *SPD*, 1652–3, p. 76.
57. Ibid, p. 89.
58. Ibid, p. 215.
59. Ibid, pp. 260, 280.
60. *SPD*, 1653–4, pp. 327, 451.
61. Latimer, *Annals*, p. 257.

62. Ibid, pp. 257–8.

63. *SPD*, 1655, p. 256; *SPD*, 1655–6, p. 344.

64. *SPD*, 1655–6, p. 344.

65. Hill, *Upside Down*, p. 75.

66. Kem, *Orders given out*, p. 11.

67. Anon, *A Letter from sixteen*, p. 7.

68. Hill, *Upside Down*, p. 121.

69. Ibid, p. 245.

70. Ibid, p. 263.

71. Latimer, *Annals*, p. 270.

72. Ibid.

73. Hill, *Upside Down*, pp. 264–5.

74. Latimer, *Annals*, p. 214.

75. Ibid, pp. 217–18, 219–20, 226–7, 231–2, 235–8, 263–4, 272–3.

76. *SPD*, 1656–7, p. 48.

77. *SPD*, 1653–4, p. 570.

78. McGrath, *Merchants and Merchandise*, pp. 286–7, 294.

79. Ibid, pp. 280–1.

80. Ibid, p. xxi.

81. Ibid, pp. 284–7.

    Wine: 1612–13

      820 tuns, 1,822 butts, 9 hogsheads, 2 tierce

    Wine: 1654–5

      1,402 butts, 1 hogshead, 49 pipes, 1 quarter cask, 1 tierce

    Tobacco: 1612–13

      324 lbs

    Tobacco: 1654–5

      1 chest, 3,440 hogsheads, 4,109 rolls, 120 hand rolls, 780 small rolls

    Sugar: 1612–13

      1514 cwt

    Sugar: 1654–5

      342 barrels, 533 butts, 87 casks, 2 small casks, 229 chests, 4 small chests, 2 fardles, 10 fetches, 1,336 hogsheads, 60 pipes, 143 puncheons, 8 tierce

82. *SPD*, 1657–8, p. 352.

83. *SPD*, 1659–60, p. 42; addressed to Col. Hagget, Nathaniel Collins, Edward Tyson, Thomas Ellys, Samuel Clarke and John Harper.

84. Ibid, p. 50.

85. Ibid, p. 68.

86. Ibid, p. 195.

87. Ibid, p. 280.

88. Ibid, p. 374.

Bibliography

STATE PAPERS DOMESTIC

Charles I: vols 4–23
Commonwealth: vols 1–13
Committee for the Advance of Money: vols 1–3
Committee for Compounding of Delinquents: vols 1–5
Charles II: vols 1–4

CONTEMPORARY NEWS-SHEETS AND SIMILAR

Certain Informations
Exceeding True News
Mercurius Aulicus
Mercurius Britannicus
Mercurius Belgicus

PAMPHLETS AND BOOKS

Adair, J., *Cheriton 1644* (London, 1973)

Aldworth, R., *A letter sent to the right worshipful William Lenthall esquire, speaker in the commons house of Parliament from the mayor of Bristol and others whose names are hereunto subscribed intimating the free benevolence of the city of Bristol for the relief of the Protestants of Ireland* (London, 1643)

——, *Copy of a letter from the lord mayor of Bristol* (London, 1643)

Anonymous, *An abstract of some letters sent from Dorchester to some friends in London* (London, 1642)

Anonymous, *The association, agreement and protestation of the counties of Somerset, Dorset, Cornwall and Devon* (Lichfield, 1644)

Anonymous, *A brief relation abstracted out of several letters of a most hellish cruel and bloody plot against the city of Bristol* (London, 1643)

Anonymous, *A collection of sundry petitions presented to the king's most excellent majesty, as also to the most honourable houses now assembled in Parliament* (York, 1642)

Anonymous, *A copy of the commission of array granted from his majesty to the Marquis of Hertford* (London, 1642)

Anonymous, *The Earl of Essex his letter to master speaker* (Oxford, 1643)

Anonymous, *Heads of some notes of the city scout from the army* (London, 1645)

Anonymous, *The humble petition of the city of Bristol for an accommodation of peace between his majesty and the honourable the high court of Parliament* (Oxford, 1643)

Anonymous, *A letter from Exeter sent by the deputy-lieutenants of Somerset* (London, 1642)

Anonymous, *A letter from sixteen gentlemen of Kent, also the remonstrance and petition of diverse honest inhabitants of the city of Bristol and adjacent villages to his excellency Thomas Fairfax and the honourable council of the army* (London, 1648)

Anonymous, *More good news from Ireland* (London, 1642)

Anonymous, *A relation of all the passages and proceedings in Somerset and Bristol, with their valiant resolution to fight for king and parliament* (London, 1642)

Anonymous, *Several examinations and confessions of the treacherous conspirators against the city of Bristol* (London, 1643)

Anonymous, *The Somerset petition with an answer in defence of the Parliament against the same petition, and others of that malignant and dangerous nature* (London, 1642)

Anonymous, *Strong motives: or loving and modest advice unto petitioners for Presbyterian government* (London, 1645)

Anonymous, *The tragedy of the king's army's fidelity since their coming to Bristol* (London, 1643)

Anonymous, *A true and exact relation of the proceedings of the Marquis of Hertford* (London, 1642)

Anonymous, *A true and joyful relation of two famous battles* (London, 1642)

Anonymous, *A true relation of the great and glorious victory through God's providence obtained by Sir William Waller, Sir Arthur Hasillrig and others of the Parliament's forces* (London, 1643)

Anonymous, *A true relation of the late fight between Sir William Waller's forces and those sent from Oxford* (London, 1643)

Anonymous, *Two letters, the one from Lord Digby to the Queen's majesty the other from Mr Thomas Elliott to the Lord Digby* (London, 1642)

Anonymous, *Two state martyrs: or the murder of master Robert Yoemans and master George Boucher citizens of Bristol* (London, 1643)

Archibald, E.H.H., *Wooden fighting ships of the Royal Navy* (London, 1968)

Ash, J., *A perfect relation of all the passages and proceedings of the Marquis of Hertford, the Lord Paulet, and the rest of the cavaliers that were with them in the west* (London, 1643)

——, J. *A second letter sent from John Ash esquire, a member of the house of commons to the honourable William Lenthall esquire, speaker to the house of commons in Parliament* (London, 1642)

Ashley-Cooper, A., *A copy of the King's message sent by the Duke of Lennox* (London, 1644)

Atkyns, R., 'The Vindication' (ed. Young, P.) in *Military Memoirs of the Civil War* (London, 1967)

Ayler, G.E., *The interregnum: the quest for settlement 1646–1660* (London, 1974)

Ball, J., *A declaration from the city of Bristol: sent by M: John Ball in Bristol to M: James Nicolls a merchant in Fenchurch Street London* (London, 1642)

Bamfield, J., *Colonel Joseph Bamfield's apology written by himself and printed at his desire* (Holland, 1685)

Baynton, W., *Letter to the Earl of Pembroke* (London, 1643)

Bedford, S., *A brief relation of the taking of Bridgwater by the Parliament forces under the command of Sir Thomas Fairfax* (London, 1645)

Betty, J.H., *Bristol observed: visitors' impressions of Bristol from Doomsday to the Blitz* (Bristol, 1989)

Bowells, M., *The proceedings of the army under the command of Sir Thomas Fairfax from the first of August to the seventh of the same* (London, 1645)

——, *A continuation of the proceedings of the army under the command of Sir Thomas Fairfax* (London, 1643)

Cantile, N., *History of the army medical department* (London, 1976)

Clarendon, Earl of, *History of the great rebellion*, 6 vols (Oxford, 1717)

Cromwell, O., *Lieut-General Cromwell's letter to the house of commons of all the particulars of the taking of the city of Bristol* (London, 1645)

Damer-Powell, J.W., *Bristol privateers and ships of war* (Bristol, 1930)

Davies, G., 'The Parliamentary Army under the Earl of Essex', *English Historical Review* (1934)

Davy, H., *The true copy of a letter sent from an inhabitant of Bridgwater* (London, 1643)

Dring, T., *A catalogue of the lords, knights and gentlemen that have compounded for their estates* (London, 1655)

Dunne (Snr), Manuscript History of Bristol (Bristol Central Library, no date)

Eddershaw, D., *Civil war in Oxfordshire* (Stroud, 1995)

Ede-Barrett, S., *The storm of Bristol: De Gomme's account* (Leeds, 1988)

Fairfax, T., *A letter sent to the honourable William Lenthall Esquire, speaker to the honourable house of commons: concerning the routing of Col Goring's army near Bridgwater* (London, 1645)

——, *A letter sent to the right honourable William Lenthall Esquire, speaker to the honourable house of commons: concerning the raising of the siege of Taunton by the Parliament's army* (London, 1645)

——, *Memoirs of northern actions* (Harrogate, 1810)

——, *A true relation of a victory obtained over the king's forces by Sir Thomas Fairfax being fought near Langport in Somersetshire* (London, 1645)

——, *Two letters: the one sent to the right honourable, the lord Fairfax by Sir Thomas Fairfax his son commander in chief of Parliament's forces* (London, 1645)

Farr, G., *Shipbuilding in Bristol* (London, 1977)

Fiennes, N., *An extraordinary delivery from a cruel plot* (London, 1643)

——, *Col Fiennes letter to my Lord General concerning Bristol* (London, 1643)

——, *N. Fiennes, his reply to a pamphlet entitled: an answer to Col Fiennes relation concerning his surrender of Bristol* (London, 1643)

——, *A relation made in the house of commons by Col Nathaniel Fiennes concerning the surrender of the city and castle of Bristol* (London, 1643)

Firth, C., *Cromwell's army* (London, 1921)

——, *Regimental history of Cromwell's army* (Oxford, 1940)

—— & Rait, R., *Acts and ordinances of the interregnum* (Oxford, 1911)

Gardiner, S.R., *History of the great civil war*, 4 vols, (London, 1893)

de Gomme, B., 'The siege and capture of Bristol by the royalist forces in 1643', ed. Firth, C., *Journal of Army Historical Research* vol. IV, 1927

Grinsell, L.V., *The Bristol mint: a historical outline* (Bristol, 1972)

——, *The Bristol mint: the history and coinage* (Bristol, 1986)

Hibbert, C., *Cavaliers and Roundheads* (London, 1993)

Hill, C., *The world turned upside down* (London, 1991)

Hogg, I., *English artillery, 1326–1716* (London, 1963)

Hopton, R., *Bellum Civile* (Taunton, 1902)

Horner, J., *Marquis of Hertford, his letter sent to the Queen in Holland* (London, 1642)

Hutton, R., *The Royalist war effort* (London, 1982)

Iremaine, S., *An exact relation of Prince Rupert his marching out of Bristol, the 11 of this inst. September 1645, according to articles of agreement between him and the right honourable Sir Thomas Fairfax* (London, 1645)

Kem, S., *Orders given out: the word stand fast, as it was lately delivered in a farewell sermon by Major Samuel Kem to the officers and soldiers of his regiment in Bristol* (London, 1647)

Kitson, F., *Prince Rupert* (London, 1996)

Langrish, H., *A full declaration of all particulars of the march of the forces under Col Fiennes to Bristol and their carriage upon the enemies approach* (London, 1643)

Latham, R.C., *Bristol charters 1509–1899* (Bristol, 1947)

Latimer, J., *The annals of Bristol in the seventeenth century* (Bath, 1970)

Lilburn, J., *A more full relation of the great battle fought between Sir Thomas Fairfax and Goring on Thursday last 1645. Made in the House of Commons* (London, 1645)

Lloyd, D., *Memoirs of the lives, actions, sufferings and deaths of those noble, reverend and exceptional persons that suffered by death, sequestration, decimation or otherwise for the Protestant religion and the great principle thereof allegiance to their sovereign in the late intestine wars* (London, 1668)

Luke, S. (ed. Philip, I.G.), *Journal of Sir Samuel Luke* (Oxford, 1947, 1950, 1952–4)

Lynch, J.P., 'Bristol shipping and royalist naval power during the English Civil War', *The Mariners Mirror*, vol. 84, no. 3 (August 1998)

Markham, C.R., *Lord Fairfax: commander in chief of the army of the Parliament of England* (London, 1870)

McGrath, P., 'Merchant Venturers and Bristol shipping in the early seventeenth century', *The Mariners Mirror*, vol. 36, no. 1 (1950)

——, *Merchants and merchandise in seventeenth-century Bristol* (Bristol, 1955)

——, *Bristol in the Civil War* (Bristol, 1991)

——, 'Bristol and the Civil War' in Richardson, R.C. *The English Civil Wars: local aspects* (Stroud, 1997)

Needham, *Check to the checker of Britannicus* (London, 1644)

Newcomen, M., *A sermon, tending to set forth the right use of the disasters that befell our armies* (London, 1644)

Newman, P.R., *Royalist officers in England and Wales* (London, 1981)

Nott, H.E., *The deposition books of Bristol, 1643–1647* (Bristol, 1937)

—— & Ralph, E., *The deposition books of Bristol, 1650–1654* (Bristol, 1948)

Ollard, R., *War without an enemy* (London, 1976)

Parker, G., 'Tyndall's Park Bristol, Fort Royal and the Fort House therein', *Transactions of the Bristol and Gloucestershire Archaeological Society* (1929)

Parliament, *A declaration of the lords and commons assembled in parliament for the prevention of a most horrid, wicked and unnatural design, pursued by Sir Ralph Hopton and his adherents, rebels and traitors in a warlike manner in Devon and Cornwall* (London, 16 January 1643)

——, *A declaration of the lords and commons assembled in parliament for the raising of all power and force as well trained bands as others, in several counties of this kingdom* (London, 10 August 1642)

——, *An ordinance of the lords and commons assembled in parliament for the association of Wiltshire, Dorset, Somerset, Devon, Cornwall and the cities of Bristol and Exeter and the town and county of Poole* (London, 1644)

——, *An ordinance of the lords and commons for the constitution and appointment of Sergeant Major Philip Skippon governor of Bristol* (London, 1645)

Peachy, S., *The storming of Bristol* (Bristol, 1993)

—— & Turton, A., *Old Robin's Foote* (Leigh-on-Sea, 1987)

——, *The fall of the west*, vols 5 and 6 (Bristol, 1994)

Peters, H., *God's doings and man's duty opened in a sermon preached before both houses of parliament, the lord mayor and aldermen of the city of London and the assembled devines at the last thanksgiving day 2 April* (London, 1646)

——, *Mr Peters' report from the army to the parliament made Saturday 26 July 1645* (London, 1645)

——, *Mr Peters' report from Bristol made to the house of commons from Sir Thomas Fairfax* (London, 1645)

Philerenus, *Mercurius Hibernicus: or a discourse of the late insurrection in Ireland* (Bristol, 1644)

Porter, S., *Destruction in the English Civil Wars* (Stroud, 1997)

Powell, J., *The navy in the English Civil War* (London, 1962)

Proud, J., *A true and sad relation of diverse passages in Somersetshire between the country and the cavaliers concerning the militia and the commission of array* (London, 1643)

Prynne, W., *The popish royal favourite, or a full discovery of his majesties extraordinary favours to and protection of notorious papists, priests and Jesuits* (London, 1643)

——, *A check to Brittanicus for his flattery and prevarication in justifying the conduct of Nathaniel Fiennes* (London, 1644)

—— & Walker, C. *A true and full relation of the prosecution, arraignment, trial and condemnation of Nathaniel Fiennes, late Colonel and governor of the city of Bristol* (London, 1643)

Rainsborough, T., *A true relation of the storming of Bristol* (London, 1645)

Richardson, R.C., *The English Civil Wars: local aspects* (Stroud, 1997)

Robinson, A., *A shocking history of Bristol* (Bristol, 1973)

Robinson, R., *The sieges of Bristol during the civil war* (Bristol, 1868)

Rodgers, H.C., *Battles and generals of the civil war* (London, 1966)

Roe, *Military Memoir of Colonel John Birch*, ed. Webb, T.W. (London, 1873)

Ross, E.E., 'Map of the Bristol defences during the civil war', *Professional Papers of the Corps of Royal Engineers*, vol. XIII (1887)

Roy, I., *Royalist Ordinance Papers* (Oxford, 1964 and 1975)

Rupert, *A declaration of his highness Prince Rupert with a narration of the state and condition of the city and garrison of Bristol when his highness came hither* (London, 1645)

Russell, C., *The causes of the English Civil War* (Oxford, 1990)

Russell, J., *Civil war defences of Bristol: their archaeology and topography* (Bristol, 1995)

Ryder, I., *An English army for Ireland* (Leigh-on-Sea, 1987)

Ryves, B., *Mercurius Rusticus: the countries complaint, recounting the sad events of the late unparalleled rebellion* (London, 1643)

Sacks, D.H., 'The corporate town and the English state: Bristol's "little businesses" 1625–41', *Past and Present*, no. 110

Sanderson, W., *A complete history of the life and reign of King Charles* (London, 1658)

Sellers, W.C. & Yeatman, R.J., *1066 and All That* (London, 1996)

Seyer, S., *Memoirs historical and topographical of Bristol and its neighbours* (Bristol, 1823)

Smith, W., *Several letters of great importance and good success largely obtained against the Fellowship of Bristol by Captain William Smith, Captain of his majesties ship called Swallow, now in service for King and Parliament* (London, 1643)

Sprigg, J., *Anglia Rediviva* (London, 1647 and Oxford, 1854)

Stewell, J., *An answer to the purchasers of the lands late of Sir John Stewell, by Act of Parliament exposed to sale for his treason* (London, 1654)

Stewart, C., *His majesties declaration to all his loving subjects after his victories over lord Fairfax in the north and Sir William Waller in the west and the taking of Bristol by his majesties forces* (London, 1643)

Symonds, R., *Diary of the marches of the Royalist army* (London, 1859)

T.P., *Eban Ezar, as a thankful remembrance of God's great goodness upon the city of Bristol* (London, 1643)

T.W., *The copy of a letter sent from Bristol* (London, 1643)

Thomas, P.W., *Sir John Birkenhead 1617–1679* (Oxford, 1969)

Tombs, J., *Jehovah Jireh: or God's providence in delivering the godly opened in two sermons in the city of Bristol, on the day of public thanksgiving in that city, March 14 1643* (London, 1643)

Turner, E., 'Remarks on the military history of Bristol in the seventeenth century', *Archaeologica*, vol. XIV (1803)

Underdown, D., *Civil War in Somerset* (Newton Abbott, 1973)

——, *Revel, riot and rebellion* (Oxford, 1987)

Vanes, J., *The overseas trade of Bristol in the sixteenth century* (Bristol, 1979)

Walker, C., *An answer to Col Nathaniel Fiennes relation concerning his surrender of the city and castle of Bristol* (London, 1643)

——, *Check to Britannicus* (London, 1644)

—— & Prynne, W., *Articles of impeachment and accusation exhibited against Col Nathaniel Fiennes* (London, 1643)

Wedgwood, C.V., *The king's war* (London, 1967)

Woolrich, A.P., *Printing in Bristol* (Bristol, 1986)

Young, P., *Edgehill* (London, 1967)

——, *Marston Moor* (London, 1967)

—— & Holmes, D., *A military history of the civil war* (London, 1974)

Index